NIGHT'S BLACK AGENTS

Night's Black Agents

Witches, Wizards and the Dead in the Ancient World

Daniel Ogden

hambledon
continuum

Hambledon Continuum is an imprint of Continuum Books

Continuum UK
The Tower Building
11 York Road
London SE1 7NX

Continuum US
80 Maiden Lane
Suite 704
New York, NY 10038

www.continuumbooks.com

Copyright © Daniel Ogden, 2008

All rights reserved. No part of this publication may be reproduced or transmitted in any form or by any means, electronic or mechanical, including photocopying, recording or any information storage or retrieval system, without prior permission from the publishers.

First published 2008

British Library Cataloguing-in-Publication Data
A catalogue record for this book is available from the British Library.

ISBN 9781847250339

Typeset by YHT Ltd, London.
Printed and bound in Great Britain by MPG Books Ltd, Bodmin, Cornwall

わが最愛の妻
江里子に

Contents

List of Figures ix
Introduction 1

1 The First Wicked Witches of the West? 7
   At the dawn of the classical tradition: Circe 7
   Circe and the birth of the mage 21
   The emergence of Medea 27
   Conclusion 35

2 Roman Gothic: the Witches of the Latin Tradition 39
   In the background: Hellenistic literature and indigenous Roman magic 39
   Latin poetry: Canidia, Erictho and friends 45
   Latin novels: Meroe, Panthia and others 56
   Folk traditions of modern Italy 71
   Conclusion 75

3 Babylon and Memphis: the Sorcerers of the Imperial Age 77
   The conglomerated magical peoples of Asia: Persians, Medes, Mages, Babylonians, Chaldaeans, Assyrians and Syrians 77
   Egyptian priest-sorcerers 91
   Judaeo-Christian exorcists 100
   The Neo-Pythagoreans: Arignotus, Apollonius and Alexander 104
   Conclusion 113

4 Hidden Stories: Grimoires, Amulets and Curse Tablets 115
   Grimoires: the Greek Magical Papyri 115
   Circles of protection: amulets 129
   Curse tablets and binding spells 138
   Conclusion 144

5 Across the Divide: Love and Sex between the Living and the Dead	146
Love beyond the grave	146
New love between the living and the dead	160
Conclusion	169
Notes	170
Bibliography	197
Index	218

List of Figures

(*Between pages 114 and 115*)

Figure *1.1* Circe mixes the magic potion she hopes will turn Odysseus into a pig. Burlesque image.
Figure *1.2* Odysseus challenges Circe with his sword. A pig-man attends.
Figure *1.3* Circe attended by ass-men.
Figure *1.4* Medea uses herbs to inflict sleep on the unsleeping serpent that guards the golden fleece.
Figure *1.5* Medea pets, charms or feeds the fleece-guarding serpent, here with three heads.
Figure *1.6* Medea, wand in hand, rejuvenates Jason in her cauldron. The Argonauts come running.
Figure *1.7* Medea rejuvenates an old ram in her cauldron. A demonstration for an elderly Jason.
Figure *2.1* Naked witches bind and draw down the moon: 'Hear me, Lady Moon'.
Figure *3.1* Coin of Ionopolis. Glycon coils around the neck of Ionopolis personified in the fashion in which he coiled around that of Alexander of Abonouteichos.
Figure *3.2* Cult image of Glycon, the human-faced and lion-tailed prophetic serpent sponsored by Alexander of Abonouteichos.

Introduction

Let us open with two vignettes:

> The hag Meroe hails from Thessaly, traditional home of witches in the ancient world. She is an expert in 'binding' magic and we learn that she has sealed a baby into its mother's womb for nine years. She enslaves a young man, Socrates, to her by sleeping with him just once. When Socrates is rescued by a friend, Meroe sets off in pursuit with an equally horrid companion, Panthia. They attack the hotel room in which the fugitives are holed up, bursting the door from its hinges. Meroe slits the throat of her former slave as he sleeps and draws his heart out through the wound, but then she reanimates him temporarily by replacing the organ with a magical sponge. Before they leave they empty their bladders over the terrified rescuer, who has been hiding under the bed. As they depart, the door is magically restored to its hinges. The rescuer is amazed, in his terror, to find his friend seemingly still alive, but the following day, as the friend takes a drink of water, the sponge leaps out of his throat and he is left dead for good ...

***

> Polycritus, an Aetolian magistrate dies, leaving his wife pregnant. When the child is born it is found to be a hermaphrodite, which the horrified Aeolians take as a terrible portent. As they debate what to do with the child to free themselves of the doom it appears to bring upon their state (burn it alive?), its father's ghost manifests itself, seizes the baby, tears it apart limb from limb and devours it in front of them. He then disappears, leaving only the head uneaten. The head then speaks prophecies of the very doom the Aetolians had been dreading ...

These two scenes, with their grotesque witches and dread ghosts, serve well to indicate the subject matter of this book (the former scene will be discussed in Chapter 2, the latter in Chapter 5). The book's fundamental brief is to provide a readable and accessible introduction to the world of magic and witchcraft in antiquity, and also to the ghosts often associated with it. This is most easily and most honestly done by foregrounding the lively literary and documentary evidence for these subjects. In this we encounter the ancient equivalents to, and indeed often the actual prototypes of, the cherished ingredients of the modern horror movie: the witch, beautiful and ugly, the sorcerer, the ghost and its haunted house, the werewolf, the dragon, the vampire, the zombie, the Frankenstein's monster and even the Island of Dr Moreau. This range of subject matter is well encapsulated by Shakespeare's phrase 'night's black agents' (*Macbeth* Act iii, Scene 2), although it is important to note that the ancient world had no conception of 'black magic' as such. For the most part I have chosen to incorporate this evidence in the form of managed paraphrase rather than direct quotation, so as not to break the flow of exposition or argument, or to confuse or distract readers by burying the more important information in the less important, or with jarring changes of tone or, for that matter, with too many discontinuities of text. The most significant exception to this rule falls in Chapter 4, where arguments about the correspondences between narratives in the literary texts and narratives or quasi-narratives in the documentary texts of magic depend upon at least a limited degree of direct quotation. The book seeks to embrace a wide range of material, but there is no respect in which it aspires to be exhaustive. It is divided into five strongly themed chapters, but within these I have assumed the licence to write quite discursively, and in this fashion, a somewhat piecemeal one, to broaden the book's scope.[1]

The book also has a second and consonant aim, and this is to draw out the full significance of the narrative texts under consideration for the history of ancient magic. These texts, whether ostensibly fictive or historical, incorporate and rehearse a great many traditional tales and even international folktales. Such tales did not just report or manipulate beliefs about ancient magic, they were fundamentally constitutive of them. Put simply, the reason the ancients knew that magic worked was less because they objectively observed it in operation, and more because they were used to hearing such good tales of witches and sorcerers putting it into practice. These tales could work on two levels. On the one hand they had a direct probative value as reported examples of successful magical practice, however fantastical they might be. But on the other hand, and more importantly, by ensuring their own viral repetition and dissemination with their panoplies of engaging motifs, they lodged themselves firmly in the popular imagination. In this way, and more insidiously, they constructed and encoded compelling and plausible templates for thinking about magical behaviour, and perhaps even for practising magic. The traditional and folktale background of these tales accounts in large part for the continuing ability of the texts that preserve them to captivate the modern reader with immediacy. This book can therefore be said to be about *magic-making* in two distinct senses: the texts that form its subject matter in one sense describe the making of magic in antiquity, but in another sense it is they themselves that made the magic, or at any rate the system of beliefs about it and its thought-world.

An ancillary aim of the book is to present in more accessible form a number of arguments and connections I have developed in less accessible form elsewhere. It is accordingly for reasons of efficiency, rather than of vainglory, that I refer readers on to my own publications more often than is customary for me, albeit still rather less often than is customary for others in the field. Many, but by no means all, of the texts discussed in this book are reproduced in full, formal translations in my sourcebook, *Magic, Witchcraft and Ghosts in the Greek and Roman worlds* (New York, 2002a). Citations for the ancient texts are, where appropriate, accompanied by the their serial number in the sourcebook, in the fashion '= *MWG* no ...'.

Readers will be grateful and relieved to be spared the narcissistic posturings about the definition of magic in an ancient context that ritually populate the introductions to parallel books, not to mention the childish, ponderous rehearsals of doxography that attend them. Their befuddled authors confuse the attempt to give final definition to an abstract concept, ancient or modern, which is self-evidently impossible, with the delineation of a coherent core of source-material for study, which, in this case, is easy. This is why these introductions, for all the brilliant and innovative insights they proudly defend, are all followed by the same old stock-in-trade: the witches, mages and sorcerers of Classical and early Christian literature, amulets, curse tablets and the Greek Magical Papyri. This is hardly surprising, because, despite the very different textures of these groups of documents, the thematic coherence between them is emphatic: ancient literature shows us witches (figures described by the terms *pharmakis* in Greek, *venefica*, *saga* in Latin), mages and sorcerers (figures described by the terms *magos, goēs, pharmakeus, epōidos* in Greek, *magus, veneficus* in Latin) doing the same things, and it wraps them up in a strong tradition with a tight nexus of repeated motifs. Amongst the things they are shown to do are the using of recipe books and the making of amulets and curse tablets. The formularies or grimoires of the Greek Magical Papyri regard themselves as the work of the mages and offer, amongst other things, recipes for what the literary sources show us witches, mages and sorcerers doing, and indeed recipes for the manufacture of curse tablets and amulets. The amulets and the curse tablets that survive answer well to those described and prescribed in the literary texts and in the magical formularies. The core source-material to be discussed in response to the terms *mageia* (Greek) and *magia* (Latin), the ancient abstract terms built upon *magos* and *magus*, accordingly delineates itself, despite the open-endedness of these terms. For practical purposes, to withhold from the same core source-material the similarly open-ended modern English abstract term 'magic', which itself derives directly from *mageia* and *magia*, is merely precious.

Like the modern English abstract term 'magic', the ancient abstract terms *mageia* and *magia*, together with the dependent terms listed above, were words that people used, and they could use them in any way they liked, with the result that they must always elude final definition. Leaving aside questions of whether the general concepts associated with the terms evolved over a thousand years, and of whether Latin usages generally differed significantly from Greek ones, the terms were characteristically deployed in a tendentious, contentious and competitive fashion. So it is, for example, that the Hippocratic author of *On the Sacred Disease* brands his medical competitors as mages for making dietary prescriptions for the cure of epilepsy, before proceeding to make dietary prescriptions for the cure of it himself. So it is too that the Platonic Socrates scorns the manipulation of souls, the revelation of underworld secrets and the challenging of conventional morality that he holds to be characteristic of mages. Yet he himself contrives to do all these things, and no doubt the Athenian in the street would have been hard-pressed to distinguish Socrates from his mages. In a different way, an implicitly competitive and contentious cast of mind also underlies the attempts of ancient writers to generate their own definitions or histories of magic, and to derive it or differentiate it from other fields of expertise or imposture, as is the case, for example, with the elder Pliny, Apuleius and Tertullian. Often too the key words of ancient magic were imbued with strong connotations of charlatanry: are we then to say that a *goēs* was someone who exhibited special powers, or almost the opposite of this, someone who claimed special powers but in fact possessed no power at all, other, perhaps, than that to deceive? In short, the attempt to give final definition the terms magic, *mageia* or *magia*, etc. is fruitless. It can be fruitful only to ask such questions as, 'When X uses the term *mageia* in particular context Y, what does he mean by it, and what is he trying to achieve by it?"[2]

So why has the problem of magic-definition, which is either impossible or trivial, but nothing in between, become so fetishized? Why, given its fatuity, is the magic-definition industry in such rude health? The chief responsibility lies with the New Magic, of which I now offer, in tribute to the elder Pliny, a brief history. The New Magic was the creation of a group of scholars who, over the last couple of decades, have conspired to appropriate the study of ancient magic. Hitherto the subject had resided with scholars of technical skill and profound learning. But these New Magicians, devoid of the same skills, or at any rate falling far short in them, were obliged to establish other credentials to license their entry into the field. This is where the craft of magic-definition and its associated theorizing, that hall of smoke and mirrors, took its rise. This was their great contribution to the study of ancient magic, this marvellous science cobbled together from fragments of philosophy contemptible to philosophers, fragments of anthropology contemptible to anthropologists, fragments of psychology contemptible to all, and the whole of it risible to anyone with an elementary grasp of the nature of language. The great deceased scholars of the Old Magic were accorded the pious veneration that only true successors may offer. Those with the poor taste to remain alive were dismissed as plodders, or more often occluded in silence together with their works, embarrassing madwomen shoved off into the attic.

The combination of weak philology with arbitrary theorizing has been corrosive. It has produced a wholly unsympathetic history of ancient magic that no one in antiquity could have found intelligible, and within which none of the ancients could have located themselves, their beliefs or their own experiences. And so whatever its claim to truth, its value as history is nugatory. But in one regard, it may be conceded, the New Magicians are very much in tune with the spirit of ancient magic as it was practised and as it was conceived. They have come to identify themselves with ancient sorcerers and to project their work on the model of their craft. Their own writings are sonorously cast as offering mystical revelation. But those with the temerity to write without leave in their jealously guarded subject-area are indignantly branded as dangerous trespassers in the field into which the New Magicians have themselves intruded. For their special craft, illusory and insubstantial as it is, does not admit of transmission by rational learning or instruction, but only by a process of direct initiation from master to apprentice. This magic circle of the enlightened, this happy band of itinerant specialists, now affronts the world with volume after volume of conference proceedings spun out of ever more self-reflexive and self-congratulatory *s'entendre-parler*. The hefty, rambling grimoires of the Greek Magical Papyri, deeply layered in meta-magic, are not so far in the past. The study of magic has become, like its ancient practice, a means to power, a power deeply consoling for those fortunate enough to have achieved it, for all that it exists only in their own imaginations.

1

The First Wicked Witches of the West?

At the dawn of the classical tradition: Circe

The first portrait of a witch in Greek literature, and therefore in the western tradition, is that of Circe 'of the beautiful tresses' in Homer's *Odyssey*. The poem is thought to have reached the form in which we have it in around the seventh century BC.[1]

Circe is the daughter of the Sun and of Perse. Odysseus and his companions arrive, lost, on her wooded island of Aeaea as they are attempting to sail back home to Ithaca after the Trojan War. After the men have beached their ships and rested on the shore for two days, Odysseus decides on the third day to explore the island to see if he can discover any sign of habitation. From a craggy vantage point he espies smoke rising from what will turn out to be Circe's house in the distance. Odysseus hesitates about whether to go and investigate, and decides first to return to his companions on the shore and share a meal with them. On his way back a massive stag runs across his path. Odysseus manages to spear it, and then carries the carcass back to the shore, where he and his crew enjoy a glorious meal from it. On the fourth day Odysseus puts it to his men that they must investigate the house if they are to have any hope of finding the directions they need to continue their voyage. The men are stricken with foreboding after their recent encounters with two man-eating sets of giants, the Cyclopes and the Laestrygonians. Odysseus divides his men into two groups, one to be led by himself, and the other to be led by Eurylochus. Lots are shaken in a helmet, and it falls to Eurylochus and his team of 22 men to investigate. They weep as they set off.

When the party comes to the house they find it, to their initial terror, surrounded by mountain wolves and lions, 'which Circe herself had enchanted, for she had given them evil drugs (*pharmaka*)'. But these normally wild animals fawn upon the men, standing on their hind legs and wagging their tales, like dogs asking for titbits from the table. From the doorway the men can hear Circe within as she sings a lovely song whilst working at her loom. One of the men, Polites, heartened by this, encourages the others to call out to her, which they do. She invites them in, and the whole party follows her inside, except for Eurylochus himself, who stays back suspecting a trick. Circe seats the men and prepares for them a potage of cheese, grain, honey and wine, but she mixes into it baleful drugs to make them forget their homeland completely. When they have drunk it down she strikes them with her wand and shuts them into pigsties. They have the heads, voices, bristles and bodies of pigs, but their minds remain unchanged. As they weep in their pens, Circe casts acorns and cornel fruit before them to eat.

Eurylochus rushes back to Odysseus on the shore with the news that the rest of his team has disappeared inside the house and failed to emerge. Odysseus arms himself with his sword and asks Eurylochus to guide him back to it. The latter, in terror, refuses to accompany him, so Odysseus makes his own way. Just before he arrives at Circe's house the god Hermes manifests himself before him in the form of a young man. He tells him what has become of his colleagues, and warns him that the same will happen to him unless he takes precautions. He picks a protective plant from the ground for Odysseus, *mōly*, and this, as he tells him, will defend him against Circe's potage. It has a milky flower and a black root. It is difficult for men to pick, but easy for the gods. He also tells Odysseus that when Circe strikes him with her wand he should draw his sword and rush on her as if he intends to kill her. At this she will be frightened and invite Odysseus to her bed. Odysseus should accept the invitation, so that she will free his companions and offer him hospitality, but he must first make her swear a great oath by the blessed gods that she will not contrive any more evil against him, lest she should render him 'cowardly and unmanly' once he has taken his clothes off. Hermes leaves him and Odysseus proceeds to Circe's door. Like his men before him, he is invited in, seated, and given the same enchanted potage, but to no effect (Figure 1.1). When Circe duly strikes him with her wand and commands him to go to the pigsty to lie with his companions, Odysseus leaps at her with his sword as if intending to kill her (Figure 1.2), but Circe grabs his knees and supplicates him. She tells him that, since he has been able to evade the power of her drugs, she recognizes him to be Odysseus, whose arrival had long been prophesied to her by Hermes. She invites him to bed, so that they may learn to trust each other, but Odysseus compels her to swear the oath before he joins her.

When Odysseus rises from her bed, Circe's nymph-maids heat water in a cauldron, from which he is given a warm bath before being oiled and clothed. They and the housekeeper prepare a sumptuous meal for him, with thrones covered in purple and silver tables laden with golden baskets of food. Honeyed wine is poured into golden cups from a silver bowl. Circe sees that Odysseus has no appetite and asks him why, reassuring him that she will abide by her strong oath not to trick him again, whereupon Odysseus protests that he cannot enjoy his food until she has restored his companions to human form. This Circe does, by rubbing them with an ointment. This causes their bristles to fall out and they become men again, younger and more attractive than before. They recognize Odysseus and grab hold of his hand, lamenting their sufferings in retrospect, and even Circe feels pity. At Circe's behest, Odysseus brings back Eurylochus and the others from the ships to join them in the feast. Eurylochus himself is reluctant at first, protesting that Circe will turn them all into pigs, wolves or lions. Odysseus and his companions then tarry a year with Circe and her luxuries before they bestir themselves to press on with their journey.

Circe now tells them that to complete their journey to Ithaca they must visit the House of Hades, in order to gain directions home from the ghost of the prophet Tiresias. She gives them instructions as to how to find their way there (it is located beyond Ocean at the confluence of the rivers Acheron, Cocytus and Pyriphlegethon) and further tells them how to call up the ghosts once there and keep them under control. Odysseus must dig a pit, pour libations around it to all the dead, with honey-milk, sweet wine and water, and sprinkle barley, then pray to the dead, promising to sacrifice a cow to them upon his eventual return to Ithaca, and additionally a black sheep to Tiresias himself. Right away he must sacrifice a pair of black sheep, a male and a female, turning their heads down towards the underworld, but turning his own head back. Thereupon the ghosts will rise, and Odysseus must have his companions flay the carcass and burn the body to Hades and Persephone. He must use his sword to ward other ghosts from the pit until he has made his enquiries of the ghost of Tiresias.

As Odysseus and his crew make to leave, his youngest sailor, Elpenor, who has been sleeping off drink on the roof of the house, falls off it and breaks his neck. When Odysseus and his men arrive at their ship by the shore, they find that Circe has somehow managed to pass ahead of them unseen and leave there for them the pair of black sheep they will need.[2]

Odysseus and his men arrive at the point to which they have been directed and follow Circe's instructions. But before Odysseus can talk to the ghost of Tiresias the ghost of the newly dead Elpenor butts in, uninvited. His body has not yet been buried by Circe and it still lies in her house unwept. He tells Odysseus what has happened and begs him to return to Circe's island and complete the rites of burial for him, so that he will not become a cause of anger for the gods towards him. Odysseus promises to do this, and proceeds to talk to Tiresias and then to many ghosts of friends and family.[3]

After finishing his consultation of the dead, Odysseus and his men return to Circe's island and duly bury Elpenor. Circe entertains them lavishly once again before sending them on the remainder of their journey. Circe now gives Odysseus directions for completing his journey to Ithaca herself, and that too in rather greater detail than had been supplied by the ghost of Tiresias. After this Odysseus and his men leave her island for good, initially with the benefit of a favouring wind that Circe has contrived for them.[4]

Like its sister-poem the *Iliad*, the *Odyssey* is the final product of a long and conservative tradition of oral poetry, characterized by formulaic composition at the levels of the short phrase and the large narrative episode alike. The poems are thought to have reached their final form, that in which they were eventually to be committed to writing, at some point early in the seventh century BC. Much of the poems' content is of considerably greater antiquity than this, and the world they describe retains a strong, if distorted, connection with that of the Mycenaean culture that flourished in Greece c. 1500–1000 BC, and which is known to us from the archaeological remains of its superb citadels and palaces, and from its palace records in the Linear B script. But some part at least of the poems' content reaches back even into the Proto-Indo-European Age (c. 4000 BC), the age before the differentiation of the languages of the Indo-European family. We know this from the chance survival of what can be seen to be the identical poetic phrase in both Homeric Greek and Sanskrit Vedic poetry, once the sound changes of the respective languages have been taken into account. The *Iliad*'s *kleos aphthiton* and the *Rig Veda*'s *śrávas . . . ákṣitam* are both direct derivatives of the Proto-Indo-European phrase *$*klewos\ n̥d^hg^{wh}itom$*, 'undying renown'.[5]

The *Odyssey*'s long genesis within a formulaic tradition means that many of its individual episodes are structured in similar ways and shaped by similar motifs. The poem's most striking recurring pattern is that of the deceitful and ensnaring welcome of a man or men by a woman, women or a female entity of some sort. A chain of episodes of this type ultimately forms a paradoxical continuum between the charming teenage ingénue Nausicaa and the poem's most terrible monster, the marine vortex Charybdis. These females form very suitable foils for the hero Odysseus, who is himself a trickster amongst men. Circe, with her switchback good-and-evil nature, can be seen to fall somewhere near the centre of this continuum.

At the positive pole of the continuum is the gentle princess Nausicaa. She rescues Odysseus when he is washed ashore on her island of Phaeacia. She bathes him, feeds him, clothes him and takes him to her city. She has been sent to the shore by Athene in hopes of finding a husband, and the succour she affords Odysseus is motivated not least by the fact that he, accordingly, takes her fancy. But she is not without her little deceits. She lies to her father Alcinous about her reasons for wanting to go to the shore in the first place, and then she lies to the Phaeacian public by dissociating herself from Odysseus as she escorts him back to the city. Secondly, Odysseus' wife Penelope is compelled in his prolonged absence to welcome hordes of suitors into his house, albeit very much against her will, and permit them to devour his estate and live well at his expense. But she must detain them there in their multitude if she is to avoid taking any one of them as replacement husband, and this she contrives to do with a distinctive trick. She tells them that she will choose a husband from amongst them when she has completed the weaving – an activity that is in itself particularly associated with deceit and trickery – of a shroud for her father-in-law Laertes. She weaves it in front of the suitors by day, but secretly unpicks it by night, so that the work is never done. She also employs a trick to test the identity of Odysseus, finally returned to her, by asking a servant before him to move the bed that he himself had secretly made immovable. Thirdly, when Helen, together with her husband Menelaus, welcomes Odysseus' son Telemachus in her palace at Sparta, she is the perfect hostess and she provides them with fine food and wine. But when the conversation becomes melancholy, she secretly slips a drug given to her by the Egyptian queen Polydamna into the wine to make the company forget all thoughts of sadness. For all that Helen's action here is benign, a sinister note is sounded: it is observed that Egypt proliferates in drugs, wholesome and poisonous alike. And we may note that even Helen's good drugs make men forget themselves, if only in a small way, as do Circe's.[6]

And so we pass on to more ambivalent and then to more nasty female characters. In the fourth place the nymph Calypso welcomes Odysseus on her island of Ogygia when he is shipwrecked there. She lavishes all luxuries and comforts upon him, sleeps with him and wishes to marry him, but then keeps him with her for seven years against his will by slightly mysterious means that we will discuss shortly, before being compelled to release him by the gods. It is Calypso that Circe herself, whose tricks we have laid out, most strongly resembles, not least as being a beautiful and powerful female, the owner of a private island, and the bed-partner of Odysseus: she can be considered to occupy the fifth place in the continuum. In the sixth place, the mysterious Sirens sing an enchanting song of welcome, inviting passing sailors to come and rest on their island, but the welcome they receive when they turn in is explicitly contrasted with that they would receive at home: the sailors are trapped on the Sirens' island forever by their song, and starve to death. The Sirens sit on piles of mouldering bones. (They are not given any physical description in the *Odyssey*, but in archaic art the Sirens are typically represented as bird-women.) In the seventh place, when Odysseus and his men reach the land of the giant Laestrygonians, the first of the race they encounter is a huge girl. They ask her for directions to the ruler's house, which she supplies, and they proceed on their way. What she omits to tell them is that the ruler, who is her father Antiphates, will also attempt to eat them, and this indeed is what ensues. The most terrible female opponents faced by Odysseus and his crew are, in eighth and ninth places, Scylla and Charybdis. They lurk on either side of a narrow strait the crew must negotiate (in later times the strait was traditionally identified with the Straits of Messina). Scylla is described as inhabiting a cliff-face cave, within which half her body is buried. Twelve legs dangle forth, and six heads project, each with a triple row of teeth, and she barks. In art, in a fashion partly compatible with her Homeric description, she is typically represented as human in form down to the waist, and thence a serpent (i.e. an 'anguipede'), or a tangle of serpents. From her front project six fierce dog-heads. Charybdis, whilst explicitly presented as a female monster, is described as a marine whirlpool or vortex. She sucks men and ships deep inside herself only to spew them out again. Perhaps we should think of her as some sort of massive, abstract, elemental vagina. In classical Athens the name Charybdis was held to be a suitable nickname for a prostitute who bled men dry both sexually and financially. Scylla and Charybdis operate as a deceitful pair. Whilst Charybdis distracts Odysseus' sailors with her swirlings, Scylla swoops down and seizes six of his crew, one with each of her heads.[7]

The Homeric poems can also be seen to preserve traditional material of great antiquity in other ways. Several of the tales told in them resemble tales told in the traditions of the Near East, as is even more demonstrably the case with the Hesiodic *Theogony*, thought to be of a similar final date to the Homeric poems. This does not necessarily mean (a common misapprehension) that the Greeks simply borrowed stories from their Near Eastern neighbours and contacts, but it does show that, to some extent, they participated with them in a story-telling community. The geographical extent of this community suggests that the tales it shared were of considerable vintage.[8]

Circe herself seems to exhibit particular affinities with a goddess type popular in the narratives and the imagery alike of Greece and the Near East, that is, the *potnia thērōn*, 'Mistress of Animals'. In iconography a Mistress of Animals' goddess is shown as a standing figure flanked on either side by wild animals that rear up and fawn upon her, and so express her mastery over them. Archaic images of Artemis often depict her in this way. One Near-Eastern goddess so depicted is Ishtar. In the standard Akkadian version of the *Gilgamesh* epic, which emerged as we know it around the turn of the third to the second millennium BC, Ishtar attempts to seduce Gilgamesh. She promises that the mountain will bear him fruit, that his ewes and nanny-goats will be fecund, and that his other animals will be vigorous. But Gilgamesh rejects her advances, reminding her of the doom that her former lovers have met. She turned a chief shepherd into a wolf, and his own herdsmen hunted him down. She invited the gardener Ishullanu to touch her vulva before striking him and turning him into a frog. Gilgamesh speaks too of the unwelcome varieties of subjection she has inflicted upon the animals she has loved, these too perhaps human in origin: she broke the wing of the *allallu*-bird; she condemned the strong lion to the hunter's pit, and the horse to the whip. Broadly congruent with this is the representation of Aphrodite, Ishtar's sometime Greek counterpart, in the *Homeric Hymn to Aphrodite*. In this text, which is of slightly later composition than the *Odyssey* despite its Homeric attribution, wild animals fawn upon Aphrodite like tame dogs: 'Aphrodite came to Ida of the many springs, Ida the mother of beasts, and she made straight for the house across the mountain. And there followed after her, fawning upon her, grey wolves and fierce-eyed lions, bears and swift leopards, hungry for deer. She delighted in her heart to see them, and cast desire into their breasts, and they all lay together, two-by-two in the shady haunts.' We are told that she takes a human lover, Anchises, the father of Aeneas, only to render him 'feeble' (*amenēnos*). Subsequent sources specify that she rendered him paraplegic. The Homeric Circe corresponds with this goddess-type in three ways. First, her house is surrounded by fawning wild animals (although the animals are only explicitly said to fawn upon Odysseus' visiting companions, rather than Circe herself). Secondly, she transforms men into animals. Thirdly, there is a threat that she may in some way cripple or blight a lover by sleeping with him, rendering him 'cowardly and unmanned'.[9]

Circe (as to some extent Ishtar too) can also and more importantly be located in the context of 'witch'-figures in a large group of widely diffused 'folktales', 'migratory tales' or 'international tales', the roots of which must be rather more ancient than those of the Mistress-of-Animals figure. In his standard *Motif-Index of Folk-Literature* Stith Thompson catalogues precisely 100 principal motifs involving 'witches' (for all that he does not concern himself with any formal definition of the term). Of these around a quarter could be said to be of some relevance to the Circe narrative, with the following fourteen of them being of particular importance for it:

G210	witches render themselves invisible
G211	witches in the forms of animals
G224	witches' salve
G225	witches control animals as familiars
G242	witches fly through the air
G251	witches make soul-flights
G263	witches injure, enchant or transform victims, in particular into animals
G264	witches entice men with an offer of love and then desert or destroy them: 'La Belle Dame sans Merci'
G265	witches cause animals to behave unnaturally
G269	witches cause persons to fall from height
G272	witches' powers compromised by steel
G275	witches overcome by threat of sword
G283	witches raise winds
G299	witches calls up spirits of the dead and cause them to walk on water

Most important of all is a series of international tales in which a witch transforms men into animals until she is overcome by a hero or even a heroine. Thus in a Corsican tale recorded by Ortoli six brothers in turn encounter a witch in a forest who tricks them into putting on a magic ring, turns them into goats and pens them up. Their sister comes in search of them and, advised by a good fairy, declines to put the ring on, kills the witch and so restores her brothers to human form. Circe's name (*Kirkē*) is usually thought to derive from *kirkos*, 'hawk', although nothing is made of any hawkish identity or attribute in the *Odyssey* narrative. Nonetheless, it may be worth noting that the witches of international folktale commonly transform themselves into raptors.[10]

Such then, is the background to the *Odyssey*'s portrait of Circe, but, whatever the archaeology of the narrative or elements of it, it is self-evidently true that it must have been fully meaningful and coherent to its audience at the point at which it reached its final form. With this in mind, let us examine the character and extent of Circe's powers as they are portrayed in the text.

The Circe that this audience met, and which we meet still, is, first and foremost, a woman who works with *pharmaka* (plural; the singular is *pharmakon*). This, the term from which our own word 'pharmacy' is derived, signified in the first instance drugs or poisons, and at some point it came to acquire a more general meaning of 'spells'. Homer gives Circe the summary epithet *polypharmakos*, 'of the many drugs or spells', and her use of drugs or poisons is well demonstrated in her focal trick, that of her transformation of the men into pigs and back into men again. She achieves the first transformation with a potion imbued with baleful *pharmaka*, a wand and a verbal command or spell, and she achieves the second with an ointment made from another *pharmakon*.[11]

Beyond pigs, what is the range of Circe's transformations of men into animals? It is likely that the tame wolves and lions that fawn upon Odysseus' men as they approach Circe's house are also men transformed. That is certainly Eurylochus' guess. Odysseus tells us that Circe had bewitched the animals (*katethelxen*) and given them evil *pharmaka*. In antiquity itself this was apparently understood to mean that Circe had derived the lions and the wolves from men. The alternative, less plausible, explanation is that these creatures are just original wild animals, and that the effect of Circe's *pharmaka* upon them has merely been to tame them, presumably so that she may protect herself, her household and her herds from their depredations. But in that case it is not so easy to explain why the *pharmaka* Circe uses are described as 'evil' (*kaka*). They may, just about, be 'evil' from the perspective of her potential victims amongst wild animals, anxious to retain their wild state, if we can imagine that such a perspective was held to be significant. Or perhaps the term 'evil' should be understood as no more than a formulaic epithet without particular force in its immediate context. But on the assumption that the lions and wolves are indeed men transformed, then the meaning of their fawning upon Odysseus' companions should be interpreted as an attempt to warn them of the fate that awaits them, should they encounter Circe, or as an appeal to them for help in reversing their own transformed state, or even perhaps as an expression of longing for their own lost human forms.[12]

The later tradition at any rate was familiar with the notion that Circe turned her visitors into a range of different animals. Numerous images, mainly on vases, survive showing Circe accompanied by creatures half-man, half-pig. Most of these creatures have human bodies and pig-heads (Figure 1.2, again), but other configurations are occasionally found. Sometimes it appears that the painters are showing us Odysseus' men in the process of transformation and caught between the two forms, but sometimes it seems that the composite form is rather the painter's way of showing us a pig that is a man within. However, some Attic black-figure vases of *c.* 510 BC show a seated Circe stirring her potage and surrounded by men metamorphosing into other forms. On one she sits between two men with asses' heads (Figure 1.3). On another she is surrounded by three men, one with a pig's head, another with a lion's head, and a third with a bull's head (a sort of minotaur, therefore). Apollonius of Rhodes, writing *c.* 270–245 BC, seems to have drawn inspiration from images of this kind. When he brings the fleeing Jason and Medea to Circe's island, as they seek purification for the murder of Medea's brother Apsyrtus, they find it full of beings made up from the jumbled body-parts of different creatures, à la *Island of Dr Moreau*. Apollodorus, writing in the first or second century AD, tells that Circe transformed Odysseus' own men into a variety of pigs, lions, wolves and asses.[13]

What is the purpose of all these transformations? There is no obvious reason in the immediate context of the tale as to why Circe should have transformed men into lions and wolves. And perhaps, paradoxically, this is the reason she is made to do it: it is precisely an act of inscrutable, arbitrary cruelty, which well befits the Circe we first encounter. In this respect Circe initially bears a thematic resemblance to the Sirens, who invite sailors to their island with welcoming song, only to trap them there to starve to death once they have come (and note that Polites is reassured that a pleasant welcome awaits by Circe's singing at the loom). The effect of this characterization is all the more keenly felt in retrospect after Odysseus has challenged Circe and she transforms herself into a welcoming, friendly and humane woman.

Why, more specifically, does Circe transform Odysseus' own men into pigs? Here the answer must be more sinister still. There is only one purpose for which pigs are kept in the Homeric world, as indeed in the modern, for all that it is not explicitly advertised at this point in the text: to be eaten. Circe, then, plans to eat Odysseus' companions in due course. In this way she is revealed to be a close thematic relative of the terrible man-eating giants Odysseus has already encountered on his voyage, the Cyclopes and the Laestrygonians. This point was well appreciated in the medieval age when elements of the *Odyssey* were taken up in the storytelling traditions of the Middle East. They eventually found their way, perhaps via Persia and India, into the stories of the voyages of Sinbad the Sailor in *The Arabian Nights* or *The Thousand Nights and One Night* (*Alf Layla wa-Layla*), as the collection of tales is more properly known. The Sinbad stories are thought to have found the form more or less in which we know them *c.* 900 AD, in the Abbasid period. In his *Third Voyage* Sinbad finds himself stranded on the island of a monstrous giant who gradually devours his way through Sinbad's crew. Sinbad escapes by blinding him (in his two eyes) with red-hot iron spits, before taking to a raft to escape. The wounded giant calls another giant to his aid, a female one yet more horrible, and together they pelt Sinbad's retreating raft with rocks. This tale evidently wraps together quite tightly the Homeric tales of the one-eyed Cyclopes and the Laestrygonians, with the female yet more horrible reminiscent in particular of the latter episode. In the *Fourth Voyage* Sinbad's fellow merchants encounter a race of cannibal 'Magians'. These anoint them with coconut oil and feed them a strange food which both compels them to continue to eat until they are fat and deprives them of their senses, whereupon they are driven out into the fields to be kept as cattle until it is their time to be eaten, either roasted or raw. Sinbad alone holds back and so remains unaffected and so is, in due course, able to escape. This tale similarly wraps up the Homeric tale of Odysseus' encounter with the Lotus Eaters, who feed on the enervating lotus and have no thoughts of doing anything else, with the Circe episode. But in this case there is no attempt to disguise the nature of the eventual fate of the drugged victims.[14]

Given the latent motif of cannibalism, a yet more terrible implication lurks. If Circe did indeed create the wolves and the lions, as well as her pigs, out of men, then we are invited to infer that she has created all the animals on the island out of men. This will then include the magnificent stag killed by Odysseus and eaten with relish by him and his men, who will therefore have been tricked into cannibalism themselves. Was this proud stag once a commensurately stout warrior? And what, furthermore, of all the feasts that Odysseus and his companions go on to enjoy with Circe over the year they remain with her? These are explicitly said to include meat, and indeed it would have been strange if they did not. And this consideration perhaps explains why it is that Odysseus makes such an emphatic point of refusing to touch Circe's food until he has seen his companions returned to human form: he needs to reassure himself that the feast he is about to enjoy is not made out of them!'[15]

So much then, for animal transformations. What of Circe's other powers? Seemingly she has the power of rejuvenation. When she returns Odysseus' men to human form, she renders them younger than they were before. Here it may be worth noting that rejuvenation was a speciality of Circe's sister and that other great witch of early Greek literature, to whom we will turn shortly, Medea.[16]

Furthermore, Circe has either the power to render herself invisible or the power to teleport herself through space, or indeed both. Homer describes the manner in which Circe leaves the black sheep by Odysseus' boat in the following terms: 'But whilst we were coming to our swift ship and the shore of the sea, grieving and shedding heavy tears, Circe in the meantime made her own way and tethered a ram and a black ewe beside the ship, easily slipping past us. For who could see with his own eyes a god going to and fro, if the god did not wish it?' The precise significance of these words is not clear, and they can bear either interpretation.[17]

Circe is also a mistress of erotic magic. This is revealed in Hermes' instructions to Odysseus before he sleeps with her: 'But bid her swear a great oath by the blessed gods not to devise any other evil woe for you yourself, lest she make you cowardly and unmanly when you have taken your clothes off.' These lines seem to be suggestive of the threat of erotic magic, whereby a witch can enslave a man to her by sleeping with him once. As we will see in the following chapter, Apuleius' terrible witch Meroe was subsequently able to enslave Socrates to her and reduce him to abject beggary merely by sleeping with him just once. Apuleius knew his Homer, so his text is more valuable here for offering an implicit reading of the Circe episode rather than for attesting continuity in erotic-magical culture across eight centuries. But we can find further traces of this sort of erotic-magical notion elsewhere in the *Odyssey*: Calypso, the nymph who keeps the lost Odysseus by her side on her island for seven years, is a close doublet of Circe in important respects, as we have seen. The terms in which Homer describes Odysseus' relationship with Calypso may seem paradoxical: 'His sweet life was melting away as he grieved about returning, since the nymph did not please him any longer. To be sure, he would spend the night beside her under compulsion in her hollow caves: she was willing, but he was not.' In what way is Odysseus compelled to make love to Calypso, whom he does not desire? There is no indication of any physical constraint or of any threats on the nymph's part. The sort of compulsion exercised in erotic magic seems to offer the best solution. We have already noted the parallelism between Circe, who traps visiting sailors on her island by transforming them into animals, and the Sirens who trap passing sailors on their island with their enchanting song (and indeed Circe and Calypso too sing their own lovely songs). This also could be seen as a variety of erotic magic, and it was indeed explicitly viewed as such by Xenophon, whose Socrates indentifies the Sirens' song with an incantation, and compares it with love-potions (*philtra*). It has been contended that in the subsequent classical world women's erotic magic against men could be seen as feminizing in effect – i.e., perhaps, as rendering men 'cowardly and unmanly'?[18]

And, finally, Circe is a mistress of necromancy. It is often overlooked that it is Circe that provides Odysseus with minute instructions for getting to the House of Hades, where he must consult the ghost of Tiresias for directions for his journey home. She also provides him with detailed instructions as to how to call up the ghosts once there, and how to manage them once they have risen. And indeed she even provides him with the pair of black sheep he will need to sacrifice within the course of the necromantic rite. This is more than sufficient to render her a mistress of necromancy, much as is the Sibyl who leads Virgil's Aeneas down into the underworld, and Lucan's Erictho who reanimates a corpse for Lucan's Sextus Pompey. But her involvement seemingly goes further still. When Odysseus returns to her island, Circe already knows what the ghost of Tiresias has told him during his consultation, particularly in relation to Thrinacia. Somehow, despite appearances, she has been secretly present throughout the consultation (we know at any rate that she can travel instantaneously and unseen), or has been observing it at long distance. The figure of Elpenor also gives us pause for thought. Why is it that the now proactively helpful Circe should leave Elpenor unburied in her house, with the result that his restless ghost interrupts Odysseus' consultation of the ghost of Tiresias to complain and to bring him back to the island to bury him himself? Perhaps because in alternative versions of the story within the Homeric tradition Odysseus did not get his directions from the ghost of Tiresias, whose prophetic abilities have to be explained a little awkwardly by the fact that he had been a prophet in life, but from the ghost of Elpenor, whose prophetic abilities were explained by the fact that, as unburied, he belonged to the still vigorous, restless dead who wandered between the realm of the dead and that of the living, and could therefore bring arcane information back from the one to the other. Such a hypothesis suggests, in the first instance, that Circe has deliberately left Elpenor's body unburied, so that Odysseus will have a suitable ghost to consult. In the second instance, it suggests that Circe herself – perhaps showing one last vestige of the old heartless, inscrutable and destructive Circe – may even have contrived his death in the first place for the same reason (note again Thompson's motif no. G269).[19]

We should also take note of the magic used against Circe, namely the *mōly* given to Odysseus by Hermes. Whilst this is not part of Circe's own repertoire, it might be considered to reflect it in an indirect way, as Circe's magic is counteracted in its own terms, with a cropped plant. And as we will see, the cropping of plants to obtain their drugs was subsequently to be held to be a defining activity of the witch in general, and not least of Circe's own sister Medea. Theophrastus, writing in the late fourth or early third century BC, identified *mōly* as garlic. The obvious understanding of it is that Odysseus eats the plant as an antidote to the magic potion Circe is going to feed him. In his subsequent version of the story Apollodorus explicitly has Odysseus throw the *mōly* into the potage to neutralize it before drinking it. But it remains remotely conceivable that Odysseus rather wears it as a protective talisman or phylactery. Certainly plants could be incorporated into amulets much later on in the Greek magical tradition. The fourth century AD amulet instruction book *Cyranides*, for example, gives instructions for the manufacture of a ring-amulet to exorcise or avert demons, which involves enclosing a sprig of mullein under the stone, and for another, to bestow sexual attractiveness, which involves enclosing a sprig of rocket under the ring's stone.[20]

For the post-Homeric tradition it was Circe's animal transformations that retained the greatest interest. We have seen the manifestations of this on pots and in the works of Apollonius of Rhodes and Apollodorus. In his *Metamorphoses* of 8 AD, Ovid tells of her partial transformation of Scylla, her rival in love, into the monster we have already met. She turns Scylla's loins into their familiar nest of dog-heads by poisoning the pool into which the girl strides to bathe. Ovid also tells, at length, of

Circe's transformation of Picus, who has scorned her love, into a woodpecker. We must bear in mind Apollodorus' report that Circe transformed Odysseus' men into a variety of pigs, lions, wolves and asses when we contemplate the accounts of what subsequently happened to Polites, the man to whom, in the *Odyssey*, the cautious Eurylochus relinquishes leadership of the group of sailors that enter Circe's house. Writing in the mid-second century AD, Pausanias tells how Polites got himself drunk at Temesa in southern Italy and raped a virgin of the city. The angry locals stoned him to death. This gave rise to a terrible ghost, known as the Hero, who terrorized the city. The people were compelled to build him a shrine and give him the prettiest virgin of each year to be his wife. This continued until Euthymus of Locri fell in love with the latest girl to be offered and ambushed the Hero as he came to collect her, chasing him once and for all into the sea. Pausanias saw a painting of the scene, in which the ghost was portrayed as 'dreadfully black' and as clothed in a wolfskin. This ghostly lycanthropy was, presumably, a lurking vestige of a lupine transformation by Circe.[21]

Circe and the birth of the mage

After reading the foregoing summary and exegesis of the *Odyssey*'s Circe episode many readers may be surprised to learn that the prevailing opinion of Classical scholarship is that Homer's Circe should *not* be considered a witch. The case has been put in its most influential form by Matthew Dickie. With some justice, he regards the ancient concepts of witchcraft and magic as identical with each other, and, a little more contentiously, also as broadly identical with the modern concepts of the same. But he holds that this unitary concept did not crystallize until the later fifth century BC, over two centuries after the Homeric poems are believed to have reached their final form. So, although Circe may look like a witch to us, and although she certainly was regarded as a paradigmatic witch throughout the later Classical tradition, Dickie excludes her from the realm of magic on the ground that the concept of 'magic' was not a category that informed the thinking behind the *Odyssey*.[22]

Now, for Dickie the crystallization of the concept of 'magic' in the later fifth century BC is demonstrated in the following fashion. He assembles a syndrome of activities uncontroversially regarded as magical throughout the remainder of pagan antiquity and shows that they are all attributed already in the later fifth century to individuals described by terms that would later be uncontroversially applied to magical specialists. The terms in question are *magoi* ('mages') *goētes* ('sorcerers') *pharmakeis* ('poisoners', 'spell-casters', male), *pharmakides* ('poisoners', 'spell-casters' or 'witches', female) and *epōidoí* ('charmers'). The activities he holds to be key to the syndrome, which we shall call the 'mage paradigm' may be tabulated (with some additional examples) as follows:[23]

1. **Control of sun, moon and weather.** Herodotus, writing *c.* 425 BC, has Persian mages (*magoi*) and sorcerers (*goētes*) combine to appease a storm by sacrifice. In Aristophanes' comic play *Clouds*, composed in 423 BC, the old bumpkin Strepsiades supposes that he might be able to avoid paying the interest on his debts, which falls due with the new moon, if he can buy a Thessalian witch (*pharmakis*) to draw it down for him, so that he can keep it locked up in a helmet-crest case. (Unfortunately we can tell nothing of the activities of the drunken, man-mad-sow of a witch, *pharmakis*, referred to Aristophanes' fellow comic poet Pherecrates, who seems to have written in the 430s–420s BC.) The Hippocratic treatise *On the Sacred Disease*, written in the late fifth or early fourth century BC, speaks of mages claiming to know how to draw down the moon, make the sun disappear, create bad weather and good, rains and droughts, make the sea impassable and render the land sterile.[24]

2. **Prolongation of life, bestowal of immortality.** In Euripides' *Suppliants*, written, it is believed, *c.* 423 BC, Iphis expresses contempt in a passing reference for people who seek to extend their lifespan with 'drinks and mageries (*mageumata*).' This could be a reference to the curing of fatal diseases or to the extension of one's fated span, or both.[25]

3. **Incantations and purifications.** Gorgias' *Encomium of Helen*, probably composed in the later fifth century (he made a big splash in Athens in 427 BC), but potentially as late as *c.* 380 BC, draws a very strong analogy between rhetoricians on the one hand and mages (*magoi*) and sorcerers (*goētes*) on the other, and he associates incantations that deceive the soul with both of the latter. In Euripides' *Iphigenia in Tauris*, written seemingly shortly before 412 BC, a messenger reports that Iphigenia cried aloud and made an incantation of foreign songs, practising magic (*mageuousa*), as if purifying a murder. Again according to the Hippocratic text *On the Sacred Disease*, the mages offer incantations and purifications against disease.[26]

4. **Initiation.** In Euripides' *Bacchae*, written shortly before the poet's death in 406 BC, the god Dionysus, who seeks to impose initiation on the Thebans, is described as a sorcerer-charmer (*goēs epōidos*) from the land of Lydia and said to introduce wicked and unwholesome rites. The association

of mages with initiation could be taken back a century, if trust could be placed in the puzzling words that the second-century AD Clement of Alexandria seems to attribute to Heraclitus, who wrote *c*. 500 BC. Clement seems to imply that Heraclitus had asserted that 'Night-wanderers, mages (*magoi*), bacchants, Lenaeans and mystery-initiates' were 'initiated into men's customary mysteries in unhallowed fashion'.[27]

5. **Making men disappear.** In Euripides' *Orestes*, produced in 408 BC, a Phrygian slave supposes that her disappearance was due either to the 'spells [*pharmaka*] of mages [*magoi*] or to her being stolen away by the gods'.[28]

However, this same syndrome technique can be used to demonstrate equally well, and indeed actually rather better, that the concept of 'magic' was indeed already underpinning the portrayal of Circe in the *Odyssey*. Indeed the syndrome is more successfully demonstrated in Circe's case because, inevitably, the full range of activities is attributed to a single individual, rather than to individuals ranged under a series of descriptive terms that may in theory at any rate still have denoted rather different things in the late fifth century BC.

1. **Control of sun, moon and weather.** Circe sends favourable winds, first to help Odysseus' voyage to the House of Hades, and then to help him on the remainder of his journey. Whether or not she is able to control the sun, she is able to direct Odysseus, at any rate, to the land of Night where the sun never shines.[29]

2. **Prolongation of life, bestowal of immortality.** Under Circe's instructions, Odysseus has acquired a double life, by visiting the realm of the dead, Hades, and returning from it. We may note that Circe's close doublet Calypso offers to make Odysseus immortal. Circe is also capable of rejuvenation. When she transforms Odysseus' companions back to being humans from pigs, we are explicitly told that they are 'younger than before'.[30]

3. **Incantations and purifications.** Circe's (failed) spell to transform Odysseus into a pig includes a verbal element, the command to go to the sty. And she instructs Odysseus in the prayer he should make to the dead to bring them up.[31]

4. **Initiation.** Circe sends Odysseus for an anticipatory visit to the underworld, the characteristic and fundamental conceit of mystery-initiation.[32]

5. **Making men disappear.** Circe travels invisibly when leaving the black sheep for Odysseus and his men to sacrifice to the dead.[33]

Indeed, it is possible to go beyond Dickie's list and expand the range of activities subsequently regarded as magical and already attributed to 'mages' in the later fifth century with the important categories of the summoning up of ghosts, divination and transformation.

6. **The summoning up of ghosts.** Herodotus strongly implies that the Medio-Persian mages (*magoi*) were believed to be able to call up the dead. When the Persian king Xerxes paused at Troy as he brought his army to Greece for the great invasion of 480 BC, his mages poured libations to the heroes of the Trojan War buried on the plain: 'Because they had done this, terror fell upon the encamped army during the night.' As often with matters of the supernatural, Herodotus avoids committing himself to a final interpretation of this event. He may imply that ghosts actually were called up and that these directly inflicted terror on the army. Or he may mean that the army terrified itself by fretting, perhaps erroneously, that the mages had called up the ghosts. But in either case, it is clear that in Herodotus' mind the summoning up of ghosts was an activity to be associated with mages. (For what it is worth, the notion that Persian mages should have been pouring libations is in itself verisimilitudinous from a Persian perspective: the Persepolis tablets refer to a mage, *makuš*, Irdakurradduš, receiving wine to make a libation for a *lan* ceremony.) In view of this, we may well wonder whether the group of Persian elders with whom Atossa calls up the ghost of the dead king Darius in Aeschylus' *Persians* of 472 BC are also supposed to be read as mages, for all the word is not applied to them; a 'mage Arabos' may, however, feature in a roll-call of the Persian dead. In a passing reference to the lamentations of sorcerers (*goētes*) in the *Choephoroe* of 458 BC Aeschylus may also imply that they had the ability to control the movements of ghosts.[34]

7. **Divination.** Herodotus makes dream-interpretation one of the specializations of Medio-Persian mages (*magoi*), and he has Xerxes' mages obtain some other kind of divination by sacrificing white horses to the river Strymon. In Sophocles' *Oedipus Tyrannus*, probably written between c. 415 and 406 BC, Oedipus abuses the seer Tiresias, whose prophecies displease him, as a mage (*magos*) and a beggar-priest (*agyrtēs*).[35]

8. **Transformation.** A fragment of the anonymous epic poem *Phoronis*, perhaps composed in the late sixth century or early fifth BC, refers to the Idaean Dactyls as sorcerers (*goētes*) in the light of their metalworking. Pherecydes of Athens, whose traditional floruit is c. 456 BC, spoke of them as both *goētes* and *pharmakeis*. Herodotus refers to the people of the Neuri as *goētes* in their aspect of being able to transform themselves into wolves. Hellanicus, writing at some point towards the end of the fifth century BC, may also have applied the same term to the Dactyls.[36]

Again, Circe can be seen to be a mistress of activities in all three of these categories:

6. **The summoning up of ghosts.** Circe gives Odysseus detailed instruction in this art.[37]
7. **Divination.** Odysseus' purpose in summoning the ghosts will be to effect a divination.
8. **Transformation.** Circe transforms Odysseus' companions into pigs, and almost certainly also turns men into wolves, lions and stags.[38]

But we can also point to a further activity that was uncontroversially regarded as magical in the subsequent period, and which is already attributed to the Homeric Circe, but not, as it happens, to individuals badged under the terms in question in the later fifth century:

9. **Erotic attraction.** As we have seen, Odysseus must protect himself against Circe's erotic-attraction magic.[39]

This information is tabulated in chronological order in Table 1.1 (see pages 36–8). Two strong and far-reaching conclusions derive from it. The first is that Dickie's central thesis must be turned on its head. The Odyssean Circe's claim to be considered a witch and as part of the history of magic is not merely as strong as that of the mages of the late fifth century BC, but it is actually stronger. The second and corollary conclusion is even more important. We must not look to the new male magical practitioners of late fifth-century Athens for the first defining template of magic and witchcraft: rather, we must look to Circe. Circe does not retrospectively become a witch because she broadly anticipates the mage paradigm. Rather, the paradigm that she herself offers must have shaped the development of the concept of the mage. In public consciousness at any rate, and perhaps too in actuality, male magic was a secondary development of and a response to female witchcraft.

At last, let us consider the terminology the *Odyssey* applies to Circe. It is true, to put it simply, that she is repeatedly described as a 'goddess' and that she is not described by any of the terms that were subsequently applied to witches or sorcerers. Does this undermine the case laid out here? Not at all. First, for all that the terms 'witch' and 'goddess' both in their own way define supernaturally powerful females, the terms do not belong within the same category and do not therefore inevitably conflict with each other. Just as a mortal woman may be a witch or not, so a goddess may be a witch or not, or at any rate may use witchcraft. The *Iliad* makes the point well with its description of the great goddess

Aphrodite's embroidered band (*kestos himas*), a bra-like erotic amulet which she can lend to other goddesses when the occasion calls.[40]

Secondly, we have in any case argued that the representation of Circe is subject to many pressures and to the forces of many traditions, and that one of the traditions that impacts upon her representation is that of the mistress-of-animals type goddess. We might be tempted to think that Circe is in the process of mutating out of an old original mistress-of-animals type goddess into a more modern, seventh-century witch. But actually we have no reason whatsoever to think that her identity as a witch is any more recent than any other aspect of her characterization.

Thirdly, the fact that the poem applies to Circe neither of the two terms that were subsequently to become the normal ones for 'witch' is not a difficulty. Both these terms are derived from *pharmaka*, 'drugs' or 'spells'. *Pharmakis* is first attested in Aristophanes' *Clouds* of 423 BC, *pharmakeutria* in the title of Theocritus' poem on Simaetha, which was composed in the 270s BC (discussed in the following chapter). If the composers of the *Odyssey* knew the latter word, they could not have used it, because it could not have fitted into the poem's hexameter metre. Metrical considerations alone would not, however, have excluded the use of *pharmakis*. But if the word did already exist in the era of Homeric composition, and there is no reason to suppose that it did, it need never have been taken up into the highly traditional and restrictive set of verbal formulas upon which the epics depended for their construction and propagation.

That said, a strong case can be made that the poem twice ventures to describe Circe in terms that either reach towards or anticipate the term *pharmakis* within the strictures and possibilities of the language available to it. First, Polites describes Circe as 'either a goddess or a woman'. In immediate context this phrase may appropriately express his doubt about the identity of a female whom he has apparently encountered so far only in voice. But more generally the phrase looks like an attempt to describe someone who in a sense straddles both camps, a woman, perhaps, with powers of the sort one would normally associate rather with a goddess. Here it is particularly noteworthy that the characterization of Circe as divine is in fact not completely carried through. We recall that, on Hermes' instructions, Circe is made to swear a great oath by the blessed gods that she will not contrive any more evil against him. Gods do not themselves swear oaths by the gods. Secondly, Circe is described by the epithet, as we have seen, *poly-pharmakos*, 'of the many drugs or spells', which is also built on the term *pharmaka*. It would seem disingenuous to attempt to dissociate *poly-pharmakos* and *pharmakis* in meaning. We may also note the other female specialist in drugs mentioned in the *Odyssey*, the queen of king Thōn of Egypt who gave to Helen some of the drugs produced in that country, which are both beneficial and deleterious. Her name, *Poly-damna*, means 'Subduing many', and is presumably a speaking name descriptive of the powers that are hers by virtue of her drugs.[41]

The emergence of Medea

The greatest witch of Classical tradition was to be Medea (*Mēdeia*), whose name signifies intelligence, and in a way anticipates one of the common Latin terms for 'witch', *saga*, 'wise woman'. We can be sure that Medea too flourished in her role as a witch long before the emergence of the mage-paradigm in the fifth century. However, no early source for Medea or her magical activities in the round survives in coherent form. So, before we reconstruct the earlier traditions about her, we shall begin with a summary account of her career constructed from a range of later, more coherent sources, the first of which is Euripides' tragedy *Medea* of 431 BC, and the most substantial of which is Apollonius of Rhodes' Hellenistic epic *Argonautica* of c. 270–245 BC.[42]

Medea is the daughter of Aeetes, king of Colchis in modern Georgia at the eastern end of the Black Sea, and Hecate, his wife skilled in the use of drugs. She is either sister or niece to Circe. When the Argonauts arrive in Colchis in search of the golden fleece, Medea falls in love with their leader Jason and so resolves to help him. She uses her drugs first to make an ointment with which to coat Jason and his weapons, so that he will be both strong and invincible as he faces the tasks imposed upon him by her father. These tasks are to yoke his brazen fiery bulls and then to use them to sow a field with the teeth of the serpent of Ares. As these are sown, warriors spring up from them at once to challenge Jason.

Medea then uses her drugs against the unsleeping serpent that guards the fleece, so that Jason can steal it. She enjoys a special affinity with the serpent. She casts sleep upon it either by sprinkling the drugs over its eyes with a sprig of juniper, or by feeding it a drink or solid food imbued with soporific drugs (Figure 1.4).

The fleece secured, Medea abandons Colchis to elope with Jason and his Argonauts. Initially pursued by her brother Apsyrtus, they ambush him and murder him, burying him at Absoris. On the return journey to Jason's home city of Iolcus they stop off in Crete where they are challenged by Talos, the bronze giant, either humanoid or bull in form, who guards the island. Medea destroys him, according to the more familiar accounts, either by casting the evil eye upon him, or by maddening him with her drugs. Either way, the bewitched Talos dashes his ankle on a jagged rock and breaks open a vein, from which his animating fluid, *ichōr*, then drains out. According to a third variant, she tricks him into believing that she will make him immortal, and so he allows her to drain out his *ichōr*, in preparation for the rite that she declines to complete.

Back in Iolcus Medea does, however, complete the rejuvenation of Jason's elderly father Aeson, either by chopping him up and boiling him in her cauldron with her special drugs, or by draining his old blood out of him and pumping into his veins fresh blood from her cauldron, infused with drugs. According to some accounts she also applies the same rejuvenation process to Jason himself and to the nurses of Dionysus, presumably in one of these ways.

Medea now embarks upon an elaborate plan to revenge Jason upon the wicked king Pelias, who dispatched him on the dangerous mission to get the fleece and who has usurped his father's throne. She first inveigles her way into the palace by using her drugs to transform herself into an old woman. She anoints her hair to turn it grey. She inserts further drugs into a hollow statue of Artemis and uses it to inflict a frenzy upon all she encounters. She offers to rejuvenate Pelias himself. She gives initial proof of her abilities by washing the drugs from her own skin with pure water. She then offers further proof by having Pelias' daughters (the 'Peliades') help her hack up an old ram, which she then boils in her cauldron with her drugs, until a fresh young lamb – or the simulacrum of one – leaps out from it. This persuades the girls to hack their father to death as he slumbers in a deep sleep induced again by Medea, but Medea then declines to proceed with the rite, or does so but fails to add the critical drugs to the cauldron.

Chased out of Iolcus by Pelias's son, Jason and Medea make their home in Corinth. After some years, and the birth of children, Jason abandons the marriage to marry instead princess Glauce, daughter of Creon, king of Corinth. The scorned Medea, banished from Corinth by Creon as an obvious precaution, sends her rival a wedding dress she has treated with her harmful drugs. As soon as Glauce tries it on, it bursts into flames and devours her. As her father embraces the corpse, the flames engulf his flesh also. In an alternative version, Medea enters the palace herself, after (again) altering her appearance with drugs, and uses a special root to set fire to it, one that cannot be extinguished once kindled. Glauce and Creon perish in the flames. Jason himself she punishes by killing the children they share. Medea escapes from Corinth in a chariot of the Sun drawn by winged serpents.

Passing briefly through Thebes, Medea uses her drugs to cure Heracles of the madness that has descended upon him. After this she moves on to Athens, where she marries king Aegeus. There she perceives Aegeus' returning son Theseus to be a threat to her, and so she attempts to poison him with a cup of aconite. Aegeus, recognizing his son at the last minute, dashes it from his hands. Medea now escapes in a magical cloud and flees on to Colchis. En route she stops off at Absoris, where she delivers the city of a plague of snakes by gathering them together and hurling them into her brother's tomb, where they can continue to live, so long as they never leave it. Back in Asia, she gives birth to Medus, the progenitor of the Median or Persian race.

We can see at once that a tight group of themes recurs here in these gloriously rich traditions: Medea's exploitation of drugs, many of them applied externally (to make Jason invincible; to change her own appearance, twice; to burn up Glauce and Creon); magical rejuvenations (Aeson, Jason, nurses of Dionysus, ram); deliberately botched magical rejuvenations (Talos, Pelias); the infliction or relief of madness (Talos, Heracles); control of serpents (lotion to protect against the serpent-teeth warriors; the unsleeping guardian of the fleece; the chariot of the Sun; Absoris).

This, then, is the figure of Medea that, in general terms, the Greek world knew at least from the early Hellenistic period onwards. But what can we know of the traditions bearing upon Medea in the archaic and early classical period? For all that our evidence here is scrappy and murky, it is cumulatively sufficient to show that certainly by the sixth century BC, and long, at any rate, before the emergence of the mage paradigm in the fifth century, Medea was well established as a powerful woman who used drugs to achieve a range of effects. The evidence for this too is tabulated in Table 1.1.

We find a prototype for Medea, direct or indirect, in the *Iliad*'s intriguing passing reference to a woman with a name built on the same root as Medea's, although she belongs to a different family: '... the warrior Moulios. He was the son-in-law of Augeias, and was married to his eldest daughter, blonde Agamede (*Aga-mēdē*), who knew all the drugs (*pharmaka*) that the broad earth grows.' The prefix *aga-* is merely intensive: Agamede is, accordingly, 'very intelligent.'[43]

The earliest good evidence for Medea proper is iconographic: two Etruscan pots. An amphora of *c.* 660–640 BC is illustrated with a crude but winning image of a large, three-headed serpent being petted or calmed, or perhaps fed (although there is no indication of a bowl or box as in later images) by a woman in a long cloak, which also veils her head (Figure 1.5). And an *olpē* of around 630 BC gives us another woman wearing a long cloak which is inscribed with an Etruscan version of Medea's name, Metaia. Metaia stands before a low, diamond-patterned pillar and waves a short wand with a ring-shaped head over a cauldron, out of which a young man, evidently freshly rejuvenated, pulls himself, levering himself up by its handles. Rather more puzzling in this image is the running file of six young men behind Medea, seemingly carrying under their left arms a rolled-up textile inscribed with the retrograde word or name *kanna*. The first man raises his right arm high, possibly in alarm, or perhaps, advisedly or otherwise, to arrest Medea. The long textile can surely only be a ship's sail, which invites us to think that the men are Argonauts. This may imply, though it need not, that the man rejuvenated is Jason as opposed to Aeson (Figure 1.6).[44]

The traditional *floruit* of the elegiac poet Mimnermus was 632-629 BC. A fragment of his work includes the observation that Jason could not have brought the fleece back from Aea, i.e. Colchis, without the help of a female individual, whose name is not preserved. This almost certainly refers to the help given him by Medea: the Etruscan amphora gives us good reason to think so. At any rate Mimnermus' reference to Colchis under the name 'Aea' forges a link with the Homeric Circe's island of Aeaea.[45]

Medea makes brief appearances in five early epic sources. Unfortunately question marks hang over the dating of all these texts (or the relevant portions thereof), but they are now usually thought to derive from around the mid-sixth century. First, she is mentioned as the desirable wife Jason brings back to Iolcus with him in the Hesiodic *Theogony*. She is the niece of Circe, who is now the daughter of Perseis, and the mother of Medeios. The associated reference to Pelias as hubristic, wicked and violent may imply that she was the agent of his comeuppance, although we are told nothing of the means by which this was achieved. The *Theogony* as a whole is traditionally seen as a mid-seventh-century work, though there is a strong case for suspecting that the mention of Medeios at any rate, whose sole *raison d'être* was to be the ancestor of the Medes, cannot antedate the middle of the sixth century, when this people first came to the Greeks' awareness. Secondly, in a fragment of the *Corinthiaca* ascribed to Eumelus, Medea is a native-born Corinthian who has been summoned back from Iolcus with Jason to become queen. She kills her own children by burying them in the sanctuary of Hera in hopes that they will thus become immortal. This at least has the smack of something akin to a magical operation (we recall that the extension of life is something attributed to the mages of the later fifth century). Thirdly, Creophylus, supposed author of the *The Siege of Oechalia*, is said to have told that Medea killed Creon with drugs (*pharmakois*). Fourthly, one of the few surviving fragments of the *Nostoi* or *Returns* tells us how 'she at once made Aeson into a dear youthful, boy, stripping off his old age with clever cunning, boiling many drugs [*pharmaka*] in golden cauldrons.' Fifthly, Medea and Jason were the subjects of an extended section of the *Naupactia*. Five of the poem's surviving fragments bear upon them, but suggest a series of events in Colchis rather differently sequenced to those in Apollonius, and nothing said of Medea in the fragments happens to bear upon any magical activities.[46]

We are on much firmer ground when we come to a series of pots produced in Athens from *c.* 520 BC. These depict Medea's rejuvenation of a ram by cutting it up and boiling it in a cauldron, in a deceitful display of expertise to the daughters of Pelias. The lyric poet Simonides is said to have lived to the age of almost 90, from 556 to 467 BC. At some point within this lifetime, and perhaps at a period associated with this new flurry of images, he wrote a poem in which he told that Medea rejuvenated Jason himself by boiling him up.[47]

As we move into the fifth century we encounter an important flurry of evidence towards the middle of it, and one which broadly coincides with the first significant evidence for the mage paradigm. First, a beautiful Attic red-figure vase of *c.* 470 BC shows Medea standing with ram in cauldron before an elderly man with white hair. We might have assumed this to represent the deceitful demonstration before Pelias, were the old man not accompanied by the legend 'Jason' (Figure 1.7). He too, then, must have been offered a ram-demonstration before undergoing rejuvenation treatment. Secondly, Pindar wrote his fourth *Pythian Ode* for Arcesilas of Cyrene in 462 BC. This contains an extended disquisition on the Argonautic legend. His passing reference to Medea as the killer of Pelias tells us nothing of how she was imagined to have done this, though the obvious supposition is that she contrived the murder in the fashion already indicated by the ram pots. More importantly, Pindar expands Medea's drug-based magical portfolio for us. He tells us that Medea made up a lotion of drugs in an olive-oil base (*pharmakōsaisa*) and anointed Jason with it to protect him during the tasks set for Jason by her father, namely the yoking of the fiery bulls and the battle with the warriors grown from the serpent's teeth. He also here makes the first mention of an instrument of magic that was to become famous in the Classical tradition, the *iynx*-wheel, a tool of erotic attraction. Paradoxically, however, this is not found in Medea's hands. Rather, Pindar tells that Aphrodite gave it to Jason in order to seduce Medea so that she would help him. Whilst we cannot use this as direct evidence for Medea's own magical portfolio, we may nonetheless take it as indirect evidence for the sort of figure she is imagined to be: Jason seemingly uses corresponding magical means to win to his side a magical specialist, much as Odysseus uses his *mōly* to win Circe. It is an oddity that, for all that Medea was destined to become antiquity's single most paradigmatic witch figure, she was never herself credited in any significant fashion with the performance of the variety of spell that was the most characteristic of witches in general, namely that of erotic attraction. Thirdly, in his tragedy (or possibly satyr play) *Nurses of Dionysus*, written at some point between 499 and his death in 456 BC, Aeschylus told that Medea boiled the god's nurses and rejuvenated them. Fourthly, Pherecydes speaks of Medea's killing of Pelias (method unspecified) and of her rejuvenation of Jason by boiling. It was in the following year, 455 BC, that Euripides produced his *Peliades*. Unfortunately none of the surviving fragments of this play indicate anything about the manner of Pelias' killing in it. Fifthly, there then begins from about 450 BC a series of pots in which Medea is shown using drugs in a different way again, namely to poison Theseus. Perhaps the *Aegeus* play of Sophocles or that of the same name by Euripides coincided with these scenes.[48]

An Attic vase of the [*c.*] 450-425 BC period illustrates Medea's destruction of Talos. Here Talos, of larger than human size, collapses. Jason kneels to remove the plug from his ankle, assisted by a small figure of Thanatos (Death). Behind Jason Medea leans forward, bowl in hand. Almost certainly we have here the first witness to Medea's use of the evil eye against Talos, but it is also strongly indicated that drugs have also somehow been employed in his destruction. This anticipates the version of his death preserved only rather later in the literary record, by the first- or second-century AD Apollodorus, who tells that Medea inflicted madness upon Talos through the medium of drugs (or, perhaps, spells: *pharmaka* once more).[49]

In 431 Euripides produced his famous *Medea*. In this play Medea's magical powers are very much played down so that she can be portrayed as a woman with limited and desperate choices in the face of suffering. But they do lurk, and once again they are powers derived from drugs. First, she tells Aegeus that she knows of drugs (*pharmaka*) that will enable her to cure his infertility. Then she gives Glauce, her rival for Jason's love, a wedding dress which she has impregnated with other drugs (*pharmaka*, again). When Glauce tries it on, it bursts into flame, killing both her and her father Creon when he attempts to embrace her corpse. It is possible that Euripides' play had elements in common with the *Medea* of Neophron, which may (or may not) have preceded it by a few years, but that play's surviving fragments do not happen to address any magical issues.[50]

From c. 415 BC a series of pots puts Medea at the centre of the scene in which Jason takes the golden fleece guarded by the unsleeping dragon. She is shown either with a little casket, evidently one in which she keeps her drugs, or actually feeding her drugs to the snake from a bowl. These images unquestioningly salute the version of the tale subsequently attested in literature in which the snake was drugged to sleep by Medea so that Jason could take the fleece (Figure 1.4, again).[51]

With rare exceptions it is impossible to date the tragedies of Sophocles within his long career, which spanned from 468 to 406 BC. At some points within this period he wrote three tragedies bearing upon Medea. Nothing pertaining to magic survives from the *Colchides* (*Women of Colchis*) or *Skythai* (*Scythian Women*), but his *Rhizotomoi* or *Root-cutters* is of great interest. The three surviving fragments of this play convey a vivid picture of Medea 'root-cutting', collecting her drugs. In the first Medea crops evil plants whilst turning her head away, so that their noxious smell will not kill her, and then, covering her eyes with her hand, drains their cloudy white juice into bronze jars. We are also told that Medea keeps chests (no doubt like the ones she holds in some of the dragon images) in which she stores roots which she has reaped naked, with bronze sickles, whilst crying out and howling. In the second fragment the chorus of root-cutting women, after whom the play is named, evidently a sympathetic group of like-minded supporters for Medea, pray to Hecate of the crossroads. In the third an unnamed male character melts a doll with fire, possibly as part of an oath-taking rite, but rather more probably, given the play's magical context, as an act of erotic attraction magic. Indeed the character is most likely to be none other than Jason himself, using an alternative variety of erotic magic to the *iynx*-wheel to seduce the great witch.[52]

This review of evidence speaks strongly in favour of Medea having been well established as a rounded witch figure long before the emergence of the mage paradigm. As we reach the end of the sixth century, and the point at which the evidence for the 'mage paradigm' only begins to emerge, and that too with uncertainty, we already have in Medea a figure who is certainly known as a general expert in drugs; who is certainly known to have rejuvenated Aeson and a ram with drugs, and almost certainly too Jason; who is certainly known to have killed with drugs and to have sought, at any rate, to extend life; and who is probably known to have helped Jason steal the fleece, either with drugs of invincibility or with drugs that induce sleep. Significant and substantial evidence for the mage paradigm only really begins to emerge with Herodotus, whose work was published *c.* 425 BC. By this time Medea was now certainly known to have used drugs to make Jason invincible, to induce sleep upon the fleece-guarding dragon, to exploit the evil eye, to poison, and to kill by incendiary means. She was also by this time known to have indirect associations with Hecate and with the erotic-attraction tools of the *iynx* and the melting wax doll.

And so the case of Medea, like that of Circe, demonstrates clearly that the witch paradigm flourished long before the mage paradigm, and reinforces the likelihood that the latter was derivative of the former. And this is what the ancients themselves believed, for what it is worth. As we have seen, the Hesiodic *Theogony* implicitly derives the people of the Medes (*Mēdoi*), the people of the original mages, from her son Medeios. A similar argument underlies Herodotus' subsequent assertion that the Medes derived their name directly from Medea after she fled to them from Athens. And no doubt too the fact that Circe was the daughter of Perse (*Odyssey*) or Perseis (*Theogony*) helped to justify in the Greeks' mind the association of mages with the Medes' dominant neighbour-race, the Persians (*Persai*). We may further note that Sophocles seemingly derived the origin of another magical race, the Chaldaeans, whom we shall meet in Chapter 3, from the Colchian Medea too.[53]

Whilst it is possible to trace the emergence of the mage paradigm, the point of emergence of the witch paradigm, which comes to us already fully formed in Homer, is lost in prehistory and the distant roots of folktale, if indeed there ever was such a thing as a point of emergence. But it is not difficult to explain the logic behind the Greek witch paradigm. For the drug-based activities of Circe and Medea represent for the most part an imaginative extension of the skills, crafts and roles traditionally associated with women, used either for good or ill: cooking, nursing and cosmetics. Circe transforms Odysseus' men with the food that she has prepared for them. Medea rejuvenates Aeson, Jason and the ram through the very act of cooking in a cauldron, as if making a stew, and she sends the unsleeping dragon to sleep by feeding it. The ointment that Circe rubs over the pigs to restore them to men and the ointment that Medea rubs over Jason to render him invincible are suggestive of healing salves or massage oils.

Conclusion

This chapter has been devoted principally to the first two great magical figures of the ancient tradition, the two sister-witches Circe and Medea. Both of these women, evidently in large part figures from ancient folklore, derived their powers mainly from plants and herbs. The Homeric *Odyssey* already preserves for us a rounded portrait of Circe and the range of her activities, but the early tradition relating to Medea must be reassembled rather more awkwardly from passing or fragmentary references in early texts and from illustrated pots. What is crucial is that the range of powers and concerns attributed to Circe already in the *Odyssey* matches almost exactly those attributed to sorcerers and to mages, when we first begin to hear about them, in rather scrappy fashion, in the fifth century BC, almost two centuries subsequently. It is apparent, therefore, that the recent fad for beginning the story of ancient magic only in the fifth century BC and with these men is misguided. The developing notions about male mages and sorcerers in the fifth century BC were fundamentally shaped in response to and indeed largely to mirror already well-established ideas about female witchcraft. This may be considered an overdue victory, of sorts, for women's history – should historians of women wish to claim it. It is impossible to know anything for sure about witchcraft and its representation in the age before the Homeric poems (whatever that might be), given that they are Greece's earliest surviving works of literature. But the witchcraft practised by Circe and Medea gives every sign of being rooted in folklore and folktale. It is in the latter that the makers of magic are themselves made.

Table 1.1: Powers attributed to early witches, mages etc.: a summary chronology

Date	Circe, Medea and Witches	Mages and Sorcerers
c. 700 BC	Homer, *Odyssey*: Circe knows drugs, controls weather, extends and renews life, makes incantations, manages a proto-initiation, manages summoning and control of ghosts and divination, changes forms, makes disappear, has the power of erotic attraction. Note also drugs of Polydamna and Helen.	
c. 700	Homer, *Iliad*: Agamede knows drugs	
c. 660–640	Pot: Medea pets/ charms/ drugs three-headed serpent?	
632–629	Mimnermus: Medea helps Jason take the fleece – by drugging the snake?	
c. 630	Pot: Medea (Metaia) rejuvenates Jason in cauldron	
c. 550	Hesiod, *Theogony*: Medea punishes Pelias and is mother to Medeios	
c. 550	Eumelus, *Corinthiaca*: Medea seeks to extend the life of her children	
c. 550	?Creophylus: Medea kills Creon with drugs	
c. 550	*Nostoi*: Medea rejuvenates Aeson with drugs	
from c. 520	Pots: Medea rejuvenates ram in cauldron	
530–467	Simonides: Medea rejuvenates Jason in cauldron	
c. 500		?Heraclitus: mages associated with initiation
c. 500		*Phoronis*: Dactyls as sorcerers transmute forms
472		Aeschylus, *Persians*: Persian elders (mages?) summon ghosts; [mage Arabos/ Magos the Arab]
468–406	Sophocles, *Rhizotomoi*: Medea collects noxious plants. Associated with prayers to Hecate and spells of erotic attraction.	[Sophocles, *Rhizotomoi*: a man – a Jason? – uses doll in erotic magical rite?]

THE FIRST WICKED WITCHES OF THE WEST? 37

Date	Circe, Medea and Witches	Mages and Sorcerers
468–406		[Sophocles, *Tympanistai*: Colchian-Chaldaean-Syrian man]
462	Pindar: Medea renders Jason invincible with drugs and kills Pelias – with drugs trick?	[Pindar: Jason uses *iynx*]
458		Aeschylus, *Choephoroe*: sorcerers control ghosts?
c. 456	Pherecydes: Medea rejuvenates Jason in cauldron and kills Pelias – with drugs trick?	Pherecydes: Dactyls as sorcerers transmute forms
455	Euripides, *Peliades*: Medea kills Pelias – with drugs trick?	
from c. 450	Pots: Medea poisons Theseus with drugs	
c. 450–425	Pot: Medea destroys Talos with evil eye and drugs	
c. 440?		[Xanthus of Lydia: the succession of Persian mages from Zoroaster; their incest and wife-swapping]
430s–420s	Pherecrates: drunken witch	
431	Euripides, *Medea*: Medea cures infertility with drugs, kills with incendiary drugs	
c. 427?		Gorgias, *Encomium*: deceptive incantations of mages and sorcerers
c. 425		Herodotus: mages make incantations, summon ghosts, interpret dreams, make divinations; mages and sorcerers control weather; sorcerers change forms; they are derived from Medea
from c. 425	Pots: Medea casts sleep on serpent with drugs	
423	Aristophanes, *Clouds*: Thessalian witch draws down the moon	
423		Euripides, *Suppliants*: mages heal diseases or bestow immortality
415–406		Sophocles, *Oedipus Tyrannus*: mages as diviners
412		Euripides, *Iphigeneia in Tauris*: mages purify a murder
408		Euripides, *Orestes*: mages make men disappear

Date	Circe, Medea and Witches	Mages and Sorcerers
c. 406		Euripides, *Bacchae*: sorcerers and charmers initiate
c. 400		Hippocrates, *Sacred Disease*: mages control weather, cure disease
c. 400		Hellanicus: sorcerers change forms

Note: references to men – but not mages or sorcerers – performing magic operations, and references to mages or Chaldaeans which are of interest without referring to magical operations, are enclosed in square brackets.

2

Roman Gothic: The Witches of the Latin Tradition

In the background: Hellenistic literature and indigenous Roman magic

Relatively little survives of the Greek literature of the Hellenistic age, which was separated from the Classical world by the career of Alexander and extended to the fall of Egypt's last Macedonian monarch, the great Cleopatra, i.e. 323 BC to 30 BC. But from it we do have two substantial portraits of witches, and these were produced by poets who both worked in the court at Alexandria under the patronage of Cleopatra's illustrious ancestor Ptolemy II Philadelphus. One is Apollonius of Rhodes' portrait of Medea, diffused across the two later books of his Jason epic, *Argonautica*, and which formed the basis for our summary of Medea's career in the first chapter. The second is a fascinating poem, *The Witch* (*Pharmakeutria*) or *The Witches* (*Pharmakeutriai*: both singular and plural versions are handed down), composed in the 270s BC by Theocritus.[1]

This poem takes the form of a monologue by Simaetha, into which elements of magical incantation are integrated. The monologue describes in detail Simaetha's multiple spells to recover the love of Delphis and recounts the circumstances that have led her to make them. Simaetha is evidently a free woman living independently. The setting of the poem is not clear, but some of the names employed in the poem, Delphis and Philinus, may indicate the island of Cos. As she tells us, Simaetha first encountered Delphis as she went out to see a procession for Artemis, and she fell in love with him at first sight. The love had a debilitating effect on her: her heart was stricken with fire, she lost her mind, became feverish and took to her bed for ten days. Her skin turned yellow, she wasted away and her hair started to come out. She did the rounds of all the old women that she knew that were adept in incantations, but, apparently, could find no release. So she decided that she must have Delphis and sent her slave-girl Thestylis to his gymnasium to invite him to her house. He came, and as he stepped over her threshold, she grew rigid, like a doll. Delphis professed, perhaps only as a courtesy, that he had been planning to come to woo her of his own accord, and told Simaetha that she had rescued him half-burned from the fire of Eros. In no time at all they lay down together to make love, and, with hot faces, warmed skin on skin. Thereafter Delphis would visit Simaetha three or four times a day, often leaving his oil-flask with her. But at the time of the poem's action Simaetha has not seen Delphis for eleven days, and now the mother of Philista has come to her with the news that Delphis is in love with some unknown person.

And so Simaetha embarks upon a rite to bring Delphis back to her, with the help of Thestylis. It has many complex elements, which are best conveyed in tabulated form:

1. **Prayer.** The earlier part of Simaetha's monologue partly resembles a prayer. She calls upon the Moon, Underworld Hecate and Artemis, three closely related deities. However, when, in the course of the rite, dogs are heard to bark at the crossroads and so indicate Hecate's approach, Simaetha commands Thestylis to rattle a bronze instrument at once, an apotropaic device by which the women protect themselves from the awful presence of the goddess.
2. **Magic wheel.** The focus of Simaetha's spell is a 'magic wheel', an *iynx*, a metal wheel spun on a looped thread to attract its victim. She repeatedly apostrophizes her wheel with the words '*Iynx*, draw this man to my house', and the phrase comes to serve as a kind of refrain within the context of the poem. The *iynx* may or may not be identical with another whirling metallic object also apostrophized by Simaetha, a bronze *rhombos*.[2]
3. **Sympathetic and part-for-whole burning.** A number of things go into the fire Simaetha has kindled to induce a 'sympathetic' burning desire for her in Delphis' body. She has Thestylis sprinkle barley-grains into it and declare as she does so, 'I sprinkle the bones of Delphis', whilst she herself burns a bay leaf and prays that Delphis' flesh may shrivel in flames like the leaf. And so too Simaetha puts a wax doll into the fire, as she prays that Delphis should similarly be melted by love. Into the fire also goes a bit of cloth from Delphis' cloak: this represents rather a part-for-whole technique. It is trusted that the burning action of the fire on this small part of Delphis' person (in the widest sense) might somehow be transmitted to the whole from which it derives. The bran that goes into the fire is described as a 'sacrifice'.
4. **Further sympathetic techniques.** Other items too are exploited for sympathy. Simaetha prays that Delphis should whirl round at her

door like her whirling *rhombos*. She also prays that Delphis should go crazy with love for her like the mares and the foals that eat the Hippomanes or 'horse-madness' plant in Arcadia and then rave over the hills. Simaetha bids Thestylis knead some herbs whilst asserting that she is kneading the bones of Delphis; this is to be done at his threshold, a common place for the deposition of magical apparatuses.[3]

5. **Love philtre.** Simaetha declares that she will give Delphis a love-philtre on the following day in which the active ingredient will be a powdered lizard. It is not clear whether, in talking of the Hippomanes, she actually has some of the plant in her possession and intends to make a draught of it for him (or indeed to use it against him in any other way).

6. **Erotic separation magic.** Simaetha deploys erotic-separation magic in praying that Delphis should 'forget' whoever lies beside him at present: 'Whether a woman lies beside him or a man, may he forget the person as utterly as they say Theseus once forgot fair-tressed Ariadne on Dia.' Here Simaetha uses two magical techniques. First, she describes her putative rival with an 'exhaustive dichotomies' formula, 'whether man or woman', of the sort found commonly in the curse tablets. And secondly she deploys a historiola or 'mini-story', with a one-sentence narration of Theseus' abandonment of his lover Ariadne. Historiolas will be discussed more fully in Chapter 4. Here we may note that the narrative of past action is supposed, somehow, to leave the impress of its historical pattern of action on the present and the future. However, the inclusion of the qualifying phrase 'they say' adds an intriguing twist to the presentation of the historiola. This kind of phrase is familiarly used in Hellenistic and Latin poetry when introducing deferential and passing allusions to the mythological repertoire, but its use here, while enhancing the poem's poetic sheen, is somewhat undermining of the historiola. For if the historiola is to have any efficacy, then the action it narrates must, surely, belong in the realm of actuality and of certainty, and not in the realm of vague or disputable tradition. We also may note that Simaetha also makes appeal to the force of history, in a sense, by appealing to Hecate to ensure that her drugs are no less powerful than those of the great witches of the past, Circe, Medea and Perimede.

7. **Poison.** If all else fails, Simaetha is determined, so it seems, to kill Delphis, or at any rate bring him to the point of death ('the gates of

Hades') using evil drugs, the power of which she learned from an Assyrian stranger.

Theocritus' text is an ostentatiously and self-consciously literary confection, and this is exemplified not least by Simaetha's allusions to Circe, Medea and Perimede. The name Perimede stands in a similar relation to the name of Medea as does the name Agamede, which, as we have seen, is given by the *Iliad* to a woman skilled in drugs. Whether or not Theocritus invented the name Perimede in this context, he almost certainly held her to be identical with Medea, just as he presumably did Agamede, and so the differentiation between Medea and Perimede on Simaetha's lips is probably a literary joke. Concomitantly with this, Theocritus does not, it seems, set out to document a particular, complete and unified magical rite as might have been practised in reality. Rather, he weaves together a diverse series of love-magic practices that would never in reality have been employed all at once.[4]

The poem thrives, as poems do, on ambiguities, the chief of which is Simaetha's status as a witch, despite the seeming assertion of this status in the poem's titles. In some ways she seems to be an accomplished and expert witch in her own right: such may be indicated by the proliferation of spell-types she employs, and by the confidence with which she issues her commands to Thestylis. On the other hand, she speaks of herself doing the rounds of wise old women for help when she first fell in love with Delphis, presumably not so long before. And in this case her concatenation of diverse varieties of love magic could be read rather as indicative of the unchecked exuberance of the amateur. Her instruction at the hands of an Assyrian master (it is rare, incidentally, to find mention of magical expertise being transferred between people of different gender) could be read either way. The way in which Simaetha describes her own passionate love for Delphis, with reference (repeatedly) to her experience of a feverish burning and with reference to being reduced to a doll-like state, leads one to suspect that she may herself have been the victim of a spell of fire-and-doll-based sympathetic magic made by or on behalf of Delphis. If Delphis' remarks about his intention to come wooing are to be taken as sincere, then he might have prepared his ground this way. Whilst we might be surprised to find accomplished witches themselves rendered the victims of erotic magic, we may recall that no less than Medea herself, the greatest witch of them all, was successfully made the victim of Jason's *iynx*-led love magic, with the help of Aphrodite.[5]

Simaetha's respectability status is also ambiguous. In recent years it has become fashionable to make the reductive claim that she is a prostitute *tout court*, but this cannot be right. The strongest evidence in support of the notion is perhaps to be found in her reference to her friend or associate Philista as 'our flute player', flute-playing being a craft often associated with prostitutes. One might otherwise point to her supposed boldness in accosting Delphis for a relationship, but then, as she herself says, she was overwhelmed by love. And indeed it is noteworthy that throughout her substantial monologue Simaetha speaks only of love and nowhere of money, although elsewhere in Greek literature money is shown to be, unsurprisingly, the principal interest of prostitutes. Moreover, by Simaetha's own account she gave her virginity to Delphis, so whatever her source of income as a seemingly independent free woman before meeting him, it wasn't prostitution. As she says too, she expected him to marry her: 'I am ablaze over him who has made me a wretched, wicked, despicable non-virgin, instead of a wife.' This sentence above all shows how Simaetha's respectability status teeters on the brink: if Delphis returns to her and marries her, she will be fine. If he does not, then she may find her marriage-chances vitiated with others too. In that case her only options for love with others may be in the role of, if not quite a prostitute, then at any rate that of a mistress, and it is in this unresolved crisis that the poem's poignancy lies.[6]

It was to the Greek literature of the Hellenistic age that the developing literature of Rome looked for models in the first instance, and the earliest extant account of a witch at work in Latin literature is in fact directly and closely modelled on Theocritus' poem. This is the similarly incantatory monologue Virgil composed for his own unnamed Simaetha-like figure in his *Eclogues*, published in 39 BC. She seeks the return not of a Delphis, but of a Daphnis, and is aided by a slave-girl now named Amaryllis. Again a range of erotic-magical rites is deployed, with particular focus being given first to a binding rite involving a knotted string of three colours. Then we hear of a pair of voodoo dolls, one of clay and one of wax, cast into the flames so that the first grows hard whilst the second melts. The analogy between the second doll and Daphnis is made clear, and, as in Theocritus, bay leaves and grain are also burned. A historiola is deployed too: the speaker asks that Daphnis be made to resemble a lovesick heifer. She also refers to the power of spells to draw down the moon, a commonplace of erotic magic, but she does not seem to attempt this directly herself (Figure 2.1). Appeal is made again to the precedent of Circe and, via a reference to the magical plants picked in Pontus (the Black Sea), to Medea. Virgil's monologue ends on a more upbeat note than Theocritus'. An unexpected omen from the altar suggests that the spells might be successful, and the terrifying howling of Hecate's dogs as she approaches in Theocritus' poem is replaced by the friendly barking of the household dog Hylax, 'Barker', at the gate, seemingly in welcome of the returning Daphnis.[7]

Undoubtedly Rome will have had a magical culture of its own before it became submerged under Greek ideas and borrowings. Few traces of it remain, but some that do are tantalizing. The ancient Roman law code of the *Twelve Tables*, reputedly compiled in 451 BC, forbade, in the seventh table, the singing of an 'evil incantation' (*malum carmen*) and the charming away of another man's crops (*excantatio cultorum*). If one can trust the story that Calpurnius Piso, writing in the later second century BC, told of the trial of the freedman C. Furius Cresimus for crop-charming, one can understand that this crime was made manifest not by the instantaneous teleportation of crops from one field to another, but by the insidious purloining of the vigour of one's neighbour's crops, so that one's own thrived whilst his failed to do so. Cresimus was acquitted when he was able to demonstrate that the magic he had used to make his crops thrive was none other than hard work. Writing *c*. 160 BC, the elder Cato recorded a cure for a dislocation or fracture. According to his instructions, one is to take a green reed, four or five feet long, split it down the middle, and have two men apply it to one's hips. One is then to begin an incantation until the reeds come together: *motas vaeta daries dardares astataries dissunapiter*. Next one is to wave a knife over the reeds and cut them short with it on both right and left sides. The reed pieces are then to be bound tight around the dislocation or fracture. The incantation is to be repeated on a daily basis. An alternative one is also supplied: *huat haut haut istasis tarsis ardannabou dannaustra*. Some elements of this procedure are of course readily intelligible from a modern medical point of view. The two incantations as preserved were meaningless in the Latin of Cato's day, and probably any other day, though individual words may have feinted towards significance. The unintelligibility of these incantations is not, lest we think it, any guarantee of peculiar antiquity, but the strikingly repetitive series of jangling syllables and sounds from which they are constructed may well be. Indeed, it may well be a guarantee that the incantation derived ultimately from the Proto-Indo-European Age. Repetitive and jangling incantations for the healing of dislocations or fractures are found in several diverse Indo-European daughter languages (for all that the words of these incantations do not share common roots). From Old High German we have the expression *ben zi bena, bluot zi bluoda, lid zi geliden* (bone to bone, blood to blood, limb to limb). From Irish we have *ault fri halt di, féith fri féth* ('joint to joint, sinew to sinew'). From Sanskrit we have *sáṃ te majjá bhavatu sá u te páruṣa páruḥ* ('marrow with marrow should be together and joint with joint'). Even from Hittite we have *hastai-kan hastai handan* ('bone [is] attached to bone'). In the light of this, we cannot doubt that phraseology of this sort underlies Cato's formulas, and that they once specified more intelligibly the reconnection of like part to like part. Nothing comparable survives in the Greek tradition, though the brief Homeric description of the medical care given to the boy Odysseus' wounded thigh gives pause for thought. The *Odyssey* tells that the sons of Autolycus bound his leg and staunched the blood with an incantation: would this too have been of the jangling, repetitive variety?[8]

Latin poetry: Canidia, Erictho and friends

Less than a decade after Virgil's poem, we encounter for the first time in extant Latin literature an example of the variety of witch that was to come to dominate the Latin tradition. These witches exhibit a distinctive syndrome of characteristics. They are typically old hags, wicked, drunken, and they are primarily motivated by their lust for attractive young men. They manipulate poisons, drugs and other recherché magical substances, sometimes in cauldrons. They collect noxious herbs and human body parts, the latter sometimes from the mouths of wolves, with which to effect their spells. They put the gods under constraint. They control the physical environment in large scale, sea and land alike: mountains are levelled, rivers are sent backwards, forests are made to walk, crops are charmed from one field into another. The earth is opened up to release ghosts. They also control the elements and the skies: winds, clouds, rain, sun (and therefore day and night) and moon. The last is also drawn down for erotic purposes. They can shape-shift, most commonly into wolves. The witches are often given a Thessalian derivation or connection. Circe and Medea are projected as their archetypes. Hecate is often cited as their patron. In love poetry in particular the witch is also often seen in the role of a bawd in control of the young prostitutes that are the object of the poets' lust. But here perhaps we should think of bawds being assimilated to witches, rather than vice versa. As hags producing drug-magic in cauldrons, the witches of Latin poetry are the true antecedents of the modern western Halloween-style witch, for all that we hear nothing of crook-noses, warts, green skin, pointy hats, flying broomsticks or black cats.[9]

This first hag-witch is the Canidia of Horace. She was clearly a well-established figure in Horace's repertoire by 30 BC. Her name, suitably enough for a hag, means 'Grey-haired'. She appears in a cycle of six poems distributed across three different books, taking a prominent role in three of them. In the three poems in which she receives only a passing reference, her name is a byword for poisoning: in one Canidia threatens her enemies with poison; in another Horace compares garlic to her poisons; the third poem combines and redeploys the themes of poison and garlic-breath to give us Fundanius running away from an elaborate feast as if Canidia had breathed over it.[10]

The poem in which Canidia first takes a major role is spoken by a fig-wood statue of Priapus. Such statues, with their huge erect phalluses, emblematic of fertility, served to protect gardens and vineyards from birds and thieves. The former they deterred as scarecrows, the latter with their implicit threat of violent buggery or forced fellatio (*irrumatio*). The statue tells how he presides over and protects a new park on Rome's Esquiline hill. This has recently been built over a paupers' cemetery in which the bodies of the poor and indeed of slaves were hurled – inadequately – into mass graves, and bleached bones lay exposed on the surface. In consequence, this Priapus has to deal with an unexpected variety of intruder, the witches who come by moonlight in search of body-parts for their spells and poisons, and the destructive herbs that like to grow in land of this sort. He relates how Canidia came one night, with her elder colleague Sagana, whose name is derived from *saga*, 'wise woman' or 'witch', to practise her magic.

The spell, as Priapus narrates it, seems to change direction and purpose as it proceeds. Canidia arrives in a black dress, girt up, shoeless and with her hair unbound. It was notionally customary for witches to cull their herbs by moonlight in unbound or naked state (as we have seen with Sophocles' Medea), and so the reader is perhaps at first invited to infer that this is her purpose. But though she does indeed begin to dig up the earth with her fingernails, it transpires to be for a different end. The women make a pit into which they pour blood from a lamb jugulated with their own teeth. Their goal, rather, is to make an offering to the ghosts of the dead so that they can receive, as we are told, necromantic divinations from them. But then the spell now mutates again into an erotic one, presumably one that will be powered by the ghosts summoned up. The witches draw forth a pair of dolls, familiar accoutrements of erotic magic, a larger woollen one and a smaller wax one. The larger doll is made to dominate the smaller one, which is given a suppliant pose, and which is evidently emblematic of the person to be seduced. It is eventually cast into a fire to melt, so that its victim may burn with sympathetic desire. They invoke Hecate and another underworld power, the Fury Tisiphone. The dogs and snakes associated with them manifest themselves. They turn the moon blood-red and draw it down: Priapus jokes that it is trying to hide its embarrassment behind the remaining tombs. The women converse with the ghosts, and make mournful, shrill noises of the sort normally associated with ghosts themselves: evidently, they address them in their own language. Finally, they also deposit in the ground some further magical equipment of obscure purpose, a wolf's beard and a snake's tooth.

Priapus goes on to tell how, having observed all this, he belatedly returned to his task of aversion. He let out a violent fart by splitting the fig-wood of his buttocks. The two women ran off in terror letting everything fall, and not just their magical equipment. Left behind alongside their herbs and 'enchanted bonds' – binding-curse materials or perhaps amulets – are Canidia's false teeth and Sagana's outmoded wig.[11]

The second poem in which she stars presents Canidia in a yet more ghastly light. She is now accompanied not just by Sagana but also by Veia and Folia. Here she is described as Fury- or Gorgon-like, and as keeping small vipers in her unkempt hair. Sagana's hair is spiky like a sea urchin or the bristles of a wild boar, perhaps cropped short for her wig. When Horace tells us that Folia has a masculine sex drive, he may mean that her preference was for women, but it is more likely that he is referring to her vigorously active pursuit of (male) lovers. In an imprecation made to Night and Diana (i.e. Hecate), whilst gnawing her untrimmed thumbnail with her blue tooth, Canidia lets us know that her previous love potions have so far failed to compel Varus to her bed. This is despite the fact that she has used the poisons Medea herself used against Creon and Glauce, and despite the fact that she has searched out every root, however much concealed. She speculates that he has been delivered of her spells by a more knowledgeable rival witch. But now she is preparing a much more terrible draught. The four witches have stolen a young boy. They dig a hole in the ground inside a house, perhaps therefore within its peristyle, strip the boy and bury him in it up to his chin. Then, twice or three times a day they lay out a feast before him, just beyond the reach of his lips. The purpose of this is to starve him to death in such a way that his body becomes suffused with longing. When he is dead, they will dry out his bone marrow and his liver, and powder them to form the basis of a love potion, which will accordingly imbue Varus, the young man who is the object of Canidia's desire, with a burning longing for her. In drinking it Varus will, it may also be noted, be rendered cannibal (as Odysseus perhaps was by Circe). The trapped boy, now on the point of death, finally abandons his pleas for release and lays a curse of his own upon the women. The curses of the dying were regarded as particularly powerful, since they could be enacted directly by the curser's ghost as it was released. (The effect of the dying curse of Virgil's Dido upon Aeneas was particularly terrible, and ultimately culminated in the Hannibalic war.) The boy declares that as a ghost he will attack Canidia and her fellows in the night, bringing (the real) Furies along with him. He will tear frenziedly at their faces with his curving nails and deprive them of sleep through terror. A crowd will stone them in the street, and their bodies, unburied, will be scattered by wolves and birds. We are told that the witches have themselves been burning in their rites bones snatched from the mouths of ravening dogs (we will say more of this below): in their own death, we may conclude, Canidia and her colleagues will provide magical material for others of their own kind.[12]

The association of child-sacrifice – at any rate within the literary world – with magic was commonplace, as we shall see in the final chapter. But more germane to the immediate context, an epitaph of the 20s AD from Rome has been thought to offer credible and independent testimony to the reality of the sorts of practices described by Horace in his poem 50 years earlier. In this inscription Livia Julia, i.e. Livilla, the wife of Drusus, son of the emperor Tiberius, laments the loss of her three-year-old slave-boy Iucundus, the son of Gryphus and Vitalis. In the epitaph, as often in funerary inscriptions, the boy is imagined to speak on his own behalf: he tells that he was snatched away by the cruel and harmful hand of a witch (*saga manus*) and exhorts other parents to guard their children well, lest grief of this magnitude implant itself in their breasts too. If one wished to play detective, absurdly, of course, at such remove, one might wonder whether the witch's hand that snatched away Iucundus did not belong to the woman who had easiest access to him and fullest power over him, namely Livilla herself. For she was soon to be executed in AD 31 on the charge of having poisoned her husband

Drusus in AD 23. More soberly, we might think that Livilla sought to account for her slave-boy's otherwise unexplained disappearance by appeal to the imaginary world constructed by court poets of the generation before.[13]

In Canidia's third major appearance Horace portrays himself as exchanging speeches with her. First he addresses her. He presents himself as one who has formerly been a doubter of her magical abilities (such doubt is not actually evident in any extant poem), but has now been convinced, because he experiences the effects of her magic. An erotic binding spell has been depriving him of sleep and rendered him prematurely aged. His lungs are permanently tight and he cannot breathe. He burns more than Heracles when his wife Deianeira soaked his shirt in the Hydra-poisoned blood or semen of the centaur Nessus in a misfired attempt at an erotic spell. All these are clear signs that he is the victim of erotic magic, and this, of course, has been shown to be Canidia's principal concern in the other poems. It is not clear in whose favour Horace's desire has been compelled. By default, we may think Canidia herself. She is not shown to use her powers for anyone else's benefit in the other poems. Horace begs to be released at any cost, citing the precedent of Circe's reversal of her spell over Odysseus' sailors. He offers, by way of payment, to recant in new poems the slanders he has made against her in his previous poetry: he will declare that she is chaste and honest, generous and kind. The implication is that he has been saying the opposite. He will also declare that Pactumeius is her blood son. The implication is that he has previously declared him to be suppositious. But Canidia will not be placated. She declares rather that Horace will be made to die in slow agonies for his mockeries, agonies that he will not be able to cut short by suicide. This, she declares, will be an easy accomplishment for one who can animate wax effigies, draw down the moon by incantations, raise up the cremated dead and blend love potions (the declaration more or less resumes the activities attributed to her in the Priapus poem). To some extent Canidia is made to project Horace himself as a rival sorcerer: she brands him the 'high priest of Esquiline sorcery (*veneficium*)'. This allegation plays on the affinities between song and magical incantation, but also reminds us that the slander that Horace confesses (albeit ironically) to have doled out against Canidia is itself a cherished technique of ancient magic: magicians slander their victims before the gods with allegations of blasphemy, and each other before the public. The contention that one's specific activities or one's career in general had been compromised by the malice of a professional rival was a useful way of accounting for the failure of one's own spells without bringing into question the general integrity of the magical arts.[14]

As we have seen, the figure of Canidia blossoms in the Latin tradition without any extant or identifiable precedent. Whence did Horace derive his inspiration? Some, in antiquity at any rate, were inclined to find a historical figure behind Canidia. Horace's ancient commentators tell us that she was based on a Neapolitan perfume-seller and witch, Gratidia. It is implied, thereby, that the name 'Canidia' functions as a sobriquet that matches the general shape and metrical pattern of 'Gratidia', much as a generation before Catullus had famously written about Clodia under the soubriquet of 'Lesbia'. The connection with Naples seems to have been based on nothing more than the obscure reference to that city in the boy-sacrifice poem, despite the fact that it is made in connection rather with Canidia's colleague Folia, who is herself said to come rather from Ariminum (Rimini), far distant from Naples. Whether there ever was any such Gratidia, from Naples or anywhere else, must remain extremely doubtful.[15]

It is more important to locate Canidia's literary rather then her historical precedents, but in this respect too she is difficult to pin down. We can construct only limited links for her with Simaetha and the corresponding spell-maker of Virgil's *Eclogues*, but one thing these portraits do notably share is the feverish concatenation of diverse erotic-magical spell types. But whence derived the notion of the witch as hag? No extended portraits of hag-witches come down to us from Hellenistic literature, but the literature of this age did work with a concept of witches who were old women at least, and whose specializations included matters of love, as we can see from Simaetha's reference to her visits to old women to find a cure for her obsessive love for Delphis. A Hellenistic prototype may also underlie Lucian's brief second-century AD portrait of an old Syrian woman who deals in love spells (see Chapter 3). Hellenistic portraits of elderly witches may have had something of the feel of the portrait of the old bawd Gyllis by Theocritus' contemporary Herodas (although there is no suggestion that Gyllis is herself involved with witchcraft). But Canidia's gothic cruelty and morbidity has a very Roman colour, and the precedents for this colouring, if there were any, doubtless lay rather in the lost traditions of Rome and early Latin literature. This colouring remains common in the later Latin portraits of witches, as is perhaps demonstrated most graphically of all in the case of Lucan's portrait of Erictho.[16]

Lucan died in AD 65 leaving his epic on the civil war between Caesar and Pompey, *Pharsalia*, unfinished. One of the most striking scenes in this poem falls in its sixth book, set in Thessaly, the notorious home of witchcraft in Greece, where Sextus Pompey, the son of the great commander, turns to Erictho, the local mistress of the art, for a prediction of the war's outcome. Lucan's portrait of Erictho is the most elaborate, overblown and gloriously horrible portrait of a witch in classical literature.[17]

After an extended general disquisition on the subject of the Thessalian witch, Erictho herself is introduced as the most terrible of all the Thessalians. She has a particular affinity with death and the dead, specializing in the manipulation of the latter. She is on good terms with the gods of the underworld, and hears their converse. Her homes and workplaces are those of the dead. She lives in tombs and performs her rites in a cave that is itself actually an entrance to the underworld. Like the famous entrance at lake Avernus in Italian Campania, it is shrouded by a canopy of dark, light-excluding trees, and these are themselves cave-like in turn. The cave's stifling air is compared to the other famous underworld entrance at Tainaron. This is accordingly an environment into which the lords of the underworld feel comfortable in releasing ghosts for Erictho to manipulate. Erictho herself, quite appropriately, resembles the dead that are her intimates, a common conceit in the representation of those who deal with ghosts in antiquity: her face exhibits a foul and wasted decay and a 'Stygian' pallor, and her hair is matted, as that of the dead is typically envisaged to be. Like Canidia, she also resembles those other denizens of the underworld, the Furies, when she dons a parti-coloured garb of the sort they wear and ties her hair back with vipers, as she gets down to work.

With her spells Erictho brings the living to their death before their time, whilst, in macabre fashion, bringing the dead back to life. This she does not only by calling up ghosts for cursing or divination, but also by retrieving the body-parts of corpses for use in her magical operations. Body parts will serve as tools for engaging the action of the ghosts associated with them. She snatches the burning bones of babies from their funeral pyres. She opens stone sarcophagi to pluck out desiccated eyeballs and gnaw off fingernails. When invited to a funeral, she will take the opportunity to gnaw bits off the corpse's face whilst pretending to smother it in kisses. At the same time she will prise open the corpse's mouth, and by muttering into it she can send orders down to the underworld ghosts. The hanging bodies of executed criminals offer particularly rich pickings. In a memorable vignette we are told how she detaches a needed muscle from a suspended corpse by gripping it in her teeth and hanging her body-weight off it. The gore scraped from a cross, and the crucifixion nails caked in it, are also prized. Those efficacious fragments of the True Cross so prized in the medieval world are intriguingly anticipated. It was useful to be able to harness for magical purposes the peculiarly vigorous ghosts of those restless because denied due burial rites. The symbolic opposite of the bestowal of due burial rites was the casting out of a corpse to be eaten by the dogs and the birds. Accordingly, for magical purposes, the most valued body-parts were those snatched from the mouths of wild creatures. Hence, we are told, Erictho sets up camp beside exposed corpses and waits for the animals to arrive. As soon as the wolf has taken a limb she will snatch it from its mouth, before the poor creature has even had the chance to salivate. She will also manufacture corpses and ghosts of her own when the occasion calls for it. She lays still-quivering human entrails on an altar. Pregnant women are cut open so that their foetuses too can be cast into altar flames. The notion that witches deployed foetuses in their rites may dimly refract the murky trade of the female abortionist. We are given a picture of the results of such collecting in Apuleius' subsequent description of his witch Pamphile's workshop or laboratory. It contains every sort of spice, metal tablets with undecipherable inscriptions, preserved pieces of shipwrecks (the dead of which cannot achieve due burial), and body parts of all kinds, even from bodies that have already been buried: noses, fingers, pieces of flesh still clinging to crucifixion nails, gore and mutilated skulls, these twisted from the jaws of wild animals. No doubt we are to imagine that Erictho retained similar stores in her tomb-home or her cave.[18]

As we first encounter Erictho she is, we are told, devising a new kind of spell: a spell to retain the fighting of the civil war in her local territory, so that she can harvest a plentiful supply of corpses from it. This appears to be a (parodic) inversion of a more intelligible spell-type designed rather to avert war. The soldier-corpses will be particularly valuable as falling into two of the chief categories of restlessness: in many cases they will be unburied, but also, in all cases, they will be dead by violence. The corpses of the slain 'princes' themselves, Caesar and Pompey, promise to be particularly efficacious.[19]

But when the witch first speaks in response to Sextus' request for divination, we are given an impression of her strongly at odds with her gruesome build-up. She is flattered that her reputation has preceded her, and charmingly touched by Sextus' approach. And thereafter she is projected as a skilled and competent professional, kindly reassuring and keen to help her client. After laying out the capacities and limitations of her art, she explains that the obvious method to adopt is to reanimate for necromantic divination one of the corpses that lie out on recent battlefields. A reanimated body can speak in a plain and intelligible human voice, whereas a ghost summoned back independently of its body can only make the indistinct bat-like squeaking that ghosts had been imagined to make since the time of Homer.

And so she wanders out across a battlefield to select her victim. Helpfully, the wolves and the vultures are already at work on the corpses, and so have endowed them with the most sought-after form of burial deprivation. Their ghosts will, accordingly, be particularly vigorous and exploitable for magical purposes. The creatures flee before her as she arrives. She pokes the bodies about to test the qualities of their innards. The Pompeian soldier she selects, interestingly, has a cut throat. A cut throat may seem an unpromising quality for a corpse from which one wishes to press speech. But it may be that Erictho makes such a choice the better to demonstrate the extent of her power. Or it could be that the choice pays tribute to the practical-magic technique prescribed in the Greek Magical Papyri of deriving divinations from decapitated skulls (of which more in Chapter 4). Erictho throws a noose round the already compromised neck, and drags the corpse off to her cave to begin the rite. She opens up the chest with additional wounds and rinses the innards in seething blood. She then pours in moon-juice into which she has blended, in addition to her poisons, a range of ingredients that combine the theoretically possible, if bizarre, with the fantastically impossible: the foam of a rabid dog, lynx guts, hyena hump, bone marrow from snake-fed deer, ship-stopping fish (*echenais*), snake-eyes, eagle-incubated stones, Arabian flying snakes, pearl-guarding Red Sea vipers, Libyan horned-snake slough, and phoenix ashes.

Then she begins her incantation. This starts with a cry that combines a range of animalian noises, dog-barks, wolf-howlings, screeches of the screech owl and snake-hissing, with the sounds of waves dashing on rocks, woods rustling and thunder-claps. She then invokes, in what is described as a 'Thessalian spell', a protracted range of underworld powers, including Furies, Poenae (the personified 'Punishments' of the dead), Chaos, Hades, Styx, Elysium, Persephone, Hecate, Aeacus, Fates and finally Charon, whom she wryly describes as having been reduced to a worn-out old man by having to ferry so many of the dead back across the Styx in response to her own ghost-summoning spells. She pleads that she has earned a hearing with them through her criminality, which includes cannibalism and baby-sacrifice. Finally, she proceeds to her specific request: the return of the soul of the Pompeian soldier recently killed. This, she claims, should be an easier task than the return of a soul long dead and buried in the recesses of the underworld. Her mouth is foaming as she completes her incantation.

The incantation opens up clefts down into the earth, through which the ghost of the soldier returns as it continues and stands beside her (the notion that Erictho's cave is itself a sort of underworld entrance seems to have been laid aside). But the ghost refuses, in its fear, to re-enter the mangled corpse. Erictho lashes the corpse with a live snake and barks a further incantation down to the underworld through the clefts. This incantation, a more powerful one made up of angry threats to the underworld powers, constitutes what the Greek Magical Papyri term a 'second spell'. She tells the Furies Tisiphone and Megaera to harry the soul through the underworld with their whips (oddly, perhaps, since Erictho has seemingly already succeeded at least in withdrawing the soul from the underworld). She threatens them that she will turn the tables on them and subject them to the harrying pursuit they characteristically inflict on others – a fitting enough threat for the Fury-like Erictho. Comically, she threatens Hecate that she will reveal her to the gods above without her make-up on. She threatens to reveal the Mysteries of Persephone. She threatens Hades that she will open up his dark realm to the sun and blast him with daylight. Finally, she utters the most terrifying threat of all, to unleash upon the underworld gods their own underworld god, lord of a more terrible underworld below their own, a figure known as Demogorgon in other texts.

The second spell is immediately effective. The soul returns to the corpse, and its congealed gore warms up and flows through the veins again. The chest heaves and the limbs quiver. The corpse stands upright, in the most symbolic gesture of the return to life. But, stiff with rigor mortis, it does not clamber to its feet using all its limbs. Rather, it rises up directly onto its feet without bending. We are put in mind of the striking scene in F.W. Murnau's classic expressionist horror movie of 1922, *Nosferatu*, in which the Dracula figure, Count Orlok, rises from his coffin in the ship's hold as if hinged at the heels. The corpse's eyes stare open, its mouth forms a rictus grin, and the soldier returns not to a state of full life, but to the intermediate phase of dying. Erictho addresses him, and again we get a glimpse of the woman's paradoxically decent side. She reassures him that if he gives her a sure answer (in contrast with the notorious ambiguities of the Delphic oracle) to her questions, she will use her spells to put his soul beyond all accessibility to magical exploitation in the future. She then uses a spell, otherwise undescribed, with which she confers knowledge on the ghost. This is curious, and seemingly negates the fundamental tenet of necromantic divination, namely that the dead are inherently possessed of a special wisdom. The gloomy corpse weeps and responds. His prophecy, as typical of the ancient dead, is itself one of death. Indeed, he prophesies doom on all sides, noting that if Pompey is to die first, Caesar's additional span of life will be but brief. So all that is really at stake is which of the two generals will be buried by the Nile (i.e. Pompey) and which by the Tiber (i.e. Caesar). After delivering his prophecy the corpse falls silent, but with a reproachful expression asks to be returned to the state of death. Erictho is as good as her word. She builds a massive fire and marches the dead man into the flames, and so ends the divination.[20]

This is the most elaborate account of a necromantic rite to come down to us from ancient literature, and it is the earliest account of a reanimation necromancy of any kind, although we may well suspect that scenes of this type were already well established when Lucan wrote.[21]

Georg Luck has the intriguing insight that the Erictho episode may have been an inspiration for Mary Shelley's Gothic classic of 1818, *Frankenstein*, her future husband, Percy Bysshe Shelley, being an ardent admirer of Lucan. He may well be right, but the nature of the link is probably not what those more familiar with movie Frankensteins may imagine. Whilst the stiff and semi-robotic reanimation Lucan describes anticipates rather wonderfully favourite movie sequences with Boris Karloff and Christopher Lee, the novel leaves the actual awakening of the eight-foot-tall monster almost unnarrated: we hear only of the creature opening its dull, yellow eye, breathing hard and agitating its limbs in a convulsive motion. More suggestive correspondences are to be found elsewhere: in the boy Frankenstein's initial fascination with the raising of ghosts and devils; in his raiding of graves, charnel-houses, dissecting rooms and slaughter-houses to find the parts (presumably including animal parts) from which to construct his monster; in the monster's final assertion that he will destroy himself by building a pyre and walking into it; and indeed in Mary Shelley's retrospective introduction, penned in 1831, which describes the musings that led to the framing of the novel with the phrase 'perhaps a corpse would be reanimated'.[22]

Latin novels: Meroe, Panthia and others

The witchcraft found in Latin poetry shares its morbid and gruesome character with that found in the Latin novels. It can be seen that the witchcraft material in novels at any rate is strongly grounded in the folktales and folklore of Roman culture, and this may well have had some effect also on the poetic treatments.

Two of the most engaging tales of witchcraft and related phenomena to have come down to us from the Roman world are to be found in the *Satyricon* of Petronius. Petronius was Nero's 'Arbiter of Elegance', his advisor in taste, but he was compelled to suicide by the emperor in 66 AD. His once massive novel survives only in fragments, the most substantial of which is that narrating the splendid 'Dinner of Trimalchio'. This describes the lavish but ridiculous dinner laid on by the nouveau riche ex-slave Trimalchio for his fellow-freedmen guests. In the midst of these garish entertainments, Niceros and Trimalchio himself exchange a pair of fantastic tales.[23]

First, Niceros tells a tale from when he himself was still a slave. He was keen to go to visit his lover, Melissa of Tarentum, after her husband, Terentius the innkeeper, had died, and he persuaded his master's house-guest, a brave soldier, to make the trip with him. They set off before dawn, and the moon – presumably a full one – was shining like the sun. As they passed through a cemetery the solider went off to relieve himself against a tombstone, whilst Niceros occupied himself by singing and counting the stones. When he looked back at his companion, he discovered that he had taken all his clothes off and laid them down beside the road. He urinated in a circle around the clothes and suddenly became a wolf, howled and ran off into the woods. When Niceros had recovered from the shock he went to pick up the man's clothes, only to find that they had been transformed into stone. He ran off in terror to his girlfriend's house, sword drawn and hacking at the ghosts he imagined to be surrounding him. When he arrived, in a state of nervous exhaustion, Melissa told him that a wolf had just got into her flocks and begun to slaughter them, but her slave had managed to drive a spear into its neck before it escaped. Niceros was so disturbed by this that he could not sleep, and when it had become fully light he ran back home again. When he came to the place where the soldier's clothes had been turned to stone, he found it full of blood, and when he finally got home he found the soldier laid out in bed with a doctor tending to his neck. He realized that the soldier was a werewolf or, more literally, a shape-shifter (*versipellis*), and thereafter he could no longer bring himself to break bread with the man.[24]

In the wider tradition werewolves tended to straddle the divide between sorcerers and ghosts, and could be regarded as a subcategory of either. As to the former, here in Petronius' tale the werewolf evidently has a strong if undefinable relationship with the ghosts of the cemetery. The terrible ghost of Polites, who demanded the sacrifice of beautiful virgins to himself at Temesa, would appear dressed, somehow, in a wolfskin, and bearing, it seems, the name Lycas, i.e. 'Wolfy', as we saw in the first chapter. We may recall also the important role wolves could play in enhancing the restlessness and vigour of ghosts by mauling the bodies of the dead. As to the latter, Herodotus speaks of the Neuri, a race he believes may be sorcerers, and reports the tradition that they each turn themselves into wolves for a few days each year.[25]

Why does Niceros' soldier turn his clothes into stone with his urination-spell? Presumably to stop them being stolen. The elder Pliny's discussion of Arcadian werewolf lore, probably written around the same time as Petronius' novel, as it happens, seems to suggest that a werewolf's recovery of the clothes he has disrobed himself of at the point of transformation may play a critical role in his return to human form. It may be that without access to the clothes, symbolic of his humanity, the werewolf cannot recover his human shape. The point is made in an Aesopic tale, probably composed in the imperial period, in which a thief contrives to rob the innkeeper with whom he is lodging of his fine new cloak by pretending to be a werewolf. The thief sits beside the innkeeper, yawns and howls like a wolf. When the innkeeper asks him what he is doing, the thief replies that whenever he yawns three times, he becomes a man-eating wolf, and asks the innkeeper to look after his clothes, whereupon he yawns a second time. The innkeeper gets up to run away in terror, but the thief lays hold of the innkeeper's cloak, begging him to take his clothes for him, so that he does not lose them, and begins to yawn a third time. At this the innkeeper abandons his cloak to the thief in order to make good his escape. Here the thief presumably begs the innkeeper to take his clothes specifically to invoke the known lore that the werewolf must keep his clothes safe if he is to be able to recover his human form.[26]

Next Trimalchio tells a tale from a time when he himself too had been a slave-boy. His master's favourite slave-boy had died, and his mother and the rest of the household were lamenting over him in the house. Suddenly the witches (*strigae*) started to screech round about. The household included a tall, daring and strong Cappadocian slave. He drew his sword and ran out of the house to confront the witches. He managed to run one of them through the middle and a groan was heard, although nothing was seen. The big man returned within and threw himself down on the bed. His whole body was black and blue, as if he had been beaten by whips. When the other slaves had closed the door and returned to their mourning, the dead boy's mother discovered that his body had been stolen and replaced with a straw doll. As to the big man, he never did recover, but he went mad and died a few days later.[27]

The effectiveness of this tale lies in the way it is able to convey the mysterious invisibility of the witches and their activities, not least their theft of the boy's corpse, accomplished not only whilst the attention of the household slaves is distracted, but whilst the readers' is too. The sinister technique by which the Cappadocian slave is killed can be paralleled from other tales. In Lucian's *Philopseudes* we learn of a statue of Pellichus, whose offerings are stolen during the night by a Libyan slave. The statue kills the slave by turning him mad and inflicting an invisible whipping upon him every night until he dies. In Petronius' text as we have it Trimalchio offers a brief explanation of the mechanism used to inflict this kind of death on the Cappadocian: 'this was obviously because an evil hand (*mala manus*) had touched him'. It is possible that these words originated in the marginal note of an ancient commentator that has become incorporated into the main text in the manuscript tradition.[28]

But the context of these tales is as interesting as their content. Petronius does not simply tell us these tales in his own voice, but he shows us, however parodically, one sort of context in which sinister tales of the supernatural might be generated and recycled, a context, in other words, in which the templates and codes of magical activity and its effects could be worked out and reinforced in the popular imagination.

Both Niceros and Trimalchio conclude their stories with strong affirmations of the truth of their particular tales, and of the actuality of the supernatural phenomena they describe, and they beg others to believe in the same way that they do themselves. Niceros: 'Others can make up their own mind about this. But if I'm lying, may your guardian spirits exercise their wrath upon me.' Trimalchio: 'I beg you to believe it. Wise women do exist, night-women do exist, and what is up, they can make down' (the last phrase is presumably a reference to the notion that witches could draw down the moon by night). We find something similar in the Greek text to which we have just referred, Lucian's *Philopseudes*, composed a century or so after the *Satyricon*, perhaps in the 170s AD. This recounts the conversation at a symposium in the house of the rich Eucrates. In this Eucrates and his philosopher-guests attempt to persuade the unbelieving, 'adamantine-minded' Tychiades of the reality of a range of supernatural phenomena by telling him tales of their own supposed direct experiences of them. In addition to the Pellichus tale, we hear how a Babylonian instantaneously cured a slave of a fatal viper-bite by tying a fragment of a virgin's tombstone to his foot, and then burning up all the local reptiles by breathing over them. We hear how a mage from the land of the Hyperboreans in the mythical north was able to attract a woman for a besotted client by manufacturing an animated cupid doll to go and fetch her. We hear how a Jewish exorcist drove a smoky demon from a man possessed. We hear how Eucrates encountered the terrifying goddess Hecate in the woods, and was able to avert her by turning his magic ring into the palm of his hand and opening up the earth to swallow her. We hear how Hermes, escort of souls, accidentally took Cleodemus down to the underworld before his time, with the result that he could bring back to the living the news of what he saw there and forecast the imminent death of the man he had been mistaken for. We hear how Eucrates was visited by the ghost of his recently dead wife, and how she revealed to him the location of a lost item. We hear how the Pythagorean Arignotus exorcised a haunted house by locating a concealed corpse within it. And we hear the famous tale of *The Sorcerer's Apprentice*. Amongst the storytellers, Cleodemus' tone is particularly confessional and conversional.[29]

It seems that it was an established custom to tell tales of this sort at the dinner parties and symposia of the Roman empire, and one could even bring in professional storytellers, *aretalogi*. Suetonius tells that the emperor Augustus enlivened his dinners with *aretalogi*, alongside musicians, actors and acrobats, whilst Juvenal scornfully refers to Odysseus as a lying *aretalogus* as he recounts his marvellous tales of the Cyclopes and the Laestrygonians over dinner to Alcinous. The term *aretalogi* suggests that the stories of these men owed something to the Greek practice of *aretalogia*, 'aretalogy', the celebration and affirmation of divine power on the basis of personal experience. This practice is known to us chiefly from sanctuary inscriptions in which individuals protreptically describe a personal encounter with the god and its miraculous effect. The sanctuaries of healing gods, notably Asclepius, offer inscriptions in which the miraculous cures effected by their patrons are recounted. The sanctuaries of other gods offer 'confession inscriptions', in which the gods' punishment of wrongdoers and the lessons learned therefrom are related for the edification of all. We may conclude, therefore, that the stories told by the *aretalogi* typically ended with an affirmation of the truth of the events narrated, and an exhortation to the listeners to believe in the reality and power of the supernatural phenomena described. And so it seems that they must have borne a strong resemblance to the sorts of tale told in the *Satyricon* and the *Philopseudes*.[30]

Aretalogi, professional or amateur, affirmed the truth of their marvellous stories, but, perhaps in part for that very reason, seem characteristically to have been regarded as liars, at least by the educated elite. Juvenal, as we have seen, adds 'lying' (*mendax*) as an epithet to *aretalogus*. The title of Lucian's *Philopseudes*, 'Lover of Lies', offers a judgement upon the storytellers it describes. And Trimalchio, as becomes repeatedly apparent in the narrative of his dinner party, is ignorant and credulous and inhabits something of a fantasy world (for all that he remains rather likeable).

There is enough evidence here to reconstruct a key (but by no means exclusive) context for the development and rehearsal of traditional tales of witchcraft, magic, ghosts and related supernatural phenomena. Such tales, even – or perhaps especially – when told for entertainment, and even when mocked for the sake of an educated elite as they are in our texts, helped to establish or reinforce a model in the popular imagination for the workings of such supernatural phenomena.

Two of the most substantial and important documents of magic to have come down to us from classical antiquity were penned by Apuleius of Madaura in Roman North Africa. The first of these is Apuleius' defence of himself against charges of magic, the *Apology*. In this Apuleius confronts allegations of a wide variety of magical practices, the chief of which is that he has used erotic magic to seduce a rich widow. Internal evidence locates the trial in *c.* 158–9 BC. The second Apuleian document, better known and rather more accessible, is his bawdy novel, the *Metamorphoses* or *The Golden Ass*, the only Latin novel to be fully extant. As we shall see, this incorporates a series of rich and extended tales of witches and magic. It is commonly believed that the novel must have been published after the *Apology* on the basis that Apuleius' legal opponents would otherwise have cited it as a strong indication of

Apuleius' interest in the world of magic. A corollary argument adds that since the penalty Apuleius faced would have been execution, and since he lived to publish the *Metamorphoses*, he must then have been acquitted. All this is built on sand. Amongst the many counter-arguments that can be marshalled, two will suffice here. First, since we have only Apuleius' defence speech, and not the speech of the prosecution, we cannot know what the latter contained. Secondly, the only evidence that the trial ever took place is the speech itself. And yet it is a strangely ironic and self-incriminating text. The easiest conclusion is that the speech is in fact an elaborate literary and rhetorical exercise, unrelated to any historical trial, and in the first instance paying tribute to the famous *Apology* of Plato. If we step back and view the text in this way, we can see that, for all its radically different genre and tone, it forms a sort of diptych with the *Metamorphoses*, with the latter offering us, inter alia, an elaborate series of portraits of witches and witchcraft, and the former offering us, complementarily, a complex and fractured portrayal of male magical practitioners.[31]

The *Metamorphoses* is a picaresque story narrated in the first person by one 'Lucius'. Its principal narrative arc, into which many subordinate tales are fitted, describes Lucius' accidental transformation into an ass, his trials and tribulations in this form, and his eventual restoration to human shape by the goddess Isis. The basic framework (excluding the Isiac conclusion) is based on a Greek model, the *Metamorphōseōn Logoi Diaphoroi* (*MLD*), ascribed by the Byzantine scholar Photius to one 'Lucius of Patras'. This novel no longer survives, but a healthy summary of it, known as the *Onos* or *Ass*, has been handed down to us in the collections of Lucian's works. It remains possible that Lucian, whose literary floruit fell in the 170s AD, was indeed the author of the original *MLD* (whether or not he was also responsible for the summary), and that he used the name 'Lucius', which closely resembled his own, to identify himself in part with the novel's first-person narrator. He does adopt a similar technique in some of his other works, where he partly identifies himself with a speaker named Lycinus. In contrast with its Greek model, Apuleius' *Metamorphoses* has a strongly aretalogical climax, which celebrates Lucius' direct experience of the power of Isis and turns readers towards the goddess, and it also integrates a substantial amount of further aretalogical material into the narrative along the way.[32]

A witch, the wife of Hipparchus, plays a pivotal role in the *Ass*, and it is she who is indirectly responsible for Lucius' transformation. Lucius wants to find a woman interested in performing magic in hopes of seeing her make a man fly or turn him into stone. In Thessaly he finds that Hipparchus' wife is a 'mage' who pursues young men and turns her victims into animals or destroys them (the Circean heritage is clear). Lucius asks her maid Palaestra to show him her mistress performing magical spells or changing shape, and reckons that Palaestra herself is magically adept because she has aroused his desire, which had previously been exclusively homosexual. He spies on Hipparchus' wife as she transforms herself into a bird to fly to her beloved. In attempting to effect the bird transformation for Lucius himself, Palaestra accidentally transforms him into an ass instead. The remainder of the novel is devoted to Lucius' attempts to recover his human shape. All these events are duplicated in Apuleius' novel, where, by contrast with the summary *Ass*, they are richly elaborated. Here the wife of Hipparchus acquires the name Pamphile, and the slavegirl Palaestra becomes Photis. But Apuleius bolts onto his Greek model a further three substantial tales, or concatenations of tales, of witches. For all that these tales too are set in Greek Thessaly, their tone, their ghoulishness and their gothicness seem to be much more closely akin to that of the Petronian tales and to the world of Canidia and Erictho, and so it is quite likely that they are derived from, or heavily coloured by, the Latin tradition within which Apuleius worked. It is also likely that the context in which they originally thrived was a folktale or folkloric one, as suspected in the case of the Petronian tales.[33]

The first of these is the tale of the friends Socrates and Aristomenes and the witches Meroe and Panthia. The tale is told by Aristomenes to Lucius, who has fallen in with him on the road. Aristomenes is a wholesale dealer in supplies for inns. He tells Lucius how he had once rushed to Hypata in Thessaly, the well-known witch-capital, to avail himself of a cheap supply of fresh cheese, of which he had heard. But he was beaten to it by a rival wholesale dealer, Lupus. As he wandered dejectedly to Hypata's bathhouse, he found his old friend Socrates sitting on the ground, in a wretched state, only half-covered by his rags, and 'looking like a ghost'. He asked Socrates what had brought him to this state, and told him that his abandoned wife had given him up for dead. Socrates begged Aristomenes to leave him be, but he pulled him up and took him to the baths, giving him the good wash he had intended for himself. He brought him to an inn, put him to bed, and then gave him a good meal. Eventually he persuaded Socrates to tell what had happened to him. Socrates had gone to Macedonia to make money, but on his way back home he was robbed in Thessaly and relieved of all the money he had made. An elderly innkeeper, Meroe, seemingly took pity on him. She gave him a free meal and then took him to bed, but this was his undoing. He found himself enslaved to her, and he even gave her the clothes from his back that the robbers had left him with.

Socrates explained that Meroe was a witch with a wide range of powers. These were characteristically exercised in service of her erotic desire, and could be used even over great distances. She could, for example, make even people in India and Ethiopia fall in love with her. He recounted some individual examples of her power. When an innkeeper-lover of hers had strayed with another woman, she had transformed him into a beaver, so that he would bite off his own genitals, as the beaver does when pursued by hunters. Another innkeeper was her competitor in trade, and so she transformed him into a frog, so that he now swam around in a pot of his own wine, croaking polite greetings to his customers. A lawyer who opposed her in court was transformed into a ram, and continued to plead his cases in this form. When the pregnant wife of one of the lovers she had taken spoke abusively of her, she sealed up her womb. Now her womb was massively distended with a fully grown eight-year-old child trapped within. Public outrage at her activities reached such a pitch that the city decreed to stone her, but before it could do this she called up ghosts to make binding magic and sealed all the citizens up in their own homes. She would only let them out once they had sworn that they would no longer move against her. But the ringleader's house she sent flying to another town 200 miles distant, and threw it down before the city gate.

Artistomenes urged that he and Socrates should get a good night's sleep before escaping from Hypata the next day, but Socrates fell asleep before he had even finished making the case. A nervous Aristomenes pushed his bed up against the doors of the bedroom. In his anxiety he found it difficult to get to sleep, but was rudely awakened when the doors were burst open with force, and his bed turned upside down, with Artistomenes himself left sprawling underneath it. Cowering here he peeped out and observed a terrible scene. Two old women entered, one with a sponge and a sword, the other with a lamp: Meroe and her sister or colleague Panthia. With arch words, Meroe showed the sleeping Socrates to Panthia, the lover who had dared to desert her in her 'youthful innocence'. Meroe plunged the sword into Socrates' neck up to the hilt, catching the welling blood in a leather bottle. She then stuck her right hand into the wound, delved around in Socrates' innards, and pulled out his heart, whereupon he uttered a deathly gurgle. Panthia stopped the wound with the sponge and spoke an incantation over it: 'Sponge, born in the sea, pass not over a river.' The two women lifted the bed from Aristomenes, straddled over his face and evacuated their bladders, soaking him in their foul urine. As they left through the doorway the broken doors returned to their hinges, and the bolts to their positions.

Once the terrified Aristomenes had recovered his wits, he attempted to escape, fearful that he would be held responsible for his companion's murder. But he could not persuade the inn's obstreperous porter to let him out. In despair he returned to the room and determined upon suicide. But as he attempted to hang himself using the mouldy rope with which his bed had been strung, it snapped and he fell down on top of Socrates whereupon, to his amazement, his companion awoke and began hurling abuse at the porter who had come to see what all the noise was about. In delight, Aristomenes hugged Socrates, until the latter pushed him back for smelling like a public toilet. Aristomenes at once urged Socrates to get up so they could make an early start to their escape from Hypata.

As they made their way Aristomenes scrutinized Socrates' neck for a wound. He could see none, and persuaded himself that what he had witnessed the night before had all been a ghastly nightmare. However, Socrates for his own part confided in Aristomenes that he had dreamed that he had been jugulated, and his heart pulled out. The weary travellers stopped under a plane tree to take the breakfast Aristomenes had brought with him. But as Socrates tucked into his bread and cheese he began to grow as pale as boxwood. After eating, he was overtaken by an unbearable thirst. He bent over a nearby stream to drink from it, and as he did so the wound in his throat yawned open and the sponge leapt out, with a trickle of blood, and he fell dead into the water. Aristomenes dragged the body out and quickly buried it before running off. As if guilty of the murder himself, he took on the life of an exile, moved to a new part of Greece, Aetolia, and contracted a new marriage.[34]

Apuleius' narrative is itself a sophisticated product, and it exhibits an awareness of its place within a literary canon. Socrates is made to compare Meroe not merely with Medea but specifically with Medea as projected in Euripides' tragedy of that name. Meroe herself is made to compare Socrates, ironically, to Endymion, Ganymede and Odysseus, and herself to Calypso. But despite all this, as with the Petronian tales, this magical narrative too is presented to us in the form of a told story. Indeed, it is presented to us in the form of several told stories nested within each other: within his own story Lucius tells us Aristomenes' story, which in turn incorporates Socrates' story.[35]

The Odyssean notion that those who come into contact with witches do not normally return home afterwards is here expressed twice: Socrates himself, enslaved to Meroe by a single bout of sex with her, the fate with which Circe had threatened Odysseus, abandons his wife and family to live a beggarly existence in Hypata. In the end Aristomenes, too, for reasons that are not otherwise well motivated, abandons his homeland, wife and family after encountering Meroe. We will shortly meet Thelyphron, who similarly abandons his home after a particularly unfortunate encounter with other, unnamed Thessalian witches. And in turn the novel's hero, Lucius himself, after encountering Pamphile and her apprentice Photis, will give up his thoughts of returning home. Indeed, the novel culminates with him abandoning his former life to become a devotee of Isis.[36]

Aristomenes' tale shares a number of motifs with the Petronian tales, beyond those of witches and ghosts themselves. One shared motif of particular interest is that of animal-transformation. We hear of men transformed into beavers, frogs and rams, and Aristomenes himself is metaphorically transformed into a tortoise when his bed falls on top of him. An animal transformation lies at the heart of the *Metamorphoses*, in Lucius' transformation into an ass (as it did in the *MLD* before it), and the animal transformations in Aristomenes' tale anticipate and reflect that. Although we find no wolf-transformation as such, we should note that the name of the enterprising tradesman who beats Aristomenes to his cheap supply of cheese at the very beginning of his tale is none other than Lupus, 'Wolf.'

We may also note that the motif of the innkeeper insistently recurs across these tales. Here in Apuleius innkeepers tangle with witches and ghosts; in the Aesopic tale they tangle with werewolves; in the first Petronian tale they tangle with werewolves and ghosts. We may take note also of another popular tale recounted by Cicero, and later by Aelian, in which again an innkeeper tangles with a ghost. According to this, an Arcadian visitor to Megara is murdered by his innkeeper who then attempts to smuggle his body out of the city in a dung cart. But his ghost manifests itself to a citizen, or to an Arcadian friend in the city, and tells him what has happened. He is then able to stop the dung cart at the city gate and have the innkeeper arrested. Why such a prominence for innkeepers in tales of this kind? Do they serve as markers of the low-life milieu favoured by the tales? Or does their presence signal, more indirectly, that the inn was a typical forum for the telling of the tales?[37]

Before we leave Meroe, we may note that she represents ancient literature's most powerful adept in binding magic. She is said to be able to deploy binding magic in general through the exploitation of ghosts. But she can also bind in a very immediate fashion: she can bind a baby into a womb and the entire city up into its houses. It is noteworthy that the conflicts in which Meroe embroils herself, those of trade, law and love reflect the three principal situations in which ancient binding curses were deployed. Another noteworthy feature of Meroe is her ability to use her magic over vast distances. She can make distant peoples fall in love with her. She can send houses flying off hundreds of miles. With the aid of a demon she can hear slanderous speech remotely.[38]

A second tale Apuleius bolts on to the narrative core that he inherits from the *MLD* is told by Thelyphron at a highly elaborate dinner party in the house of Byrrhena. Like Aristomenes' tale, it contrives to be at once sinister and humorous. Thelyphron tells how he arrived in Larissa in Thessaly whilst touring Greece in connection with a visit to the Olympic Games. Looking for money to sustain his travel, he heard an old man making proclamation in the forum. He was looking for someone to watch over a dead man. Thelyphron asked a passer-by the meaning of this, and he was told that in Thessaly witches (*sagae mulieres*) were in the habit of nibbling bits off the faces of corpses to use for magical supplies (cf. Erictho at the funeral). Therefore, people were hired to watch corpses carefully all night long prior to their burial. They must not shift their gaze from the corpse because the witches could transform themselves into different animals – dogs, mice or even flies. They would use their spells to bury the watchers in sleep. If a watcher failed in his duty, the local law dictated that he must make good the body-parts stolen from the corpse by the sacrifice of his own corresponding ones.

Thelyphron was blithely confident and swaggered up to the old man. He agreed a high price for the job, and was warned that he would be watching the body of the son of one Larissa's first families. He was taken into the darkened house by the back way and presented to the widow, who was pretty, as he noted, even in her grief. She urged him to do his job vigilantly, whilst Thelyphron was more interested in asking her for an extra tip. He was then taken to a room where the corpse was laid out. Before seven witnesses, and a secretary to take notes, the widow worked her way over the entire corpse, demonstrating its intact state to the agreement of all, who duly signed the secretary's paper. As Thelyphron was being left in the room to do his job, he demanded a lamp, food and wine. The widow scolded him for making the latter improper demands, but had a maid bring in a large lamp for him.

And so the watch began, with Thelyphron singing to himself to stay awake, and to keep fear at bay. Suddenly a weasel crept into the room and fixed him with its bold and piercing stare. He chased it out but all at once he was overwhelmed by drowsiness and fell into a profound sleep, only to be awoken at dawn by the cockerels. In abject terror he ran to the corpse and scrutinized every part of its face in the light of the lamp. To his relief, the corpse was fully intact after all. At once the widow burst in, threw herself weeping on the corpse, and then she too checked every part of it with the lamp. Satisfied and grateful, she ordered her steward to give the watcher the pay he had earned. Gauche as ever, the unthinking Thelyphron, in poor taste and to ill omen, offered to do the job for her again any time she needed it. The enraged household bundled him out into the street.

Soon Thelyphron witnessed the corpse being carried out for a procession through the forum. An old man seized hold of the bier and made appeal to the citizens. He insisted that the dead man, his nephew, had been murdered by his wife, so that she could please her lover and plunder his estate. The crowd was inclined to believe him and began to turn against the woman, despite her repeated denials. Thereupon the old man produced one Zatchlas, whom he introduced as an Egyptian prophet. He had agreed, for a large sum, to bring back the ghost of the dead man from the underworld and to reanimate the corpse. Zatchlas was a young man, shaven bald and dressed in a linen shift and palm-leaf sandals, as Egyptian priests typically were. He laid a sprig of a mysterious herb on the corpse's mouth and another on his breast. He faced east and prayed to the rising sun. The dead man's chest swelled, an artery throbbed, and the corpse rose up. The re-inhabiting ghost complained about being dragged back from the underworld, and begged to be restored to peace. Zatchlas then threatened to invoke the Furies to torture the ghost unless it revealed the mystery of its death. With a groan the corpse addressed himself to the gathered crowds and declared that he had been poisoned by his new bride, and that he had made his bed over to her lover. The crowd was now divided, with some insisting on the immediate execution of the widow, and others protesting that no faith should be placed in the lies of a corpse.

But the corpse soon resolved the matter by delivering clear proof of veracity. He pointed out Thelyphron in the crowd and explained that, whilst he had been watching over him, the witches had come to the attack. They had shape-shifted and cast sleep upon him. They had then attempted to make the corpse rise so that they could reap it of its precious facial parts, and to this end had called its name. But its joints, already frozen in rigor mortis, were slow to respond. By chance, the dead man's watcher was his namesake, and so as the witches called 'Thelyphron', the young man, merely sleeping, and with his limbs still supple, responded to the call first. The witches brought him to the wall of the room, where they reaped his facial parts through a hole, chopping off his nose and ears, replacing them with wax prostheses to conceal their crime provisionally. The corpse joked that the money the living Thelyphron had received was not reward for work, but compensation for mutilation. The terrified man at once touched his nose, and it came off in his hand. He touched his ears, and they fell away. The crowd pointed to him and broke into laughter. He ran from the scene but could not bring himself ever to return to home again in this ridiculous state, and so remained in Thessaly. He grew his hair long to conceal his mutilated ears, and wore a linen prosthesis in place of his nose. These he seemingly now exhibits to his fellow diners in a striking conclusion to his story.[39]

Once again we are presented with a marvellous story of witchcraft as an orally recounted tale and that too at a dinner party. Thelyphron is an intriguing figure. At first he seems shy, curmudgeonly and unwilling to talk, but in the end he is rather easily persuaded to relate or, perhaps one should say, 'perform', his tale. It becomes clear from Byrrhena's address to him that Thelyphron has told his tale many times before, and is well used to doing so. She already knows that his tale will be 'charming'. And when he begins his tale, he does so with the showmanship and style of a seasoned and professional raconteur. He props himself up on the couch on which he reclines, stretches out his right arm, forming his hand into the gesture adopted by public orators. It is only, seemingly, at the very end of his story that Thelyphron makes explicit the physical consequences of his encounter with the witches upon himself. We may imagine that his mutilations are only revealed to the audience at the end of his story with a climactic flourish, as a striking and shocking denouement. It may well be that Thelyphron gives us a particularly good insight not just into the sort of story but also into the sort of showmanship one could expect from a professional *aretalogus*. One can well imagine that the final revelation of Thelyphron's mutilations might have had a striking 'aretalogical' impact, 'aretalogical' in the sense of persuading the audience of the actuality of the supernatural events and the efficacy of the powers described. Such an effect is also achieved within the tale by the animation episode. Members of the audience to it dismiss the reliability of the reanimated corpse, and consign its utterances, if not its reanimation, to the realm of charlatanry and deceit, only to be confronted with devastating proof of its truthfulness.[40]

Features we have noted in the previous tales recur in this one: witchcraft, ghosts, animal transformations (the weasel aside, transformations into dogs, mice and flies are also mentioned, saluting the novel's central theme), the theft of body-parts for spells and the failure of the victim to return home. Innkeepers make an implicit appearance in Thelyphron's initial search for money to sustain his travel.

As a poisoner, the dead man's widow is herself closely akin to a witch. It is left unclear whether she is herself one of the witches who participate in the mutilation of Thelyphron, or even the very one who turns herself into the sleep-casting weasel. The possibility is intriguingly unresolved, and helps to animate the story. It remains puzzling why, despite their ability to enter the locked room where the corpse is kept, the witches then have to withdraw outside it to carry out the work of amputation awkwardly through a small hole. Perhaps Apuleius has them do this simply in order to explain how they could have mutilated the wrong Thelyphron by mistake. For his body parts would have been of no use to them: since he was still alive, they were tied to no ghost to whom the witches could have given commands to enact their spells for them. As for the tale's sorcerer, Zatchlas, we will have more to say of him when we look at the Graeco-Roman portrayal of Egyptian sorcerers in the following chapter.

A third tale of Thessalian witchcraft that Apuleius adds to the *MLD* is found towards the end of his work. At this point ass-Lucius had passed into the ownership of a miller, whose wife had taken a boy-lover into the house. She had concealed him upon her husband's return, but Lucius had revealed his presence by stamping on his fingers. The miller had buggered him and thrown him out (this part of the tale will be familiar to readers of Boccaccio's *Decameron*). In order to recover her situation, the adulterous wife brought in a witch, 'some old crone', an expert in binding curses. She asked the witch first to pacify her husband and reconcile him to her, but, if that was not possible, to summon a ghost or demon to kill him. The witch's initial attempts to secure the husband's pacification came to nothing, and the powers she attempted to invoke held her in contempt. So, to win her exorbitant fee and to reassert her control over the powers, she turned to the route of death. At midday a decrepit old woman, barefoot and clothed in sordid rags, appeared at the mill. She was as yellow as boxwood and dreadfully emaciated. Her hair, caked in ashes, hung down over her face. She put her hand on the miller as if wishing to confide a secret to him, and drew him aside into his office. The door was put to and stayed shut for a long time. In due course the mill workers had exhausted their supplies of grain and came to the office to ask for more to work on. Their calls to the master met with no response, and they began to hammer on the door, which had been firmly bolted from within. Suspecting something amiss, they forced the door out of its hinge and made their way in. There was no sign of the woman, evidently a ghost, but the master was hanging from a roof-beam, dead already. That night the miller's own ghost in turn, wearing the noose, appeared in a dream to his daughter, who was married and living in the next town, and explained to her the full detail of his widow's adultery and sorcery, so that it could achieve its vengeance through her.[41]

Once again we find here the familiar collection of witches and ghosts. As often, this tale achieves its sinister effect by declining to narrate its shocking central event directly. We share the growing sense of concern and then the terrible discovery with the mill workers as the narrative camera follows them. The narrative remains alive by leaving us to wonder exactly how the ghost accomplished the murder: tangibly, with the strength of a revenant? Or did the ghost, rather less tangibly, inflict some sort of madness on the miller and so persuade him to take his own life? From another perspective, we may note that mere contact alone with a ghost could be sufficient to destine a man for the death (see Chapter 5). The fact that the ghost could touch the miller's arm suggests that it had a solid form, but the fact that it could then disappear from a locked room suggests, perplexingly, that by contrast it was ethereal. What did the miller make of the ghost? As an old woman with a confidential matter to discuss, she sounds very much like a bawd or a go-between, like Herodas' Gyllis, keen to earn a commission for bringing the miller into a relationship with a secret admirer, or with a courtesan.

Folk traditions of modern Italy

The worlds of witches described by Petronius and even more so Apuleius are strikingly mirrored in Carlo Levi's evocative memoir *Cristo si è fermato a Eboli* (1945), translated as *Christ Stopped at Eboli* (1947). This recounts Levi's experiences as an internal exile of the Mussolini regime during the years 1935–6 in the village of Aliano in the remote and primitive South Italian region of Lucania. In the memoir Aliano is lightly disguised under the name of Gagliano.

Over the course of his stay Levi becomes familiar with a world saturated with witches and with magic. As a doctor, he encounters much healing magic amongst the peasants. When he visits the sick he often finds a roll of paper or a metal plate around their necks inscribed with the abracadabra triangle, alongside other protective rings and amulets, the latter including old coins, wolves' teeth and toads' bones. He learns of spells for curing toothache, stomach-ache and headache. He learns of cures for jaundice involving the making of signs over the joints with a black-handled knife. He learns also of spells for transferring one's ills to another person, animal, plant or object, and for throwing off the influence of the evil eye or a bewitchment.[42]

Although he comes into close contact with at least two admitted witches, women who serve as his housekeepers, it is evident that he learns much of the nature of the world into which he has moved from the compelling lore of witchcraft and narratives of its local practice told to him by the locals. Upon his arrival Levi is advised that, as a young and able physician, the local peasant women will take a fancy to him and attempt to seduce him with love philtres. These are made of menstrual blood, into which some herbs are mixed, and over which some words of power are murmured. The witches will sneak this into his drink, his coffee or his wine, or into his food, his chocolate, sausages or bread.[43]

And indeed, as in the Latin texts, the witches' concern is primarily with the instilling of love and, when opposed in this, the infliction of death. Levi is told of a widow whose husband had been ensnared by a peasant witch with her love potions. The witch had borne him a child. When the man sought to break off the relationship, she had poisoned him. He fell sick with a protracted and mysterious illness to which the doctors were able to give no name. His strength gradually waned, his skin and face grew dark until bronze and then black, and then at last he died. Apuleius' Meroe does not seem so far away. In fulfilment of the prediction made to him upon arrival, Levi learns that one 'Maria C' has used love magic against him. This short and stubby woman, with a forehead so low that her hairline almost meets her eyebrows and with mad eyes, had already caused a man's death. The villagers' anxieties about the behaviour of others around them are projected into similar narratives. The feud between the village's two principal families is expressed in terms of Donna Caterina's concern that the three Gibilisco women are witches, and that the dark-haired beauty amongst them has bewitched her husband and wishes to marry him. Accordingly, Donna Caterina fears that she may attempt to poison her.[44]

Levi's observations on the way in which witchcraft fitted into village society are of particular interest. He notes that it is a tenet of peasant life that whenever a man and a woman are alone together, whatever their stations, they will make love. This is a law of nature, and no one can be held culpable for acting in accordance with it. Consequently, in the interests of the preservation of social order, the moral code dictates that a man and a woman should never be left alone together. The only women exempt from this rule are those who have multiple children by unidentifiable fathers, those who are sexually liberal, those who devote themselves to everything to do with love and acquiring it, that is to say, witches. And so it is that when Levi needs a housekeeper, with whom he must inevitably be alone in his house for most of time, he must hire a witch. 'Giulia Venere' comes to him first. In her day she had been a beauty. Now she is 40 and has been pregnant seventeen times by fifteen different men. She knows everything that goes on in the village. She is a mistress of potions and young girls come to her to be instructed in the art of philtres. She knows herbs and talismans, can cure illness by repeating spells, and can bring about death by incantations. Levi describes her as possessing a serpentine head, and as an animal-like spirit of the earth. When Giulia can no longer work for Levi, he is assigned another witch-housekeeper, Maria. She has the appearance of a canonical broomstick-style witch. She has a wrinkled face with long sharp nose and prominent, pointed chin.[45]

When Levi has won the confidence of Giulia, she teaches him some of her love philtres for winning the hearts of those nearby and for binding the hearts of those who are absent, and also spells for inflicting a slow death. Giulia has a spell that can reach across to loved ones over land and sea, impel them to drop everything, heed the call of love, and return to their abandoned lover. The verse is to be recited by night, as one stands in a doorway and gazes up at the star to which it is addressed:

Stella, da lontano te vuardo e da vicino te saluto,
'N faccia te vado e 'n vocca te sputo.
Stella, non face che ha da murì,
Face che ha da turnà,
E con me ha da restà.

Star, from afar I see you and from close by I greet you,
I present myself before you and I spit in your mouth.
Star, do not let him die,
But let him turn about,
And let him stay with me.[46]

One of the notions that underlies this spell is the idea that remote lovers are connected at least by the light, gaze or visibility of celestial bodies above. The terrible spell to inflict death, Levi tells, ravages a man in his vitals and gradually dries him up until he is ready for the grave. Giulia imparts it to him in secrecy on Christmas Day, the only day on which it can be transmitted.[47]

The lore and stories with which Levi is regaled feature werewolves and ghosts too. Sleepwalkers, he is told, become werewolves, and join the packs of wolves by night. When a man returns and knocks at the door the first time, his wife must not open it, for at this point he will still be a wolf and he will eat her. If she opens it on the second knock, she will see her husband with a man's body and a wolf's head (will he thus be frozen in this form?). She can only let him in on the third knock, when he is completely changed back. Here the symbolic number three and the notion that a werewolf might encounter problems with his transformation back to human form which might leave him frozen as wolf are strikingly evocative of the Petronian and Aesopic werewolf tales. The forests around are full of gnomes and sprites, the spirits of children dead before baptism. They are playful but not truly harmful. They upset wine glasses and drop washing in the dirt. If one is able to deprive one of them of his red hood he will beg for it back and one can make him guide one to buried treasure in return. The gnomes are wise and know all the secrets of the earth. Levi is told of, and indeed encounters, an ancient eunuch gravedigger. He is feared by the women, but also mocked by them. They demand of him why he leaves them to sleep on their own in bed by night. In younger days he had been a wolf-tamer, and had wandered around followed by packs of wolves. He could bring them down to the village or keep them away from it, and indeed he could control all animals. In his present incarnation the gravedigger can call up spirits from below the ground and out of the air. He has a familiar that can help him with heavy labour. He himself tells Levi how one night he had encountered a devil in the form of a goat amongst the abandoned tombs, and that he had temporarily rendered him powerless and unable to complete his journey.[48]

The coincidence of much of Levi's material with the Classical world, and in particular that of the Latin novels, is striking, but what is the significance of the coincidence? Much turns on whether Levi is to be regarded primarily as an ethnographer or as a fictive writer, although these two terms need not be completely mutually exclusive. Levi the ethnographer may be presumed to witness, if not a cultural continuity, then at least a cultural replication. Levi the fictive writer may be presumed to be self-conscious about the tradition in which he writes, and to be calquing his Lucania, at least in part, on the worlds of that tradition. Fictive gestures, certainly, are apparent at least in the coherent narrative arc into which he has shaped his experiences, and in the light disguise of the name of Aliano. For all that no explicit mention is made of Petronius or Apuleius, a positive desire on Levi's part to link the customs he sees around him with the Classical past peeps through. He speculates that some of the healing spells he encounters may derive from Classical lore, whilst likening a palindromic incantation sung to deliver children from worms to 'an ancient Roman exorcism'. Recent critical approaches to Levi's work have, predictably perhaps, tended to focus on his use of fictive techniques to 'create a reality' or indeed even to idealize and mythologize a way of life he saw to be vanishing from Italy. Yet for all this, Levi's *Christ* was initially received in Italy as a valuable contribution to ethnography, and indeed it was the catalyst for more formal ethnographic investigation in Lucania and similar areas, which, it should be noted, was broadly confirmatory of the portrait he painted.[49]

And so it is worth pursuing a number of points of interest that arise from Levi's material for the ancient world. Of these the first is the illustration of the way in which the world of witchcraft and the codes associated with it is constructed through the rehearsal of tales of its successful (or for that matter unsuccessful) practice. The warning-tales of the magical practices of the local witches with which Levi is regaled upon his arrival in the village are strikingly reminiscent of the warning-tales with which Apuleius' Lucius is regaled as he arrives in Hypata.

Secondly, and perhaps most importantly, Levi presents us with a picture of what is at any rate perceived to be a village of witches. This in itself suggests that Apuleius' presentation of Thessaly as a land in which almost every other woman is openly a witch is a theoretical possibility.

Thirdly, Levi's association between witchcraft and women who are sexually liberal is an association found widely in the Latin sources. It is of course a corollary, in Latin literature and Levi alike, of the association of witches above all with the practices of erotic magic. Dickie's recent work on magic in the ancient world advances as its principal argument the notion that there was ever a tight association between witchcraft and prostitution in antiquity. Did Levi witness the modern reflex of this, for all that, as he claims, prostitution as such did not exist in Aliano?

Fourthly, Lucanian folklore constructs a tight relationship between the worlds of witches, restless spirits and wolves and werewolves, a set of associations clearly visible in the pair of stories exchanged by Petronius' Niceros and Trimalchio.

Fifthly, the young girls of Levi's village visit Giulia Venere to be instructed in love philtres. Ovid offers us a remarkably similar vignette, situated during the Roman festival of the dead, the *Feralia*. Here an old woman sits in the midst of young girls and demonstrates to them the rites of Muta Tacita, the 'Silent Goddess'. She binds shut the mouths of her enemies by roasting the head of a fish, the mouth of which she has sewn up, sealed with pitch and pierced with a bronze needle. The spell also involves a lead curse tablet which is either bound with threads or enfolds threads from the victim's clothing.[50]

Conclusion

In this chapter we have looked at the Latin poetry of the early empire, which pullulates with elaborate portraits of witches at work, amongst whom the most winning are Horace's Canidia and Lucan's Erictho. These witches exultantly inhabit a macabre and cruel world characterized by the collection and deployment of human body parts, a world to which the term 'Gothic' in its more modern significance is aptly applied. Although, as in all things, these Latin poetic treatments owed much to the Greek and in particular to the Hellenistic Greek literary heritage, this Gothic quality is something that can not be paralleled in Greek literature, and it is hard to believe that it had thrived there. It is absent, significantly, from the two great Hellenistic witch-portraits to survive, Apollonius' portrait of Medea and from Theocritus' portrait of Simaetha. The quality seems rather to smell of the arena, and to be a product of the sensibilities of the Romans' own more bloodthirsty culture. The horrid witches of early imperial poetry are very much akin to those we find in the Latin novels when the extant tradition begins to preserve these for us, from the reign of Nero. There is much about these tales of the witches in the novels, the howling witches of Petronius, the Meroe and Panthia of Apuleius, and much about the contexts in which the tales about them are sited within the novels, to suggest that the true home of the witch-tale in Roman culture was, again, the folktale. Apuleius projects Roman Thessaly as a veritable world of witches: is this purely a literary fantasy or might it reflect the way that denizens of the Roman empire (and not just Thessaly) perceived and told stories about the world around them? The theoretical possibility of the latter, if nothing else, is suggested by accounts of the peasant culture that survived in the remoter parts of Italy before the Second World War, not least in Carlo Levi's descriptions of Lucania in *Christ Stopped at Eboli*.

This chapter has progressed forwards in chronological fashion, albeit with a considerable gap, from the Hellenistic world to interwar Italy. At the same time, and athwart this, it has taken a journey, as it were in reverse, towards varieties of literature that are seemingly in ever closer contact with the worlds of folktale and folklore upon which all cultures of magical narrative must ultimately depend.

3

Babylon and Memphis: The Sorcerers of the Imperial Age

The conglomerated magical peoples of Asia: Persians, Medes, Mages, Babylonians, Chaldaeans, Assyrians and Syrians

We saw in Chapter 1 that the Greek concept of the male mage or sorcerer was almost certainly a secondary one, developed in the course of the fifth century BC and building on that of the rather earlier concept of the female witch. We seem to find a parallel situation with extended portraits of individual practitioners, fictitious or otherwise: developed portraits of female witches flourish in our extant evidence for many centuries before we find the first *developed* portraits of male sorcerers, who do not make an appearance until well into the AD period. Before this we have already been able to enjoy richly detailed accounts of Circe, Medea, Simaetha and Canidia. This late start for the men may in part be due to an accident of source-preservation, but we may nonetheless infer that the storytellers long continued to find greater satisfaction in the detailed imagining of female practitioners rather than in that of male ones.

When Greek or Latin texts make passing references to mages or other sorts of magical practitioner, it is often difficult to tell whether they have in mind a home-grown Greek (or latterly Roman) specialist or some variety of exotic foreigner. We confront this difficulty already in most of the earliest texts bearing upon 'mages', including what may be the very first of these, the supposed Heraclitus fragment, and then again, for example, in the Hippocratic treatise *On the Sacred Disease*, which we discussed in the first chapter. Amongst the earliest texts only Herodotus' and Xanthus of Lydia's discussions indisputably relate to specialists amongst the Medes and the Persians. But when developed tales of individual mages or sorcerers, fictional or historical, do begin to appear in the literary record, these men are almost all aliens, whereas those few that can lay claim to a Greek ethnicity are presented specifically as Pythagoreans.[1]

A text that is helpfully representative of the patterns found in the wider tradition is Lucian's *Philopseudes* or *Lover of Lies*. This is a relatively short satirical dialogue probably composed in the 170s AD. In a central monologue the sceptical Tychiades tells his friend Philocles how he has just fled from a party at which philosophers of various schools had attempted to persuade him of he reality of the intervention of the supernatural in human life by bombarding him with tales drawn supposedly from their own direct experiences. These tales focus principally on encounters with ghosts and, to a greater extent, encounters with sorcerers and their marvellous achievements. The sorcerers featured are, in the order described, a Chaldaean mage, a Hyperborean mage, a Syro-Palaestinian exorcist, a Pythagorean and an Egyptian. The Hyperborean aside, the categories to which these sorcerers belong offer us a useful framework within which to review the sorcerer-tales of the imperial period.[2]

Mages and Chaldaeans had radically distinct historical origins, but they appear to have been merged in the minds of the Greeks, perhaps already in the fifth century but certainly by the age of Alexander. The historical mages of the Persian empire are now believed to have originated in Media, as Herodotus actually says they did, and to have been the priests of a local Median religion centred around the god Zurvan, and to have had nothing to do with the Persians' own principal deity, Ahura-Mazda. But Herodotus' explicit reason for connecting the mages with Media is rather his supposition that they derived their origins from the witch Medea. The historical Chaldaeans of Babylon are now believed to have been an Aramaean people who migrated to Babylon *c.* 1000 BC and became 'Babylonianized'. We first encounter them in Greek literature in Herodotus and Sophocles, by which time Babylon had long been part of the Persian empire. For Herodotus they are priests of Zeus Bel (Baal). Sophocles' fragmentary reference intrigues: he speaks of a man who is, by what may seem to us a remarkable feat, 'Colchian, Chaldaean and Syrian by race'. Colchis speaks once again and emphatically of a defining relationship with Medea. If the identification of Babylon with Syria seems hardly less alarming here, Herodotus already notes, and that too in connection with a reference to the Chaldaeans in Xerxes' army, that the Greeks use the terms 'Assyrian' and 'Syrian' interchangeably. In the subsequent tradition the Greeks and Romans came to associate the Chaldaeans with magic in general, and sometimes with astronomy and astrology in particular. There is nothing to indicate that they bore a similar significance for the Babylonians themselves.[3]

We find the two categories of mage and Chaldaean merged in a curious fragment of the *Agen*, a satyr play composed *c.* 326 BC, supposedly by one Python of Catana. Athenaeus says that it was performed for Alexander's army on the River Hydaspes, but it is rather more likely that it was an Athenian production. The play was set in Babylon. Its sole surviving fragment, which seemingly derives from the prologue, points to a reedy, birdless lake as part of the play's scene, a typical location for an oracle of the dead. Oracles of the dead were often held to be 'birdless' (*aornos*) because birds would be killed by the noxious fumes that rose from them, as most famously in the case of Lake Avernus in Italian Campania, the name of which was given a folk-etymology that derived it precisely from the Greek word *aornos*. The *Agen* fragment tells that it was here that some 'mages of the barbarians' had offered to summon up for the distraught Harpalus, Alexander's rogue general, the ghost of his dead girlfriend Pythionice. The combination of 'mages' with Babylon strongly implies an identification between mages and Chaldaeans. The link would continue to be perceived later in antiquity. The Augustan Strabo, for instance, in his list of various magical types, places Persian mages and 'Assyrian' Chaldaeans adjacently in his list; '... the Persians have their mages and necromancers, and furthermore their so-called lecanomancers and hydromancers, the Assyrians their Chaldaeans ...'. In 65 AD the poet Lucan compared the divinatory powers of 'Persian Babylon' and its mages disadvantageously to those of his corpse-reanimating witch, Erictho. In the third century AD Diogenes Laertius tells us that the young Pythagoras associated with 'Chaldaeans and mages'.[4]

In Python's play the mage-Chaldaeans summon up ghosts from the underworld so that the living may speak with them, or at any rate offer to do so. In Lucian's *Menippus* a mage-Chaldaean offers, in complementary fashion, to take a living man down to the underworld to talk with the ghosts there. The Cynic Menippus, in despair of learning the meaning of life from the philosophers amongst the living, decides that he must follow in Odysseus' footsteps and descend to the underworld to learn it from the dead Tiresias. And so he resolves to go east and find someone who can take him down into the underworld. The man he finds is Mithrobarzanes, whose name is somewhat stage-Persian from a Greek perspective. He is defined as a mage and as a disciple of Zoroaster, and it is implied that he is specifically a Mede, but he is located in Babylon, and also defined as a Chaldaean. He has long white hair and a venerable beard. After much begging and supplicating (a theme to which we will return) Menippus prevails upon him to take him down to the underworld for a price of his own choosing. First the mage subjects Menippus to prolonged rituals of purification, stretching from one new moon to the next. Each day he washes him in the Euphrates before the rising sun, recites an obscure and protracted incantation, in which he calls upon some demons and spits in his face three times. Then they go back home without looking at any of the people they meet. All they consume during this time is nuts, milk, honey-milk and the water of the Choaspes. When the time for the descent has finally come, Mithrobarzanes purifies Menippus again at the river Tigris, this time by using a torch, a squill, and another incantation. He casts a spell over his body whilst walking around it, in order to manufacture a protective barrier around him so that he will not be harmed by the ghosts. Then they walk home backwards and prepare themselves for the journey. Many of these purificatory rituals are, it seems, supposed to begin the process of separating Menippus from the living people around him, and so put him in a better position to be able to communicate with the dead. Mithrobarzanes dons the Median-style dress of a mage and gives Menippus the attributes of those Greek heroes that had famously been able to visit the underworld and return from it, the felt cap of Odysseus, the lion-skin of Heracles and the lyre of Orpheus. They then go down to the river, where Mithrobarzanes has prepared a boat loaded with sheep for sacrifice, honey-milk and all the other offerings they will need for the rite. They sail into a marsh and beyond this a deserted place, thickly wooded and sunless. There Mithrobarzanes digs a pit, jugulates the sheep and libates their blood around the edge of the pit. He holds up a torch and shouts an invocation to all the demons, the Poenae, the Furies, Hecate of the Night, dread Persephone and also to some demons with meaningless, polysyllabic foreign names. The ground is broken open by the spell, and the underworld revealed. Menippus can see the underworld lake, Pyriphlegethon, the fiery river, and the palace of Pluto. They go down within. When Charon sees Menippus' lion skin he thinks he is Heracles, and so agrees to ferry him across into the underworld proper. After a tour of all the underworld sights, Menippus finally finds Tiresias, who offers him a disappointingly banal meaning of life, namely that the life of the ordinary man is best, and that one should take nothing too seriously. Mithrobarzanes then directs Menippus out of he underworld, whilst apparently remaining behind in it himself. He points him towards a small chink of light, which turns out to be the entrance, seen from within, to Trophonius' cave-oracle in Boeotia, and so Menippus finds himself at once back in Greece.[5]

One of the most intriguing aspects of this entertaining tale is the game played with underworld space and time. Lucian does not tell us how long it took Menippus to travel to Babylon from Greece, but the distance to the city from central Greece was around 1,200 miles as the crow flies. If Menippus had been able to manage a generous 20 miles a day and had been able to travel more or less in a straight line, the journey should have taken him a good two months. Yet Menippus tells us that, after entering the underworld from the wooded area adjacent to Babylon, he travelled in it for just a day, before emerging again into the upper world through Trophonius' hole. So what is going on? Are days in the underworld, the land of eternity, much longer than days on the surface? Or are we wrong to imagine that the underworld extends *pari passu* beneath the surface world, like a massive basement? Are we rather to imagine that in stepping into the underworld one steps into some sort of different dimension?[6]

Closely akin to such necromantic practices was that of restoring the animating ghost to the dead body it had recently left, or which it was on the point of leaving. A brief report of a Iamblichus' lost novel, the *Babyloniaca* or *Babylonian Story*, a text roughly contemporary with Lucian's writing, tells us of an episode in it in which an old Chaldaean arrives to interrupt the funeral of a dead girl. He claims that she is still breathing (though it is not clear that this is in fact the case), and then raises her up, before offering prophecies.[7]

We meet another Chaldaean reanimator in Lucian's *Philopseudes*. Here the Platonist Ion tells an elaborate anecdote about a practitioner he defines initially as a Chaldaean from Babylon, and then latterly as a mage. He recounts how, when he was a lad, a strapping slave out on his father's farm, Midas, was bitten on the toe by a viper at noontime as he dressed the vines. Having bitten him, the snake then disappears back down its hole, leaving him to wail. Midas is brought from the farm to Ion's father on a stretcher. His leg is already going rotten and he is only just breathing. But a friend tells Ion's father not to worry, because he will call in for him a Babylonian, one of the Chaldaeans, and that he will cure Midas. The Babylonian duly arrives and drives the poison out of his body with an incantation. He also ties to his foot a chipping from a virgin's tombstone. Midas at once leaps to his feet, picks up the stretcher on which he has been brought and carries it back to the farm with him. Ion goes on to tell how the Chaldaean follows up this marvellous achievement. He goes out to the farm himself at dawn, recites seven sacred names from an old book and purifies the place with a sulphur torch, encircling it three times. He calls out all the reptiles within its boundaries, and they come as if drawn to the incantation. But one old dragon-snake (*drakōn*) is left behind, either because too deaf to hear the incantation, or too decrepit to obey it. The Chaldaean asserts that someone is missing, picks out the youngest snake and sends it to the dragon-snake with a message, and shortly that snake too arrives. When they are all assembled, the Chaldaean blows over them. They are all burned up by the blast at once, as the gathered audience looks on in amazement. In a joking response to Ion's tale, the sceptical Tychiades asks him whether the young snake that took the message led the old snake back by the hand, or whether the old snake had a stick with which to support himself. There was not, it seems, any established association in ancient thought between mages or Chaldaeans and snake-blasting or dragon-slaying. Almost certainly Lucian has chosen to pin this marvellous story onto a Chaldaean figure because of the established association between them and the retrieval of the dead or the near-dead from death.[8]

This is an intriguing anecdote from a number of perspectives. Lucian is almost certainly deploying Christian imagery here, and accordingly satirizing it, if only gently. The motif by which Midas picks up his own stretcher and carries it back with him will be familiar to readers of the New Testament. Furthermore, strong parallels obtain between Lucian's narrative and the earliest saintly dragon-slaying stories of the Christian tradition, which are first attested from the early third century AD, and so not long after Lucian wrote. This is the tradition that ultimately produced the famous story of St George and the Dragon, although this is not itself attested until the twelfth century AD. Of particular importance in this respect are the following motifs:[9]

1. the revivification of a victim.
2. the specialist's disposal of the dragon and sometimes too of its subordinate snakes with methods that mirror the serpents' own weaponry:
    a. fire, corresponding to the fire that ancient serpents were held to flash from their eyes, and perhaps more importantly to the fiery effect of their venom.
    b. saliva, also corresponding to serpents' venom.
    c. fumigation and human breath, corresponding both to the noxious fumes that serpents were held to emit in life and in death, and also to their supposed ability to suck down victims, whether birds from the air or oxen from the field.

With the exception of the saliva, these motifs are all found in Lucian's tale. The revivification is found in the restoration of Midas. Even if he is not technically dead, his flesh contrives to recover from a condition of mortification. In the Christian tales the revivified person is a direct victim of the dragon-snake itself, whereas in Lucian's tale it is the direct victim rather of a viper, perhaps to be seen as one of the dragon-snake's minions. The Chaldaean's act of purification with a sulphur torch utilizes both fumigation and fire. And his blowing upon the snakes to burn them up utilizes both breath and, again, fire. So it is that in the early third-century AD *Acts of Thomas*, St Thomas reanimates the body of a beautiful youth killed by a great black serpent before killing the snake with its own venom. In the fourth-century *Acts of Philip* we are told how St Philip and his team of helpers come to the land of the Snake People, the Ophianoi. First they encounter a giant, fume-emitting, spark-bellied, black snake, which is attended by a host of lesser snakes. Philip deals with it by sprinkling holy water and making the sign of the cross in the air, whereupon God blinds the dragon and its attendant snakes with flames of lightning, and send beams of light into the snakes' holes, which pulverize their eggs. In Jerome's late fourth-century *Life of Hilarion*, St Hilarion kills a giant 'boa' that has been devouring flocks, herds, farmers and shepherds at Epidaurus in Dalmatia by building a pyre, ordering the snake to mount it, and then setting fire to it. In Sozomen's *Ecclesiastical History* of the 440s AD St Donatus kills a dragon in Epirus by making the sign of the cross in the air before it, spitting into its mouth and then having its carcass burned so that it would not befoul the air. Lucian's pagan tale accordingly seems to bear precious witness to the earliest stages of development of the Christian dragon-slaying story-type.[10]

Alongside such narrative traditions of mage-Chaldaeans in the Roman empire there thrived two further varieties of tradition. The first is that of the learned lore of the mages. This seems to have derived ultimately from the work of the Hellenized Egyptian Bolus of Mendes, who wrote under the pseudonymous name of Democritus, perhaps in the second century BC.[11] This lore has left a heavy impact on the elder Pliny's *Natural History*, in which he repeats a great many cures that he ascribes to the mages. He is often openly scornful of these cures, but not always, and in any case the expansive and detailed attention he gives to them in itself speaks of an underlying respect for the mages, if not exactly of admiration. So, for example, Pliny offers us an extended discussion of the medical uses to which the mages put the hyena. The skin of its head, tied on, cures headache. Its gall cures eye inflammation. Its teeth, brought into contact, cure toothache or stomach-ache. Its marrow eases pain in the sinews. Its backbone, reduced to ash, cures gout. Its eye cures barrenness in women. One of its large teeth, worn as an amulet, can dispel the fear of ghosts. Its genitals, eaten with honey, serve as an aphrodisiac for men. The white flesh from its breast can preserve women from miscarriage. Its jawbone, powdered, can induce periods in women. Its palate can cure halitosis. A fumigation derived from the fat of its loin induces instant parturition in women. The bladder helps against urinary incontinence. The faeces the animal passes as it is killed help protect one against magical attack. The end of its intestinal tube serves as an amulet to protect one in lawsuits. If a man wears the hyena's anus as an amulet on his left arm, the woman he looks at will follow him at once.[12]

Pliny also supplies us with his own associated 'history of magic'. Magic, he contends, grew out of medicine and then incorporated into itself elements of religion and astrology. The origin of magic in medicine mirrors Pliny's own predominant interest in the healing side of it. But the assertion that astrology had a key impact on the development of magic seemingly integrates Chaldaeans into the history of magic at a point close to its birth, and this is confirmed when Pliny speaks of the early luminaries of magic, once it had been invented by Zoroaster the Persian: Apusorus and Zaratas the Medes, Marmarus and Abantiphocus the Babylonians, and Tarmoendas the Assyrian.[13]

The second tradition is that of Roman legislation. Numerous laws and edicts from the Late Republic onwards addressed the threat supposedly posed by 'Chaldaeans'. The records of these measures and the accounts of their enforcement give us a rather different image of what it was to be a Chaldaean, and one a long way from that of the genial restorer to life, the raiser of friendly ghosts and the blaster of troublesome snakes and dragons. Whilst in this legal context too they are often associated with 'mages' or other varieties of sorcerer, they are overwhelmingly identified with 'astrologers' (*astrologoi*, Greek; *mathematici*, Latin) and, in connection with this, the presumed attempt to overthrow the state. In the imperial period they are typically projected as striving to accomplish this by predicting the destined date of the current emperor's death and so encouraging his ambitious rivals to bring it about. And so it is that we hear of frequent expulsions of Chaldaeans from Rome and Italy. Thus in 139 BC the praetor Cornelius Hispalus issued a decree ordering 'Chaldaeans' to depart from the city and from

Italy within ten days on the basis that they were profiteering and fogging up weak and foolish minds with their lies and bogus readings of the stars. Acting on Augustus' behalf Agrippa expelled 'astrologers' and 'sorcerers' from the city in 33 BC. In the next generation the emperor Tiberius had Libo Drusus condemned in AD 16 for revolutionary activity against him, and compelled him to suicide. Much of the case against him consisted in the fact that he had busied himself with 'the predictions of Chaldaeans and the rites of mages'. In the wake of this incident 'astrologers' were expelled from Italy. In AD 52, under Claudius, Furius Scribonianus, the son of one Camillus who had instigated a rebellion in Dalmatia, was condemned to exile on the ground that he had consulted Chaldaeans about the date of the emperor's death; he was subsequently poisoned. After Furius Scribonianus' condemnation the 'astrologers' were again expelled from Italy. In AD 69 the emperor Vitellius once more ordered 'astrologers' out of the city and Italy by 1 October, and in so doing provoked a response from a group styling itself 'Chaldaean': 'And the Chaldaeans say, for the good of the state, may Vitellius Germanicus cease to exist before that same day.' From the *Theodosian Code* compiled in AD 438 we learn of a flurry of anti-magical legislation passed under the earlier Christian emperors. In AD 357, in particular, the emperor Constantius II had forbidden the consultation of 'astrologers' (*mathematici*), 'Chaldaeans' and mages, amongst other types of diviner.[14]

Dio Cassius, writing at the turn of the second and third centuries AD, composed for Agrippa an imaginary speech of justification for expulsions of the sort over which he had presided: the Roman state needed its traditional diviners, its augurs and *haruspices*, but it should repress sorcerers and mages (*mageutai*), because they incite men to revolution, either by telling lies, or, indeed by telling the truth. He is made to contend that foreign religious cults in general are breeding grounds for conspiracies against the state and especially against autocratic rule.[15]

This culture of repression and expulsion provided a fertile context in which entertaining and paradoxical tales about individual emperors' relations with Chaldaeans could develop, and the famously benign emperor Marcus Aurelius was the beneficiary of these, although the stories told have little to do with astrology. The *Suda* tells us that, according to some, Julian the Chaldaean, father of Julian the Theurge and the supposed author of the *Chaldaean Oracles*, was responsible for bringing about a rain miracle for him in AD 172, when his thirsty army had been facing the Quadi. A series of demons had been called upon, including Hermes Aerios. However, others attributed this miracle rather to an Egyptian sacred scribe, Harnouphis or Arnouphis. We are also told that Marcus Aurelius' wife Faustina, daughter of Antoninus Pius, fell in love with a gladiator. She fell into a protracted sickness because of her love, and eventually confessed all to her husband. He referred the matter to 'the Chaldaeans' and they advised that the gladiator should be killed, that Faustina should bathe in his blood, and that she should then sleep with her husband in this condition. The technique worked, but the unfortunate side effect was that it made of the son thus conceived, Commodus, a man more gladiator than emperor by nature. This was why he proceeded to present the Roman people with almost a thousand gladiatorial shows, and even took to the arena himself.[16]

Before it was Persian, Babylon had been Assyrian, and so it was that Assyrians too, and also Syrians, whom, as Herodotus tells us, the Greeks identified with them, also became races of magical adepts. Syria proper perhaps became even easier to associate in its own right with magic in the early Hellenistic period, when Babylon fell within the Seleucid empire, itself based in Syria. In the 270s BC Theocritus' amateur witch Simaetha tells that she has drugs of a terrible power that she keeps in a box, and that she has learned of them from an 'Assyrian stranger'. A pseudo-Aristotelian fragment, perhaps from roughly the same period, speaks of a mage coming to Athens from Syria and predicting many things about Socrates, including his violent death. And, as we have just seen, Pliny lists the Assyrian Tarmoendas as an early luminary of the magical art, alongside Medes and Babylonians.[17]

Syrians (*tout court*) were also projected as a race of magical adepts in the high Roman empire, as indeed was a more specialized variety of them, 'Syrians from Palaestine', a circumlocution for the Jews (to whose sorcerers we will give separate consideration below). We find a 'Syrian' magical master in the preface to the Hermetic handbook of magical amulets *Cyranides*, composed at some point between the first and fourth centuries AD, supposedly by one Harpocration. The preface seems to strive, in a fashion that leaves the reader somewhat confused, at once to mesh and to differentiate the magical pedigrees of Babylonia and 'Syria'. We are first told that the amulet recipes with which the book will present us were found 'engraved in Syrian letters on iron and submerged in a lake in Syria'. But we are then given a rather different tale for the discovery of the text, the location of which is explicitly Babylonia, albeit a very Seleucid Babylonia, with its cities named Seleuceia and Alexandria. Harpocration tells how he was wandering about this territory when he fell in with an old man, a Syrian by birth, who had learned to speak Greek as a prisoner of war. The old man showed Harpocration a massive stela, surrounded by three towers that extended miles up into the air, and which had been built by the giants. The locals said the stela had been brought there *from* Syria and set up to heal the men who lived in the city some four miles distant. Harpocration examined the stela and found it to be engraved with foreign letters. The old man was rather more keen to tell him about the towers, but he begged him rather to help him understand the inscriptions. He immediately agreed, and translated them into Greek for him, this translation constituting the basis of the amulet recipes that follow in the main body of the text. Some of the themes found here, an eager, wandering student, a venerable old master and an arcane magical text, are often found combined in the traditional tales attached to Egyptian sorcerers, as we shall see.[18]

As we turn to the hagiographical tradition we encounter the delightful tale of a sorcerer from Syria proper, Cyprian of Antioch, the former Seleucid capital. The tale is found in the *Lives of Saints Cyprian and Justina*. Stylistic criteria suggest that the work was composed in the mid-fourth century AD.[19]

The narrative is set in Antioch and begins by telling how the pagan virgin Justina is converted by the deacon Praylius whom she hears preaching through a window, although her parents, Aedesius and Cledonia, are initially resistant. But they themselves are converted when they experience a vision of Christ in a dream. Praylius takes the three of them off to bishop Optatus for baptism. Justina makes continual promenades to church, and as she does so, a rich, leisured young man, 'taken with the error of idols', Aglaidas, conceives a desire for her. He sends many go-betweens to seduce her, but she sends them all back with fleas in their ears and the reproof, 'I am betrothed to Christ.' An attempt at rape fails when the girl, to whom Aglaidas is holding tight, makes the sign of the cross and throws him supine on the ground, pummelling him black and blue with her fists. Then, 'following in the footsteps of her model Thecla, she went off to the house of the Lord'.

So Aglaidas tries a third tack. He approaches the mage Cyprian and agrees to pay him two talents of gold and two of silver to capture the virgin for him with his magic. Cyprian duly summons a demon through his sorceries. He asks the demon to list its achievements, to prove to him that it has sufficient ability for the task in hand. The demon makes great boasts, which include the claim to have made angels fall, to have deceived Eve, to have persuaded Cain to kill his brother, to have persuaded the Jews to make the golden calf and to have persuaded the people of Jerusalem to crucify Christ. The demon then gives Cyprian a special drug to sprinkle around the virgin's house, and undertakes thereupon to come and fetch the girl to her lover. Justina wakes during the following night and perceives the demon's attack in the form of a burning in her kidneys. She then crosses herself, invokes Jesus with a list of his achievements somewhat mirroring those claimed by the demon ('You plunged the man-killing serpent into Hell', etc.), blows upon the demon and sends it off in dishonour. The demon presents itself again to Cyprian, now in a state of crestfallen shame, and confesses that it was not able to bring the girl, because it saw 'a certain sign' and was terrified.

Cyprian laughs the demon off and summons a stronger one. This second demon, confident that it can succeed where the last failed, similarly gives Cyprian a drug to sprinkle around the girl's house, in preparation for its coming to persuade her. Cyprian dutifully does this and the demon duly arrives at the house, again in the middle of the night, to find Justina at prayer. She completes her prayer with the sign of the cross, rebukes the demon and sends it off. It similarly returns to Cyprian and confesses its failure before the sign she had made.

So Cyprian summons a yet stronger demon, the father of all demons. This one too confidently predicts success in fetching the girl. It will, it says, throw her into a turmoil amid various fevers and then, after six days, stand over her in the middle of the night and make her ready for Cyprian. The demon in due course goes off to the virgin in the form of another virgin, sits on her bed, and asks her whether her virginity is worth so much, since she is so badly afflicted. It takes her by the hand and attempts to draw her out of her door, but she recognizes the demon for what it is, makes the sign of the cross over herself, blows upon it and sends it away in dishonour, just like the first demon. So the third demon, covered in shame, reports back to Cyprian. Again it speaks of the terrible sign, and offers to tell Cyprian the nature of the sign if he will swear by its remaining powers not to abandon it. Cyprian swears as bidden. Cheered by this, the demon explains that it saw the sign of the 'crucified one' and was terrified. 'Is the crucified one more powerful than you?' asks Cyprian, and the demon concedes that he is more powerful than all, and presides over the tortures of the sinful in the underworld. Cyprian concludes that he too should therefore become a friend of the crucified one, so as to avoid such punishments. The demon remonstrates with Cyprian: will he break his oath and abandon it? Cyprian proudly asserts that he does indeed break his oath, for he need not fear the demon's powers after this demonstration of the power of the cross against it. He implies also that this demonstration has been brought home to him by the prayers of Justina. He now makes the sign of the cross himself, divorcing himself from the demon, and it slinks off in shame.

Cyprian takes his magical books to St Anthimus to burn. Anthimus at first suspects a trick on Cyprian's part, but is eventually persuaded of his sincerity. Cyprian returns home, destroys his idols and beats himself. God then sends Cyprian further signs to confirm his conversion in the form of overheard readings from the Bible. Cyprian presents himself in a church, where the deacon Asterius, similarly suspecting deceit, attempts to throw him out, but is eventually persuaded to refer him to the bishop, who agrees to instruct him. The excellent student rises quickly through the ranks, and is eventually made bishop, whereupon he makes Justina a deacon and sets her over a convent, and the story comes to an end.

Blowing upon a demon was an established Judaeo-Christian technique of demon exorcism. In the Judaeo-Christian influenced recipe for the 'Validated recipe of Pibechis for use upon those possessed by demons' found among the Greek Magical Papyri, at the climax of the spell prescribed the exorcist is to blow upon the demoniac, raising his breath from his feet up to his face, and this will expel the demon. We shall return to this recipe below.[20]

The pagan fetching spell here envisaged has some clear antecedents, as we shall see when we come to look at Lucian's tale of the Hyperborean mage and some related magical papyri in Chapter 4. The erotic-magic element of the *Cyprian* story can also be paralleled in a broad way elsewhere within the Christian tradition, for example with an episode in Jerome's *Life of St Hilarion the Hermit*, composed before 396 AD. Here a young man of Gaza fails in his attempts to seduce a 'virgin of God' and so has himself instructed in the magical arts in Memphis. He is thus enabled to insert a maddening Memphite love-demon into the girl by burying a curse-tablet under her threshold. The demon is, of course, expelled by St Hilarion. In another intriguing example Palladius, writing in 419–20 AD, tells the tale of an Egyptian who hires a sorcerer to bring to him a chaste married woman he desires, but the sorcerer contrives rather to transform her into a horse. The unfortunate woman is eventually restored to human form with holy water by St Macarius. It has been suggested that the mistaken transformation should be understood to be the result of the sorcerer having gone too far in his attempts to make her resemble a mare on heat as an icon of lust.[21]

The account of the Cyprian-and-Justina story that has become best known in the West is the Latin version found in Jacobus de Voragine's thirteenth-century *Golden Legend*. Here the roles of lover and magician are rolled into one, with Cyprian taking them both. This tale, alongside another from the *Golden Legend*, that of the sacked priest Theophilus who sells his soul to the Devil to get his job back, exerted a substantial influence on the later development of the Faust legend. On the Eastern side an intriguing item of Nachleben for Cyprian is to be found in a Coptic rag-paper magic book of the eleventh century AD. In this the Christian and fully confessional Cyprian offers up a spell of erotic attraction now powered by the angel Gabriel.[22]

In later Greek literature we find double-whammy portraits of magical adepts who combine the ethnicity of venerable magical races with the gender and other attributes of the Graeco-Roman witch. One of Lucian's engaging gossiping courtesans, Bacchis, tells her friend Melitta how she once availed herself of the love magic offered by a Syrian witch (*pharmakis*), whose flesh is still young and firm (thanks to her magic?). Her fee for her erotic-attraction spell is two drachmas and an obol, a loaf of bread, and a whole bowl of wine for her to drink all by herself. It is clear that she salutes the type of the Latin bawd-witch. She must also be provided with some magical supplies for her task: salt, sulphur, a torch and one of the man's possessions, some clothing, a boot or some of his hair, i.e., some of his 'stuff'. She hangs the stuff up on a peg and fumigates it with the sulphur, meanwhile sprinkling some of the salt over a fire. She intones the two names in question, and then she brings out a magic wheel (*rhombos*), sets it spinning and utters an incantation of foreign and terrifying names. Bacchis tells that by using this technique the woman was able to bring back her former lover Phanias to her after four months' absence, and that too despite the reproach of his colleagues and the fact that his new girlfriend, Phoebis, begged him at length to stay. The witch also has a spell to instil hatred for a love rival, which she is happy to teach the courtesans. The courtesan must watch out for the love rival's footprints, whenever she should leave any, rub them out and place her own right foot over the trace of the rival's left one, and her left one over her rival's right one, reciting the words, 'I have trodden on you and I am on top of you.' We will shortly encounter, in the case of the old woman of Bessa, a similar double-whammy portrait of a magical professional who combines the qualities of witch and oriental sorcerer, in this case an Egyptian.[23]

Egyptian priest-sorcerers

The association of Egypt with magic also came to flourish in the imperial period, but it was an old one, older indeed than that of Persia and Babylon. For already in the *Odyssey* Helen is said to have received the magical drugs with which she banishes the cares of Menelaus and Telemachus from the Egyptian Polydamna, and we are told at that point that the land of Egypt produces many such drugs, both harmful and beneficial. We may wonder whether the name of Polydamna's husband, Thōn, salutes that of the Egyptian god the later Greeks came to associate with magic, Thōth.[24]

The imperial period was to bequeath us many fine portraits of Egyptian sorcerers at work. These are typically presented as venerable priests in Egyptian terms, and consequently as shaven-headed and dressed in white linen. Already in Virgil's *Eclogue* of 39 BC we encounter an intriguing sketch of the sorcerer Moeris. This man, instructor in magic to the woman who speaks of him, just as the Assyrian had been to Simaetha, picks plants in Medea's homeland area of the Black Sea, and uses them to transform himself into a wolf, rouse ghosts from the bottom of their tombs and spirit crops away from one field into another. Since Moeris serves Herodotus as the name of a pharaoh, we can be sure that Virgil is identifying this sorcerer as Egyptian. In an act that combines difference from with deference to his model, Theocritus, Virgil flips to the other pole of oriental sorcery.[25]

Our single most elaborate portrait of an Egyptian sorcerer is to be found in the figure of Nectanebo in the Greek *Alexander Romance* ascribed pseudonymously to Callisthenes, the historian Alexander took with him on his great campaign. The earliest version of the *Alexander Romance* that we can aspire to recover from the narrative's highly complex and multi-lingual tradition is one that circulated in the third century AD. This can be reconstructed from an abbreviated Greek version of it in an eleventh-century AD Parisian codex and an Armenian translation of a fuller Greek version made in the fifth century AD. The *Romance*'s purpose in its opening chapters is to project Alexander's conquest of Egypt as the restoration of the rightful heir to the throne, after a brief period of Persian domination. To this end an elaborate fiction is developed to make Alexander the blood son not of the

Macedonian King Philip, but of the last of the pharaohs, Nectanebo II, that is, Nekht-hor-heb (reigned 349–1 BC).

Nectanebo, the *Romance* tells us, gained mastery over all peoples by magical power and could subject all the elements in the universe to himself by speech. He did not bother with armies or weapons to subdue his enemies. Rather, he would merely retreat into his palace, take a bronze bowl, which he would fill with little boats and wax models of his enemies, and then recite a spell over them whilst waving his ebony wand, and so sink their ships. But one day, when he learns that the enemies of Egypt are once more massing against it from one of his spies, he again sets up his magic bowl to cast his spell upon them, but as he does so he sees the Egyptians' own gods steering the enemy boats, and so understands that this time the conquest of Egypt is inevitable. So he disguises himself as an Egyptian priest by shaving his head and beard and sneaking out of Egypt through Pelusium, carrying as much gold as he can. After wanderings he arrives at Pella, the capital of Macedon, where he dons the linen tunic typically worn by Egyptian prophets and astrologers and sets up stall offering divinations to all comers. Meanwhile the god of the Sinopium prophesies to the Egyptians that their pharaoh will return to them in the form of a young man traversing the world, and that he will subjugate their enemies.

In Pella news of the success of Nectanebo's divinations comes to the royal palace and to the ear of Olympias, queen of King Philip, who is away on campaign. She summons him, and he falls in love with her at first sight. She asks him about the methods of divination he uses, and in response he explains that there are many varieties of diviners, dream-interpreters, omen-interpreters, augurs, prophets, Ammon-prophets, nativity-casters, mages and astrologers. He himself draws upon the techniques of all these groups, but as a supreme prophet of the Egyptian school, he is principally a 'mage and an astrologer'. He offers to make divinations for her. He produces a special 'royal tablet' with which he is able to make astrological calculations and asks Olympias for the date and hour of her birth. His immediate calculations reveal that his own stars and the queen's are in favourable conjunction, and he resolves to seduce her. He tells Olympias that she is fated to have sex with a god come to earth and to be impregnated by him, and that the child she will bear will avenge her for the wrongs done to her by Philip. The god is to be the ram-horned Ammon. He tells her that she will see the god making love to her in a dream. He then goes out into the wilderness and picks some plants suitable for the sending of dreams, and from these he makes a decoction. He makes a model of a female body from wax, inscribes it with Olympias' name and puts it in a little bed. He throws the decoction into a lamp and invokes demons to put images into Olympias' mind, so that she sees a vision of Ammon making love to her. The next morning Nectanebo tells her that she has conceived an avenger.

Olympias now tells Nectanebo that she wishes to have sex with Ammon whilst awake and in daylight. He agrees to arrange it, and asks for a chamber adjacent to Olympias' supposedly so that he can help her with his incantations if she is frightened by her experience of the god. He tells her that when the god first manifests himself to her it will be in the form of a snake slithering along the ground and hissing. He will then transform himself into horned Ammon and finally, as he embraces her, into the form of Nectanebo himself. Ammon is given the bedchamber he seeks and now sets about making his preparations. He avails himself of a snake, which he renders tame and harmless and teaches to crawl along in upright position, and a fleece, with which to disguise himself as Ammon. He then releases the snake into Olympias' chamber. When she sees it she recognizes the god, without fear, and bids her attendants withdraw. Nectanebo follows the snake into the room in his Ammon disguise, before doffing this to appear as himself and have sex with her. This becomes a regular activity. Olympias accordingly does indeed become pregnant.

Nectanebo assuages any concerns that Philip may develop about the pregnancy and its timing by sending a dream to him too by means of a sea-hawk, and this dream is interpreted for him by a Babylonian dream-interpreter as signifying that Olympias has been impregnated by Ammon. On Philip's return to Pella Nectanebo makes a further proof of his fiction by transforming himself into a giant snake and kissing her, before transforming himself again into an eagle and flying off.

When the time comes for Olympias to give birth Nectanebo attends her at the birthing stool, with the object of ensuring that her son is born at exactly the conjunction of stars that will destine him for greatness. Taking the precepts of astrology to their logical conclusion, he commands Olympias to get up and walk around to hold the baby in during unfavourable conjunctions, and then to bring the baby forth at the optimum time. Subsequently, Nectanebo is killed by the twelve-year-old Alexander, who despises astrology. As he dies, Nectanebo reveals to him and to Olympias that it is he himself who is the father of the boy.[26]

Nectanebo's magic, as we might expect from a text with a rich and complex tradition behind it, seems to merge different varieties of technique as we know them from documentary sources and indeed from other literary texts. The spells that Nectanebo makes in his bowl seem to combine the sorts of magic associated with voodoo dolls, that of binding and that of analogy, with the divinatory magic of lecanomancy ('bowl divination'). And the use of the Olympias voodoo doll seems to combine a dream-sending spell with the technology of erotic-attraction magic.

But perhaps the most interesting aspect of this account is the device with which Nectanebo makes his astronomical-astrological calculations. The *Romance*'s account of the device runs as follows:

> He produced a precious royal tablet, the form of which cannot be conveyed in words. Three bands separated its ivory, ebony, gold and silver sections. On its first circle it had the thirty-six decans, on the second the twelve zodiacal signs, on the middle one the sun and the moon. He put it on a stool. Then he opened a small box, this too of ivory, and emptied from it the seven stars and the nativity-ascendant sign, made from eight stones ... He arranged them and illuminated this little heaven by placing them in a small circle. He added a sun made from rock crystal, a moon made from adamant, a Mars of hematite, a Mercury of emerald, a Saturn of serpentine, and the nativity-ascendant sign of white marble. He said, 'Tell me, Queen, the year, month, day and hour of your birth.' She told him, and Nectanebo charted his own birth and that of Olympias, to see if their stars were in a favorable conjunction. Once he saw that they were ...[27]

The device described here bears a striking resemblance to the famous Anticythera mechanism, an astrolabe or astronomical computer found in 82 fragments in the c. 80 BC wreck of a Roman cargo ship that was discovered by sponge divers off the island of Anticythera in 1901. Our understanding of the device's functions has recently been enhanced by a new investigation of its fragments that has exploited sophisticated X-ray tomography to get a better appreciation of its gears and to reveal more of the its inscriptions. The machine, which long remained unrecognized for what it was, was constructed in the late second century BC, as we infer from the form of its inscriptions, and probably therefore along principles developed by the distinguished astronomer Hipparchus of Nicaea, whose floruit fell in the third quarter of that century. It consisted of a complex series of (perhaps) 37 crank-operated bronze gears, many of them now locked together by corrosion, and would originally have fitted into a flattish, book-like wooden box measuring

c. 31.5 x 19 x 10 cm. Both 'covers' of the 'book' opened to reveal the inscribed exterior plates and concentric reading-dials and pointers of the machine itself. Traces of inscriptions on the plates and dials relate to the 365-day calendar, the zodiac, the planets, the sun, the moon and eclipses. Recesses in the dials, would, it is thought, originally have held beads to represent stars or planets. The machine was able to express the Saros luni-solar canon, knowledge of which in the ancient world is only otherwise found in the historical Babylon. It also expressed lunar and solar eclipses, planetary movements and the rising and falling of constellations. Its gears were even capable of taking account of the moon's elliptical orbit. We may be confident that the tale of Nectanebo's tablet preserves a dim recollection of astrological computers of this general kind. Accordingly, the *Alexander Romance* offers a fascinating illustration of a populist, magical reinterpretation of something that we would regard as a piece of precocious scientific technology.[28]

We encounter intriguing portraits of Egyptian magicians in three texts of roughly the same period. All of these are strongly projected in the first instance as priests and precious preservers of ancient and arcane religion. The first is the Zatchlas of Apuleius' *Metamorphoses* (c. 150–70), whom we met in the last chapter. He is introduced as an 'Egyptian prophet'. As we saw, he reanimates a recently dead man for a large sum. He is a young man, shaven bald, dressed in linen and he wears palm-leaf sandals. He reanimates the dead Thelyphron by placing one sprig of a mysterious herb on the corpse's mouth and another on its breast, and then making a prayer to the rising sun. The second is the Pancrates of Lucian's *Philopseudes*. Pancrates is the sorcerer in Lucian's original version of the famous story of *The Sorcerer's Apprentice*, another tale in which a young man's desperate search for arcane knowledge figures prominently. He is based in Memphis, he is long and thin and snub-nosed, and has protruding lips and skinny legs. He always wears linen. He speaks his Greek with a heavy accent. He has lived in underground crypts for 23 years whilst being instructed in magic by the goddess Isis. Animals fawn upon him, as they do on Circe. He exhibits a range of magical abilities, amongst which are the ability to ride on crocodiles, the ability to animate wooden sticks for domestic service and, seemingly, the ability to disappear into thin air. We shall look in more detail at Pancrates and his famous story in the following chapter.[29]

Harder to date, but also thought to have been produced in the second century AD, is an astro-botanical treatise *On the Power of Plants*. This is pseudonymously assigned to a historical physician of the first century AD, Thessalus of Tralles. In the prologue the pretended Thessalus explains how he discovered the astrologically determined powers of plants that are to be laid out in the body of his work (note the astrological theme again). He tells how as a brilliant young medical student in Alexandria he had discovered a marvellous book of Nechepso, which contained 24 cures for all complaints, organized in accordance with the zodiac. Excited by his discovery, he prematurely writes home to his parents about it, only then to discover that he cannot get any of the cures to work. Disconsolate and bordering on the suicidal, he wanders about the land of Egypt until he comes to Diospolis – Egyptian Thebes, the country's most ancient city – where he settles and becomes familiar with many of the learned and aged chief priests who lived there. He enquires whether any of them know anything of the old magical arts. They tell them they do, but most of them, he discovers in due course, do not really know what they are talking about. However, he finds one in whom he is able to place his trust, because of the man's self-confidence and the measure of his years. He is, according to different versions of the text, a master of lecanomancy (bowl divination) or of necromancy. Thessalus persuades him to go for a walk in the deserted parts of the city, and then throws himself on his mercy. He begs to be allowed personal direct access to a god. This the man gladly consents to do, and supervises Thessalus' fasting-purification prior to the encounter. After three days of this the priest prepares at dawn to seal Thessalus, duly equipped with pen and paper, into a purified chamber. The priest then asks Thessalus whether he wishes to have his special encounter with a ghost of a dead person or a god, and without hesitation Thessalus demands to see the healing god Asclepius, somewhat to the priest's displeasure. The priest sits Thessalus opposite a throne and then causes the god to materialize upon it by pronouncing a series of secret names. He withdraws from the chamber himself, shutting Thessalus into it. The god of his own accord addresses Thessalus, and offers to answer all his questions. He explains that Nechepso's cures fail to work because, for all his brilliance and perspicuity, Nechepso had been in want of the divine revelation of the sort that Thessalus is now himself receiving, and therefore did not understand the astrologically determined times at which or the places in which the herbs had to be picked in order to be efficacious. When Asclepius has completed his exposition and has answered Thessalus' questions, it is by now midnight. Asclepius ascends directly into heaven, and Thessalus returns to his priest.[30]

We find the ideal of the necromantic Egyptian priest appealed to also in the pseudonymous *Clementine Romance*, first composed, it is thought, in the third century BC. Here the Christian Clement of Rome (supposedly) describes how as a young man he craved proof of the soul's survival of death. So he hatched a plan to go to Egypt, insinuate himself into the friendship of one of 'the hierophants of the crypts', 'prophets' or 'mages'. He would prevail upon him, offering him a great deal of money, to evocate the soul of a dead man for him in necromancy, on the pretence that he wanted to consult the ghost on a point of business, but the real purpose of the enquiry would be to observe, more simply, whether or not the soul was immortal. The young Clement was, however, dissuaded from this dangerous course of action before he could proceed with it. We shall see, in the final chapter of this book, some further examples of early Christian saints violating basic Christian doctrine in strangely pagan fashion in order to summon up ghosts.[31]

Some of the themes we have already met in connection with Egyptian magic, necromancy, crypts of instruction, magical books and the desperate search for lost, arcane knowledge, are found in another narrative, this one pseudonymously ascribed to Democritus. But here the Egyptian master has been supplanted by a master from the Asian conglomerate of magical races, specifically the Persians, and that too a dead one. The narrative is a fragment, apparently from the prologue, of the foundation text of ancient alchemy, the *Physica et Mystica* ('The natural and the mystical'). The text may be as early as the second century BC, if it was indeed written by the hellenizing Egyptian Bolus of Mendes, to whom we have already referred and who passed off many of his works under the name of Democritus, or it may be as late as the first century AD.[32]

Democritus and his associates are pursuing their researches in Memphis, under the guidance of the great Persian mage Ostanes the elder, and evidently a shrine of some sort has been playing a role in their education. Unfortunately, the great mage dies before he is able to reveal to his pupils all the secrets of alchemy, the transmutation of the nature of substances. So Democritus resorts to the obvious measure, and calls up his ghost from Hades to ask him repeatedly how to proceed with the transmutation of natures. The ghost is restrained from passing the information on by a certain demon, but it is at least able to say to Democritus, 'The books are in the shrine.' None of the pupils know anything of these books, but Ostanes' son, Ostanes the younger, is evidently aware of their existence, if not of their content. The pupils' searches of the shrine reveal nothing. But one day, when they are all feasting in it, a pillar in its temple splits open of its own accord, and the younger Ostanes finds his father's books inside it. The pupils huddle over them and find the key phrase written everywhere, 'Nature delights in nature; nature conquers nature; nature dominates nature.' This phrase crystallizes the central principles of alchemy, those of sympathy, antipathy and neutralization.[33]

In Heliodorus' fourth-century AD novel *Aethiopica* ('An Ethiopian tale') we find an implicit portrait of an Egyptian sorcerer in the words of the Egyptian priest-prophet Calasiris. When Theagenes comes to his door, he anticipates that the young man has made the familiar mistake of confusing the two varieties of Egyptian wisdom. The sort of wisdom he believes the young man to be seeking is that which can offer him help in a love affair. This is the 'common' or 'earthly' variety of Egyptian wisdom. It is lawless and often serves the pleasures of lust. Its stock-in-trade consists of ghosts, the making of circles around the dead, plants and incantations. Its occasional successes are trivial, but it carries the risk of inflicting great harm upon those that practise it. By contrast, Calasiris himself, as a priest-prophet, is rather an exponent of the pure variety of Egyptian wisdom, which is quite distinct from the earthly, corrupted version. This uncorrupted variety is practised by those of the priest-prophet caste from childhood: it looks up to the heavens, it frequents with the gods and shares in their divine nature, and devotes itself to all that is good and helpful to man. Here we can see a distinction is being ventured that seems to mimic the old Platonic distinction between 'common' or 'earthly' love and divine love. And it fixes upon Egyptian magicians' characteristic projection as priests, their characteristic association with astrology (as with Nectanebo), and their characteristic association with encounters with gods in crypts, in order to define the heavenly variety (as with Pancrates and Thessalus).[34]

The distinctions between the two forms of Egyptian wisdom that Calasiris makes here are subsequently graphically realized in one of the novel's most striking episodes, that of the 'old woman of Bessa'. As with Lucian's Syrian witch, we here find a double-whammy synthesis of an oriental-sorcerer type with a more traditional witch.

Calasiris and the ingénue-heroine Charicleia find in their wanderings a little old Egyptian woman lamenting over the body of her dead son in the midst of a corpse-strewn battlefield. She promises to guide them to the local village, if they will first withdraw a little and allow her to perform some nocturnal rites for her son. This they do. The old woman digs a pit and kindles a fire, and lays out her son's body between the two. Calasiris sleeps, but the light of the fire allows Charicleia to observe the woman's activities through the night whilst remaining unnoticed by her. The old woman makes libations into the pit of honey, milk and wine, from three bowls. She moulds a dough-cake into the form of a humanoid doll, and makes a crown of laurel and fennel for it. This too she throws into the pit. Then she works herself up into a frenzy and invokes the moon with a string of *voces magicae* or 'words of power'. She slits her own arm open with a sword, wipes some of the blood onto a laurel branch and throws this into the fire. She then bends over and sings an incantation into her son's ear, and thus rouses him and compels him to stand upright by her magic. Charicleia is by now terrified and wakes Calasiris and bids him watch with her. They see that the old woman is interrogating the corpse to learn whether her remaining son, his brother, will return home safe and sound. The corpse makes no response, but just gives an indistinct nod, an insecure hope of a favourable answer, before falling flat on its face. The old woman begins again, rolling the corpse back onto its back. She sings more powerful, more compulsive incantations and leaps back and forth between the pit and the fire, brandishing the sword. Again she uprights the corpse and interrogates it, compelling it this time to speak plainly. Charicleia, evidently as fascinated as she is terrified, begs Calasiris to approach closer with her for a better view, but he refuses: it is not holy to watch such rites, he explains, and he contrasts his own pure form of divination with the impure form being practised by the woman. At this point the corpse begins to speak in a deep, ugly voice, as if from a crypt or a cave. The dead man rebukes his mother for outrageously violating the decrees of the gods with her sorceries, and complains that she is withholding his due rites of burial and so preventing his soul from mingling with the other souls of the dead. But he then proceeds to prophesy: her other son will soon be dead, and so will she, this by way of punishment for her lawless practices. It is a further crime on her part that she performs these mysteries not in secret but in a context in which she can be observed, as she is now by the prophet and, more unforgivably, the innocent girl. When it has finished, the corpse crumples and falls. The crone is now seized with anger towards Charicleia and Calasiris for watching her, grabs her sword and rushes over the field of dead bodies to find them and kill them. But as she does so she accidentally impales herself on a projecting spear and dies, thus neatly fulfilling her dead son's prophecy.[35]

This is the third necromantic reanimation scene we have encountered, after those of Erictho and Zatchlas. We may note that it shares some distinctive elements with the others: an Egyptian context; the use of herbs; the uprighting of the corpse before it is made to speak, in a symbolic return to life; and an eventual prophecy of doom.

Already in Virgil's day we had come close to another double-whammy portrait of this sort. His Dido tells of a Massylian witch (a figment of her imagination, no doubt) who resides on the west coast of Ethiopia. The ancients held that Ethiopia extended the width of Africa to meet the Atlantic. She has many typical witch-like qualities. She can release people from love and inflict it upon them; she can halt rivers in their course and send the stars backwards; she can raise ghosts by night; she can level mountains and transplant trees. Just as Medea had put the dragon that guarded the golden fleece to sleep with her herbs, so this witch puts to sleep the dragon that guards the golden apples of the Hesperides with the opium of poppies. But like her male African counterparts, the Massylian witch is also a priestess, specifically of the temple of the Hesperides.[36]

Judaeo-Christian exorcists

Greek literature of the imperial period preserves many accounts of exorcisms of demons from possessed individuals, the demons often clearly identifiable as ghosts. The exorcists concerned are always Jewish or Christian, or projected as acting, somehow, in the Judaeo-Christian tradition. It is accordingly most likely that the pagans imported the practice of exorcism and indeed the types of narrative in which it was celebrated from Jewish culture. In addition to the Judaeo-Christian affiliation, narratives of exorcisms in ancient literature tend to follow a formulaic pattern. First, the demon is ordered out, but it initially refuses to obey. Then it is ordered out a second time, to the accompaniment of terrible threats, and it does indeed obey. Often the demon is adjured in the name of a particularly powerful sorcerer in a historical tradition. The demon is compelled to confess its name and identity, and this act is often in itself tantamount to expulsion: identifying a demon, a creature of deceit, is evidently more than half the battle. As the demon is forced out of the body it has been possessing it gives a physical token of its departure: it is visible as it departs, usually in the form of a dark figure, or it makes a noise, or it knocks over or destroys an external object on its outward flight.[37]

One of the most striking descriptions of an exorcism by a Jewish sorcerer is to be found in Josephus' *Jewish Antiquities*, published in 93–4 AD. Josephus explains that he himself witnessed the marvellous work of Eleazar, who delivered the possessed of their demons before the emperor Vespasian and his sons. He would apply a ring to the nose of the demoniac, a ring which contained a root prescribed by Solomon beneath its seal (in the fashion repeatedly described in the *Cyranides*). As the demoniac smelled the ring, Eleazar would draw the demon out of him through his nostrils. The demoniac would collapse at once. Eleazar would adjure the demon never to return, invoke the name of Solomon, and utter his incantations. In order to demonstrate the demon's exit, Eleazar would set up at a short remove a cup or bowl of water, and command the demon to overturn it as it departed. We find the technique of expelling a demon through the nose employed also in a brief fourth-century AD exorcism recipe in a text among the Greek Magical Papyri that calls itself the 'Eighth Book of Moses': 'If you say the name to a man possessed by a demon whilst applying sulphur and bitumen to his nose, the demon will give voice at once and depart.'[38]

Our earliest records of Judaeo-Christian exorcism are to be found in the New Testament. The best known case is that of the demons of Gerasa, as recounted by Mark and Luke. We are told that as Jesus arrives in Gerasa, crossing a lake in a boat, he is confronted by a man possessed by an unclean spirit, who lives amongst the tombs or on the mountains, bawling and mutilating himself with stones. The demon gives the man supernatural strength, and he is able to smash through any chains with which the Gerasenes attempt to restrain him. Jesus bids the demon depart from the man, and it begs Jesus not to torture it. Jesus compels it to confess its name, whereupon it makes the famous reply, 'My name is Legion, because we are many.' Jesus sends the demons, now revealed to be plural, out into an adjacent herd of pigs, some 2,000-strong. The herd then rushes into the nearby lake and drowns itself. The swineherds run off to the town to report the events, and people gather at the spot. They find the demoniac sitting clothed and sane beside Jesus, but they are understandably less impressed by the fate of the pigs, and they urge Jesus to leave their territory. The expulsion of a demon of ill health into an animal is a theme we will find repeated in the case of the intriguing Antaura amulet, discussed in the following chapter. There is also a sense in which the casting out of an impure thing from a human into an animal, followed by the expulsion or destruction of that animal, recalls the Jewish practice of scapegoating.[39]

One can well understand the townspeople's dismay at the financial disaster Jesus had inflicted upon them. According to Acts the townspeople of Philippi were similarly dismayed when Paul and Silas took it upon themselves to exorcise a possessing demon from a slave girl. Paul invoked the powerful name of Jesus to expel it: 'I order you to depart from her in the name of Jesus Christ'. But the demon was a prophetic one and had accordingly been making a lot of money for the slave girl's owners. When the owners saw their trade destroyed they hauled Paul and Silas before the market officials, who accordingly stripped them, beat them and threw them into gaol.[40]

Eleazar invoked the name of Solomon to frighten his demon, and Paul invoked the name of Jesus to frighten his. Both names are invoked in an exorcism spell preserved in one of the grimoires of the Greek Magical Papyri, the 'Validated recipe of Pibechis for use upon those possessed by demons'. This is found in a fourth-century AD text, perhaps a copy of second-century AD original. Despite the fact that the recipe is attributed to the legendary Egyptian sorcerer Pibechis, and the fact that it includes some Egyptianizing names amongst its *voces magicae*, it is predominantly and self-avowedly Judaeo-Christian in texture and contains many echoes of the language of the Septuagint (the terms Osrael, i.e. Israel, and Jerusalem, *inter alia*, are featured). The recipe even ends with an apostrophic exhortation to its reader and user, 'And I adjure you, the one who take up this exorcism, not to eat pork! ... Guard your purity, for this spell is Hebraic and kept safe by pure men.' The recipe provides for the manufacture of tin lamella to be hung around the demoniac's neck. This, so we are told, is something of which every demon is afraid. One is then to adjure the demon by 'the god of the Hebrews, Jesus ...' and by 'the seal of Solomon', a famous Jewish amulet. Evidently, one did not have to be a disciple of Jesus, as Paul was, to attempt to use his name in a spell of exorcism. However, according to Acts again, some itinerant exorcists, the seven sons of Sceva, the chief priest of the Jews, tried to deploy the name of Jesus in one of their exorcisms, but with disastrous results. The Ephesian demoniac upon whom they tried to use the name remained possessed, mocked them, beat them up and sent them off naked and wounded. The problem, apparently, was that they used the name without faith.[41]

The earliest pagan – or apparently pagan – account of an exorcism is found in Lucian's *Philopseudes*. Here the Platonist Ion attempts to persuade the sceptical Tychiades of the reality of ghosts or demons by reminding him of a 'Syrian from Palaestine' supposedly known to all.

This man, Ion says, takes anyone who falls down at the sight of the moon, twists their eyes and foams at the mouth, sets them back on their feet and sends them off again sound in mind, delivering them from their affliction for a large fee. Whenever he stands over the demoniacs as they lie afflicted and asks the demons whence they come into the body, the demon itself gives answer, speaking in Greek or in the language of its country of origin, and explains how and when it entered the person. The Syro-Palaestinian then adjures it to leave, and if it does not obey, he drives it out with threats. Ion tells Tychiades that he saw one of the demons leaving: it was black and smoky in colour, as ghosts were often held to be. Tychiades remains unimpressed and makes a quip to the effect that Ion is better equipped to see such murky and evanescent apparitions than he is himself, since he is used to seeing the equally murky and evanescent 'forms' of his spiritual father Plato.[42]

I say 'apparently pagan', because it is possible that Ion, for all his Platonism, is projected as a semi-Christianized individual by Lucian, who perhaps has in mind intellectuals of his own day of the sort represented by Athenagoras, who were melding Platonism and Christianity. It is also, we should recall, Ion that tells the story of the Chaldaean snake-blaster, a tale which also seems to exhibit some striking Christian imagery in the motif of the cured Midas picking up the stretcher on which he has been brought and carrying it home with him. Certainly Lucian's Byzantine commentator felt that he had Christ in his sights at this point: 'A curse on you, godless Lucian! Was my Lord and God a sophist then, and did he take fees for curing the sick? Since the earth had the capacity to open up, when you were gibbering out this rubbish, why did it not open up and swallow you down, accursed one? It can only have been because it abominated you!' It was a commonplace of Byzantine scholarship that Lucian was an anti-Christ. The *Suda*'s biographical note on him confidently continues beyond his death into the fires of Hell.[43]

Ion's description of the exorcist as a 'Syrian from Palaestine' pays tribute to a traditional way of referring to the Jews that goes back to Herodotus. More recently Ovid had used the phrase in context of the observance of the Sabbath. The archaism of the phrase no doubt appealed to Lucian, but in using it he also contrived to identify the Jewish exorcists with the wider traditions of 'Syrian' and other Asian magic, and doubtless he was not the first to do so.[44]

In view of all this it is hardly surprising that some pagans should have viewed Jesus himself as a sorcerer. In *c.* 176 AD, around the same time that Lucian wrote, the middle Platonist Celsus wrote an attack on Jesus, the *True Doctrine*, in which he equated his miracles with the acts of sorcerers who derived their craft from the Egyptians, who sold their supposedly sacred learning for a few coins in the marketplace, who expelled demons and who called up the souls of dead heroes. Celsus' work does not survive, but the Christian eunuch Origen attempted to rebut it in his *Against Celsus* of c. 249 AD. This became the most important work of Christian apologetic and survives to give us some indirect access to Celsus' arguments.[45]

And in the case of Judaeo-Christian sorcerers too we find a hint of a double-whammy female equivalent. The oldest recipe collection among the Greek Magical Papyri, dating from the first century BC, includes a prescription for an amuletic text to be worn against all types of inflammation. It is ascribed to a 'Syrian woman of Gadara' (in Palaestine).[46]

The Neo-Pythagoreans: Arignotus, Apollonius and Alexander

By the middle imperial period the legendary Pythagoras, supposedly a citizen of Samos under the tyrant Polycrates, whose supposed floruit was 535–522 BC, had himself come to be seen and projected as a full-blown mage or sorcerer. Diogenes Laertius, for instance, writing in the early third century BC, tells us both that he associated with Chaldaeans and mages, and also that he learned the Egyptian language, descended into Egyptian crypts and (presumably in them) learned the secrets of the gods. Accordingly, representations of Pythagoras' remote disciples in the imperial age, the so-called Neo-Pythagoreans, also often project them as sorcerers, be it positively, negatively or ironically.[47]

Lucian has preserved for us a pair of Pythagorean portraits of particular interest. In his *Philopseudes* we meet Arignotus, who is a typical, long-haired, ascetic Pythagorean in appearance. He claims to have cleansed a haunted house owned by one Eubatides in Corinth of its occupying ghost. The house, as he tells the tale, has with its terrors driven away all who attempted to occupy it, and in consequence has long been unoccupied and derelict. On learning of this, Arignotus takes up his Egyptian spell-books and determines to spend the night in the house, despite attempts to deter him. He settles himself down to read by the light of his lamp in the largest room. In due course the ghost materializes, ready to attack. It is squalid and long-haired (like Arignotus himself, we may think), and blacker than the dark. The ghost attacks Arignotus from all sides, transforming itself now into a dog, now a bull, now a lion. But Arignotus deploys against it his most bloodcurdling Egyptian language spell and drives the ghost down into the ground in a corner of the dark room, noting the spot where it disappears. Against the expectation of those around he emerges safe and sound from the house in the morning. He goes straight to Eubatides with the news that the house is now purified of its terrors. He takes him and a large number of others back to the house and bids them dig in the spot where he has seen the ghost go down. Some six feet under they find a mouldy and skeletal corpse. They take it out and give it proper burial elsewhere, thus laying to rest the unquiet spirit to which it had been giving rise.[48]

This sort of story was a well-loved and traditional one already in antiquity. Prior to Lucian, a partial version of it is found already in Plautus' comedy *Mostellaria* ('Haunted House') of *c.* 200 BC. This play in turn is an adaptation of a Hellenistic Greek play, *Phasma* ('Ghost'), probably by Philemon and written close to the turn of the fourth to the third century BC. Fully narrated versions of the story are found also, prior to Lucian, in a letter of the younger Pliny (AD 102), where Arignotus' role is taken by the philosopher Athenodorus, and, subsequently to Lucian, in Constantius of Lyon's *Life of St Germanus of Auxerre* of AD 480, where Arignotus' role is taken by St Germanus, and in Gregory the Great's sixth-century AD *Dialogues*, where Arignotus' role is taken by Bishop Datius of Milan.[49]

But Lucian, now speaking, or seemingly so, in his own voice, gives us a much more extended and detailed, and indeed absolutely excoriating, portrait of a real and contemporary Pythagorean sage in his *Alexander* or *The False Prophet*, which we know to have been published shortly after AD 180. Throughout Alexander is characterized in terms evocative at once of both magic and fraudulence (*goeteia, mageia, manganeia*).[50]

According to Lucian, Alexander first hatches a massive public confidence trick in cahoots with his sidekick Cocconas. They decided to base their scheme in Abonouteichos in Alexander's home region of Paphlagonia, since its people offered a fertile combination of qualities: superstition, folly and wealth. But they prepare the way for it first in Chalcedon. There, they bury some bronze tablets of their own manufacture in the foundations of a temple of Asclepius, the most ancient one in the city. These carry the prediction that Asclepius and his father Apollo will shortly move to Pontus and take up residence in Abonouteichos. They are soon discovered, and the news reaches the excited inhabitants of Abonouteichos. They vote at once to erect a temple to receive the gods and start work on the foundations.

Alexander now moves back to the city to continue the deception. He has already let his hair and beard grow long in the fashion typical of Pythagorean sages, and as seen also in the case of Lucian's Arignotus. He wears a white and purple tunic, and over it a white cloak. He claims descent from the hero Perseus and bears, accordingly, his famous attribute of the sickle-sword. The hero had many magical associations, as we shall see in the following chapter. Alexander also claims descent from Podaleirios, the healing hero who was himself a son of Asclepius. The claim may well have been that he had in fact been fathered directly by the hero. Alexander disseminates supposedly rediscovered oracles to promote his acceptance in this guise. He gives out frenzied prophecies of his own, foaming at the mouth as he does so to impress the Paphlagonians. He produces the foaming effect by chewing soapwort.

Alexander opens and empties out a goose egg, and then seals it back together using white wax and white lead, with a newborn snake inside. By night he conceals the egg in a muddy pool that has formed in the foundations of the new temple. The next morning he leaps forth into the city's marketplace wearing nothing but a golden loincloth, brandishing his Persean sickle-sword and shaking his long hair around in frenzied fashion. He brings virtually the whole city running to hear what he has to say. He climbs onto a high altar and hails the city as blessed for being on the point of receiving the manifestation of the god, and bawls meaningless foreign words, repeatedly mixing in the names of Apollo and Asclepius. He then runs to the temple site, the crowds following him, and wades into the pool singing hymns to the gods, and calls upon Asclepius to come to the city. He asks for a bowl and scoops around in the mud until he dredges up the egg. He breaks it in his hand to reveal the young snake, to the amazement of the bystanders, who raise a shout, welcome the god and call the city blessed. (It was well known that Asclepius had a tendency to migrate between his cult sites in different cities in the form of his attribute, the 'Aesculapian' snake.) The bystanders cry out prayers for riches and health. Meanwhile, Alexander carries the snake off home, and refuses to emerge for several days whilst the frantic crowds press around and the rumours of his achievement spread and grow. The crowds are joined by further hordes from outside the city.[51]

Alexander now brings out a device he has prepared earlier. This consists of a massive, beautiful, tame, adult snake, acquired from Pella, and a puppet snake-head made of linen, with a strongly human but very realistic appearance. It can be made to open and shut its mouth through the action of horse hairs, and horse hairs also control a forked black tongue that can thus be made to dart out of its mouth. He takes a seat on a couch, dresses himself in divine style and takes the snake to his bosom. He winds the snake round his neck, letting its long body hang down onto his lap and the floor below. The snake's head he tucks away into his armpit. He arranges the puppet head in such a way that it projects from the side of his beard, as if it belongs with the body of the real snake. The couch is located in a small and dimly lit room, with entrance and exit opposite. And now the crowds, who have worked themselves up into a delirium of expectation, are let into the room. They are amazed to find the tiny snake grown so huge in the space of a few days, to be so domesticated and so humanoid. But before they can have the opportunity to scrutinize it properly, they are hustled out of the exit by the continuous press of the crowds behind them. Alexander goes on to mount this display repeatedly, and particularly on those occasions when there are rich men in town. Alexander decides that the new Asclepius should be called Glycon, 'Sweetie', and manufactures an oracle to establish this. Glycon's fame soon spreads through the neighbouring regions of Bithynia, Galatia and Thrace. In the wake of this comes a burgeoning industry in the manufacture of painted plaques of Glycon, and statuettes of him in bronze and silver.

In due course Alexander contrives another wonder for Glycon. He enables him to give voice by sewing together a long tube from a series of cranes' windpipes. He feeds the tube into the puppet head, and then out through the wall behind him, from behind which an assistant speaks down it. These most special oracles are not given to any Tom, Dick or Harry, but only to the wealthiest and most generous clients. Writing shortly after 217 AD, the Christian apologist Hippolytus was to expose a similar pagan necromantic trick, in which an artificial skull was given prophetic voice with the help of a crane's windpipe. The bogus skull, folded from an ox's caul and gently glued together with wax, would then gratifyingly melt away in the heat of the incense burners around it.[52]

Lucian claims to have himself wrong-footed the complacent charlatan Alexander by submitting the same written oracular query to him under different names, only to elicit different responses for each. And this he may well have done, for such an exposure of imposture would chime well with the Lucian's own modus operandi as described in the only extant contemporary reference to him. The reference comes in Galen's commentary on the Hippocratic *Epidemics*, which survives to us only in Arabic translation. Galen describes how a contemporary named, in Arabic phonemes, LÛQIYÂNÛS discredited incompetent philosophers. He made up a book of dark meaningless sayings, which he pretended to be Heraclitus'. He passed it on to others, who took it to a famous philosopher, who managed to make sense of it. He similarly discredited some grammarians by getting them to elucidate meaningless expressions he had made up himself.[53]

Despite Lucian's attempts to undermine Alexander's reputation in deed and by word, the Glycon cult that he established survived his death and flourished in the Black Sea region and the Balkans for more than a century afterwards. We hear little more of it in literary texts, but it is well represented in epigraphy, in commemorative coins, in a range of bronze figurines of Glycon, and not least in a particularly fine marble portrait of him found in Romanian Constanza, the ancient Tomi. We learn from the coins that Glycon was supposedly born under Antoninus Pius (reigned AD 138–61). On one intriguing example, Glycon is shown as coiling round the neck of Ionopolis personified in the fashion in which Lucian tells us he coiled round Alexander's (Figure 3.1; Ionopolis was the new name Alexander persuaded the emperor to bestow upon Abonouteichos). These, the marble and the bronzes, the last of which are akin no doubt to those referred to by Lucian and will have served as both votives and souvenirs, portray Glycon as a snake with semi-humanoid face and human hair, compatibly with Lucian's description of the god. They also tell us something that Lucian does not, namely that Glycon boasted a final tail that was either bifurcated, trifurcated or leonine (Figure 3.2). A further striking testimony to the historical success of Glycon's cult is to be found in an inscription of Caesarea Trocetta in Lydia, which tells us that it was sponsored by a priest of Apollo Soter called 'Miletos, son of the Paphlagonian Glycon'. As a siring snake Glycon acted on the basis of good precedents: Alexander the Great had been sired by Zeus in the form of a gigantic snake; the emperor Augustus had been sired by Apollo in the form of a snake; it is possible that Alexander of Abonouteichos had himself been sired by Podaleirios in the form of a snake. This was perhaps the sort of phenomenon that underlay Lucian's claim that Alexander himself (as opposed to Glycon) seduced a good many wives and fathered children with them, and that their husbands were proud to boast of it. When Lucian tells us that Alexander got his tame snake from Pella, he may be alluding to the tame snake that the *Alexander Romance*'s Nectanebo deployed in Pella, that too as an agent of deception and seduction.[54]

The Lemnian L. Flavius Philostratus published his *Life* of the great Neo-Pythagorean sage Apollonius of Tyana shortly after AD 217; he was first commissioned to write it by Julia Domna, wife of the emperor Septimius Severus. The historical Apollonius's life was, it seems, approximately coterminous with the first century AD. As a Neo-Pythagorean he rejected wine, marriage and meat, and in particular devoted himself to the condemnation of blood sacrifice. His appearance was the familiar Pythagorean one: he went unshod, grew hair and beard long, and wore only linen. Appropriately, he could remember a previous incarnation. He lived for a time in the temple of Asclepius at Aegae in Cilicia, where he cured the sick. He gave his inheritance up to his relatives and urged others to give their money to the poor. He spent five years touring Asia Minor, but in complete silence, and went on to visit Persia, India and Egypt. He was arrested by Nero and Domitian but talked himself back to liberty on both occasions, and died under Nerva, with whom he was on good terms. His body rose into heaven, but he manifested himself after death to those who doubted in the afterlife. Temples were set up for him all over Asia Minor. Some parallels with the life of Jesus will already be apparent, others will emerge.[55]

By the time that Philostratus wrote, Apollonius had evidently come to be seen by many as a master mage and sorcerer. Thus Moiragenes, writing, it is thought, in the earlier second century AD, had already applied both the terms 'mage' (*magos*) and 'sorcerer' (*goēs*) to him, even defining him by the former term in the title of his work, in which he recounted how Apollonius had contrived to seduce even some distinguished philosophers with his magic. Lucian had presented him in a passing reference as the moral grandfather, as it were, of his hated Alexander, inasmuch as he was supposedly the teacher of his teacher, and portrayed him as a sort of performing conman. Philostratus' contemporary Dio Cassius memorably says of the emperor Caracalla that, 'He so rejoiced in mages and sorcerers that he bestowed praise and honour upon the Cappadocian Apollonius who flourished in the time of Domitian, and made a hero-shrine for him. Apollonius was a complete sorcerer and mage.' A similar appreciation of Apollonius' magical significance underpins his inclusion in the Greek Magical Papyri as a master upon whose authority spells may be hung. In the following chapter we shall encounter a recipe from the papyri for the manufacture of a demon assistant that calls itself the 'Old Serving

Woman of Apollonius of Tyana'. The papyrus in question hails from the fourth or fifth century AD, but is probably dependent upon a tradition of rather greater antiquity.[56]

Such, then, seems to have been the common perception of Apollonius as Philostratus wrote, and Philostratus purports to react against this perception and to write to defend his subject of these charges of magery. Despite this, the *Life* contrives to present Apollonius as someone with a striking range of affinities to mages and sorcerers. Indeed, in the early chapters he is already shown fraternizing with the mages of Babylon and Susa, the Egyptians and the Brahmins. Philostratus strives, however, to differentiate Apollonius from common-or-garden sorcerers by insisting firstly that he achieved his wonders not by magic but by wisdom, and secondly that he worked with due piety and in conjunction with the regular gods, as opposed to with the weird and wonderful demons that magicians normally compelled to their service. Thus, Philostratus tells us, whereas sorcerers claim to be able to change what is fated either by torturing ghosts, by making alien sacrifices, incantations or anointings, Apollonius, by contrast, merely followed the Fates and made prophecies about what was destined to come to pass, not by sorcery but by divine revelation.[57]

Apollonius is repeatedly portrayed as facing defensive accusations of sorcery in his own lifetime from the representatives of established shrines. In each case Apollonius demonstrates that it is rather he that enjoys the favour of the shrine's patron deity. Indeed we are offered a type-scene three times over in which Apollonius is obstructed by priests as he seeks entry to their shrine and proceeds to get the better of them. Thus when Apollonius seeks initiation into the Eleusinian mysteries, the hierophant refuses to permit it on the ground that he is a sorcerer. Apollonius observes that the hierophant's real objection to him is that, though uninitiated, he already knows more than him. The hierophant is compelled by the clamour of the crowd to agree to initiate Apollonius, but Apollonius then declines, and predicts an initiation for himself at a future date. Apollonius has a similar experience at the sanctuary of Trophonius in Lebadeia. He expresses the wish to descend to consult Trophonius 'on behalf of philosophy', but the priests obstruct him, asserting that they will not allow a sorcerer to make trial of the shrine. After forcing his way into Trophonius' cavern by night, he asks Trophonius what is the most perfect and pure philosophy, and in answer is given a book of Pythagoras' doctrines. Finally, in one of the versions Philostratus offers us of Apollonius' death, he comes to the Cretan temple of Dictynna by night. The normally noisy guard-dogs fawn upon him (compare Circe's animals), as a result of which the people in charge of the temple lock him up as a sorcerer and a robber. At midnight he throws off his bonds, runs into the temple, the doors of which open automatically for him, and disappears.[58]

The *Life* attributes to Apollonius a great many magically akin wonders. Most of these have a Judaeo-Christian flavour, and some of them seem strikingly similar to Jesus' familiar miracles. Apollonius is repeatedly shown in the performance of exorcisms. We are told, for example, about the interruption of one of Apollonius' lectures by a Corcyrean playboy possessed by a demon. As Apollonius expatiates on the subject of libation the Corcyrean youth disrupts it with loud, rude and dissolute laughter. Apollonius looks at him and sees the demon within at once. He tells him that he is possessed even though neither he nor others realize it. For this reason he laughs and cries inappropriately and behaves licentiously and as if drunk. And when Apollonius looks on the boy, the possessing ghost within emits cries of fear and anger, such as one hears from people being burned or racked. Apollonius speaks to the ghost in stern and strict fashion, in the manner of a master addressing a meddlesome slave. He bids it depart and give proof of its departure. The ghost declares that it will knock over one of the statues in the colonnade in which Apollonius is giving his talk. The statue duly rocks gently before falling over (another expensive loss, it seems). The lad then rubs his eyes as if just waking up and blinking at the sunlight. He dons the rough cloak of the philosopher and prepares himself for a life in the ascetic style of Apollonius. We will look at another example of Apollonius' exorcisms in the final chapter of this book, his exorcism from a boy of a possessing pederastic ghost.[59]

Apollonius also expels demons that manifest themselves in more monstrous form. Philostratus tells us of a plague that falls upon Ephesus, for which the Ephesians can find no remedy. They send to Apollonius and the sage responds instantaneously to their summons, teleporting himself into the city in a fashion once supposedly demonstrated by the great Pythagoras himself. He speaks reassuringly to the townspeople before leading them all to the theatre, where he comes across what appears to be an old, ragged, squinting beggar. Apollonius groups the Ephesians around the beggar and tells them to collect as many stones as they can and stone him. They are taken aback by his instructions, and think it monstrous to kill a stranger in such an unfortunate condition. The beggar himself begs for pity. But Apollonius is insistent and eventually some of the people begin to pelt him with stones. As they do so the beggar stops squinting and turns his eyes on them to reveal that they are full of fire. Thereupon all recognize that he is indeed a demon and they stone him to death so thoroughly that a heap of stones collects over his body. Apollonius asks them to wait a little while and then remove the stones to see what sort of a creature they have killed. As they do so they reveal a gigantic dog the size of a lion, spitting foam as if rabid. This, of course, is the plague demon, now destroyed. The grateful people erect a statue to Heracles the Averter on the spot of the stoning. In the final chapter again we will meet another monster defeated by Apollonius, a vampire-like Lamia.[60]

Like Jesus too, Apollonius specializes in other forms of healing, and indeed the restoration of the dead to life. Thus, when in Rome, Apollonius encounters a funeral procession. The dead girl being carried out is a new bride, the scion of a consular family, and her bier is attended by the distraught bridegroom. Apollonius speaks reassuringly to the groom and asks that the bier be set down. He asks the girl's name. But he does not use it, as the onlookers expect, for an impromptu elegy. Rather, he simply lays hold of her, speaks a few obscure words over her, and rouses her from her state of death. The girl gives voice and returns at once to her father's house. The girl's grateful relatives give Apollonius an enormous sum of money, 150,000 sesterces, but Apollonius proclaims that he gives it on to the girl for her dowry. One is reminded of Jesus' raising of Lazarus.[61]

Sometimes Apollonius' raising of the dead has a more necromantic tinge. When Apollonius comes to the plain of Troy, he is warned by the locals that the ghost of Achilles still manifests itself in terrifying form. Apollonius decides to spend the night on the hero's barrow and calls the ghost up with a spell he has learned from the Indians and with appeals to Pythagorean notions of the soul's survival of death (Philostratus reminds us that as a good Pythagorean Apollonius could not use the usual evocatory method of black-sheep sacrifice). There is an earth tremor around the barrow and a beautiful young warrior springs out of it. He is initially five cubits high, but then grows to more than twice this size (i.e. more than fifteen feet). Achilles takes the opportunity to give Apollonius a message for his native race, the Thessalians: they have been neglecting their offerings to him. They are advised to make good such offerings before he has to demonstrate his anger towards them. Apollonius undertakes to convey the message, but then begins to raise his own business with Achilles. The ghost interrupts him: it knows he wants to ask questions about the truth of the Trojan war. Achilles permits him to ask five questions of his own choosing. Dawn breaks as Achilles completes his final answer, and the ghost disappears in a flash of lightning.[62]

The correspondences between Apollonius' life and work and those of Christ are striking. They were almost exact contemporaries; they both preached against blood sacrifice; they both healed the sick; they both advocated alms for the poor; they both brushed with the Roman authorities; they both ascended into heaven; they both manifested themselves after their deaths; they both specialized in healing and exorcism miracles. These similarities did not go unnoticed in antiquity. On the basis of Philostratus' biography of Apollonius the pagan Hierocles was to write, in the early fourth century, a comparison between Apollonius and Jesus, and perhaps he was working in a tradition of comparison between the two already current in Philostratus' day. Hierocles tried to differentiate Apollonius from those who were mere sorcerers, just as Philostratus had done, whilst applying precisely this designation to Jesus' disciples. He also noted that Apollonius did not, unlike Jesus, feel the need to claim to be a god. The Christian Eusebius of Caesarea, writing in the early fourth century AD, was stung into writing a rebuttal of Hierocles' work. Hierocles's text does not survive independently, but Eusebius's reply quotes much from it and summarizes the rest. Hierocles and Eusebius alike were evidently extending the venerable tradition of debate about Jesus' own status as a sorcerer, found already, as we have seen, in the writings of the pagan Celsus and the Christian Origen.[63]

Conclusion

Developed narrative portraits of mages or sorcerers of a sort to rival those of witches emerge into the literary record, Greek and Latin, only from the first century AD. If they had thrived in the tradition from long before that time, we cannot know it. Again we might ask of those who are keen to locate the origin of magic amongst male practitioners of the Classical age of Greece why the copious remains of that era's writings have left us no substantial account of an individual mage or sorcerer. The developed sorcerer portraits of imperial literature project their subjects overwhelmingly as deriving on the one hand from a series of magical peoples overlapping (so far as the Greeks and Romans were concerned) and conglomerated in Asia, namely Persians, Medes, Mages,

Babylonians, Chaldaeans, Assyrians and Syrians, and from Egypt on the other hand. Sorcerers were also discovered in due course among the Jews, with the exorcism of the possessed recognized as their characteristic activity. The Greeks and Romans were no doubt helped to this perception first by the fact that the Jews had been known already from the Classical age as 'Syrians from Palaestine', and secondly by the fact that a great deal of Jewish religious imagery had been taken up into the tradition of the Greek Magical Papyri that first developed in Egypt during the Hellenistic age. The early imperial age also saw the rise of a more home-grown variety of sorcerer in the form of the Neo-Pythagorean sages. If, among these, Alexander of Abonouteichos owed his reputation as a sorcerer more to his perceived fraudulence than to any particular activities, Apollonius of Tyana perhaps owed his reputation rather to a range of activities strongly reminiscent of those of the Judaeo-Christian exorcists, and indeed to those of Christ himself.

Figure 1.1 Circe mixes the magic potion she hopes will turn Odysseus into a pig. Burlesque image.

Figure 1.2 Odysseus challenges Circe with his sword. A pig-man attends.

Figure 1.3 Circe attended by ass-men.

Figure 1.4 Medea uses herbs to inflict sleep on the unsleeping serpent that guards the golden fleece.

Figure 1.5 Medea pets, charms or feeds the fleece-guarding serpent, here with three heads.

Figure 1.6 Medea, wand in hand, rejuvenates Jason in her cauldron. The Argonauts come running.

Figure 1.7 Medea rejuvenates an old ram in her cauldron. A demonstration for an elderly Jason.

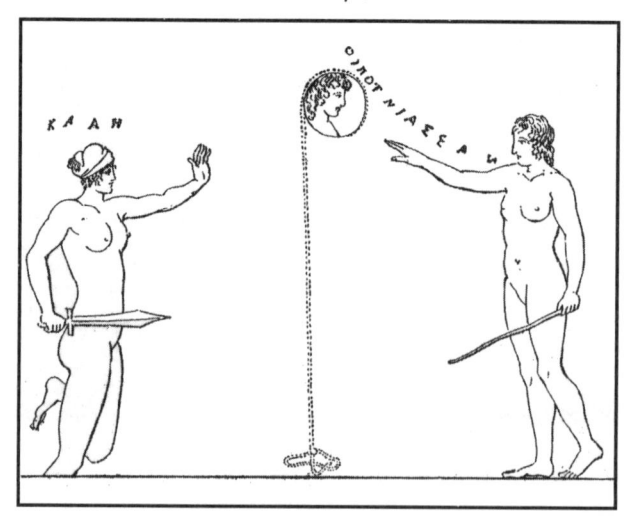

Figure 2.1 Naked witches bind and draw down the moon: 'Hear me, Lady Moon'.

Figure 3.1 Coin of Ionopolis. Glycon coils around the neck of Ionopolis personified in the fashion in which he coiled around that of Alexander of Abonouteichos.

Figure 3.2 Cult image of Glycon, the human-faced and lion-tailed prophetic serpent sponsored by Alexander of Abonouteichos.

4

Hidden Stories: Grimoires, Amulets and Curse Tablets

Grimoires: the Greek Magical Papyri

One of the richest and most important resources for the study of magic in the ancient world is a body of material conventionally known as 'The Greek Magical Papyri' or, in Latin, *Papyri Graecae Magicae* (whence the abbreviation by which they are most commonly cited, *PGM*). These are magic-related papyrus documents produced in Graeco-Roman Egypt, mostly between the second and fifth centuries AD. The corpus includes many deployed curse texts, of a sort akin to the more familiar lead curse tablets, and many deployed amuletic texts, some of which we will consider later. But the bulk of it is made up of a series of magical recipe books, 'grimoires' or 'formularies'. Many of these in turn derive ultimately from a single ancient collection, the so-called 'Theban Magical Library', which was discovered in a fourth- or fifth-century AD tomb in Western Thebes shortly before 1828. This was the year in which they were bought by the colourful antiquities dealer Giovanni Anastasi, before being broken up and sold on to the great museums of Europe in which they continue to reside. The concealment of these books in their tomb preserved them from the fate that characteristically awaited such texts: burning by the Christians, a process already recorded in and celebrated in the Book of Acts, of the late first century AD.[1]

The religious background of the recipe books is complex and syncretized, but the dominant inputs are Greek, Egyptian and Jewish, these elements being unified in a remarkably homogeneous and distinctive blend. They therefore express the cultural mix that was peculiar to the city of Alexandria in the Hellenistic period. The dearth of Latin material in the papyri is striking given that Egypt had been firmly under Roman control since 30 BC. Some of the Greek formularies contain portions written in Demotic or Coptic, and some purely Demotic and Coptic papyri have similar contents.

The oldest substantial recipe books to survive date from the first century BC. They are briefer than later documents. They show no sign of the extended descriptions of elaborate and often repetitive magical rituals and lengthy series of obscure 'abracadabra'-style *voces magicae* ('words of power'), vowel-series, word-triangles and -squares, palindromes and 'Characters' that were to become the hallmarks of the genre. But these features had come to flourish by the time of the so-called *Great Magical Papyrus in Paris*, the largest of the extant formularies, which, though in itself a copy made in the fourth century AD, is thought to reproduce a second-century original.[2]

This document usefully illustrates the structure, texture and sorts of contents typical of the mature recipe books. Its 3,274 lines comprise a wide variety of recipes in a largely random order. These recipes address such goals as: protection against death and demons and the expulsion of the latter; the attraction of lovers, the inspiration of friendship and favour, and the restraint of anger; divination by trance alone, by bowl, by lamp, or from a corpse or skull, and the inducing of dreams; the manufacture of multi-purpose charms based on Homeric verses and the Bear constellation. The book also contains a number of recipes that might be described as 'ancillary' or 'meta-magical', that is, recipes that do not in themselves accomplish any final goal but rather build towards or enable further magical activity. These include such things as prayers, hymns, consecrations, initiations and techniques for the picking of plants. A brief astrological text is also found.

We can be sure that practical use was made of such recipe books. An erotic-attraction recipe in this Paris papyrus corresponds closely (but not perfectly) with a remarkable third- or fourth-century find of magical materials, probably from Antinoopolis, which is now in the Louvre. These include a striking clay voodoo doll representing the woman Ptolemais, pierced, as per the recipe, with thirteen needles, and an extensive curse text inscribed on a thin sheet or 'lamella' of lead, in which Sarapammon, who desires Ptolemais, uses language similar to that prescribed by the recipe and invokes the ghost of Antinous (of whom more in the next chapter) against her.[3]

One of the greatest difficulties in investigating ancient magic consists in coming to terms with the dissonance that obtains between its documentary sources and its literary texts, for all their thematic links. A broad gap in feel and thought-world seemingly yawns between magic as it is projected in the documentary sources, the recipe books amongst the papyri above all, and magic as it is projected in literary texts. This applies certainly to texts of magical lore, such as are reflected in the work of Pliny (for which see Chapter 3), but even more especially to those offering narratives of magical activity. In this chapter we will attempt to construct bridges across that gap, principally by drawing attention to a few striking coincidences between recipes in the papyri and narratives of magical activity in literary texts.

First, we may note, the recipes do themselves sometimes make use of elements of narrative, or what might be termed implicit narrative. A relatively simple sort of implicit narrative common in the papyri is a future-narrative employed to lay out information and instructions about the course of a spell, particularly one that involves careful interaction or negotiation with a demon. A spell for acquiring what we might today term a 'genie', which calls itself 'The Old Serving Woman of Apollonius of Tyana' and is found in a fourth- or fifth-century AD recipe book, is a good example of this:

Old serving-woman of Apollonius of Tyana. Take the skull of Typhon [i.e. the skull of an ass, the creature sacred to Seth-Typhon], and write the following characters upon it in the blood of a black dog: [6 characters follow], SABERRA. Then go to the place, beside a river, beside the sea, or beside a cross-roads, at midnight. Place the skull on the ground, set it under your left foot, and say the following. Spell: 'EILEITHUIA MEROPE GIR-GIRO ... [etc.: many *voces magicae* follow]. Come, manifest yourself, goddess called house-warden [i.e. Nephthys].' When you have said this, you will see a woman sitting on an ass. She will be exceptionally beautiful. Her beauty will be heavenly. She will be in the fullness of her bloom in a way that defies description, and she will be young. As soon as you see this woman, throw yourself down before her and say: 'I thank you, mistress, for appearing to me. Please judge me worthy of you, and may your splendour be well-disposed towards me. Please accomplish whatever I ask of you.' The goddess will say to you, 'What is your purpose?' You reply, 'I need your services of daily-life. She will immediately get down from the ass, put off her beauty and she will become [*or*: there will appear] an old woman. And the old woman will say to you, 'I will serve you and wait upon you.' After saying this, the goddess will put on again the beauty she had put off, and will beseech you. You must say to the goddess: 'Mistress, I will make use of you yourself until I get the serving woman.' The goddess, upon hearing this, will immediately go up to the old woman [from this point on the goddess and the old women are clearly differentiated] and will take her molar tooth from her and the molar of the ass, and she gives you both of them. From that time the old woman becomes inseparable from you, unless you wish to release her. From that time on the gift of many good things will be bestowed upon you. Everything your heart desires will be accomplished through her. She will keep these things safe for you, and in particular she will understand for you whatever a person's attitude towards you is. She will tell you everything and she will never abandon you. This is the way she cherishes good will towards you. If you should ever wish it, you will be able to release her – but never do it! Take the molars from the woman and the ass. Make a fire and throw them into the fire. The old woman will wail and run off forever. Do not release her lightly, for you will find no substitute. But you will release the goddess, whenever you learn how the old woman will serve you, by saying as follows: 'MENERPHER PHIE PRACHERA LYLORI MELICHARE NECHIRA.' When she has heard this, the goddess will get on her ass and go off. Phylactery for the rite: the skull of the ass. Bind the molar of the ass with silver and the molar of the old woman with gold and wear them continuously. In this way the old woman will be inseparable from you. This rite has been successfully tested.[4]

The recipe begins by laying out direct instructions for the production of a demon assistant. First the magician is to conjure up the Egyptian goddess Nephthys, or a demon assimilated thereto. After giving instructions for this conjuring-up, the recipe passes into a more narrative mode, and comes close to telling a story in future tense. It tells, in admittedly obscure fashion, how the goddess will change form between that of a hag, in which she can be bound to serve, and that of a seductive young woman, in which she can escape the magician's clutches. The description even incorporates projected dialogue between the magician and the goddess. Somehow the magician's interaction with the goddess, if carried out aright, will compel her to manifest herself in both her forms at the same time, and the beautiful form will indenture the hag form to the magician as an assistant. We may wonder how possession of one of the old woman's teeth will bestow power over her. But we should recall that the Graeae or Phorcides of Greek myth, the demonic old women, sometimes two, sometimes three in number, shared between them a single eye and a single tooth. Perseus was able to compel these to his will by seizing not, as it happens, their significant tooth, but their significant eye. And lest we think this single old women's eye and single old women's tooth ineffectual, we must bear it in mind that the Graeae were sisters to the Gorgons, whose gaze instantly brought death, and whose heads were coiffured with snapping serpents. We must recall too that Perseus, as the supposed founder of the Persian race, had long been an iconic figure in the ancient world's imaginary history of magic. Undoubtedly his famous myth is indirectly invoked by the spell to give itself logic, meaningfulness and plausibility. Furthermore, the attribution of the spell to Apollonius of Tyana (discussed in Chapter 3) is also a means of bestowing authority and legitimacy upon it. Apollonius is evidently now being appropriated as a powerful sorcerer to whose abilities lesser ones might aspire. There is also a sense in which the invocation of Apollonius' name invites the reader to recall narratives of the great man's achievements.[5]

On occasion we do find striking relationships between papyrus recipes and literary narratives of magical rites. Let us consider here two recipes that exhibit such relationships with two of Lucian's satirical tales of magic in his *Philopseudes*, probably composed in the 170s AD. The first recipe to consider, from the fourth-century *PGM* XII, fetches for the magician a person he desires, through the agency of an Eros-doll or 'Erotion':

> **Eros-assistant. Rite of Eros, consecration and preparation.** He carries out the following functions: dream-sending and wakefulness ... For he has the power to do everything. Take some Etruscan wax and blend with it every kind of aromatic herb, and make an Eros eight fingers high, carrying a torch, and with broad base to receive offerings. Let his left hand brandish a bow and arrow. Make a Psyche in similar fashion to the Eros. When you have done all this, consecrate the doll for three days ... On the first day ... take seven creatures and throttle them: one cock, a quail, a wren, a pigeon, a turtledove, and two chicks that happen to fall into your hands. Do not make burnt sacrifices of these creatures, but hold them in your hand and throttle them, whilst offering them up to Eros, until each of the creatures is choked and their breath passes into him ... On the second day throttle a male chick before Eros and burn it in holocaust, and on the third day put another chick on the altar ... The first formula spoken with the sacrifice: 'I call upon you, on your beautiful bed, in your desirable house. Do a service for me and at all times carry whatever message I give you, to whatever place I send you, taking upon yourself the form of whatever god (or goddess) men and women revere, saying at once everything that is prescribed for you or spoken to you and deposited with you ...'[6]

The choking of a series of birds so that their breath passes into the Eros doll is evidently a mechanism not merely for animating, but more specifically for giving wing to the doll. This recipe text fairly directly embeds or anticipates a narrative in which the sorcerer manufactures an Eros doll and then sends it flying to seek out his beloved. The doll then manifests itself before the beloved in the form of the god or goddess the beloved most reveres and – inevitably successfully – persuades the beloved to submit herself (or himself) to the desires of the sorcerer. Such a narrative is realized in Lucian's satirical tale of the Hyperborean mage. This is put into the mouth of a Peripatetic philosopher Cleodemus:

> Just after his father had died and Glaucias had taken over his estate, he became enamoured of Chrysis, the wife of Demeas. He had hired me to teach him reason, and if this love had not occupied him, he would by now have known all the Peripatetic teachings... However, he did not know what to do about his love, and he let me in on the whole thing. As you would expect, since I was his teacher, I introduced that Hyperborean mage to him. The terms were a four-mina down-payment – an initial payment was needed to fund the purchase of the sacrificial victims – and then a further sixteen minas, if he got Chrysis. The mage waited for the moon to start waxing, for this is the time at which rites of this kind are usually performed. Then he dug a pit in the court within the house and at around midnight called up for us, to begin with, Alexicles, the father of Glaucias, who had died seven months earlier. The old man was angry about the love and lost his temper, but even so in the end gave him permission to pursue the affair. After that he brought up Hecate and she brought Cerberus along, and he drew down the moon. It exhibited itself in a range of different guises and kept changing its appearance. First it displayed the form of a woman, next it became a magnificent ox, and then showed itself as a puppy. Eventually, the Hyperborean fashioned an eros-doll from clay and said to it, 'Off you go, and bring Chrysis.' The clay flew aloft, and soon there she was knocking on the door. She came in and embraced Glaucias as absolutely insane with love, and she slept with him until we heard the cocks crowing. Then the moon flew back up into the heavens, Hecate dived back down under the earth and the other manifestations disappeared. We sent Chrysis off home round about dawn.[7]

This tale exhibits obvious similarities with the subsequent tale of Cyprian and Justina discussed in Chapter 3. And there, we may note, we find a further correspondence with the recipe. The third demon that Cyprian sends flying off to fetch Justina, in a role parallel to that of the Eros-doll in the recipe, transforms himself into the shape of a friendly virgin with whom Justina can identify, in order to persuade her to surrender herself to her lover. This closely resembles the Eros-doll's technique of transforming itself into the shape of the god revered by its victim for a similar purpose.[8]

The second recipe to consider is drawn from the fourth- or fifth-century AD formulary *PGM* I. It is composed in a self-consciously literary fashion, and is presented in the form of a letter of instruction from an Egyptian master-magician, referred to variously as Pnouthis and Pnouthios, to a seemingly Greek pupil, Ceryx. Some key selections from the recipe follow:

> **Demon-assistant of Pnouthis, the sacred scribe**: ... Pnouthios sends greetings to the pious Ceryx, Since I know about such things, I have prescribed this demon-assistant [sc. spell] for you, so that you should not fail in the performance of the rite. I taken over all the prescriptions left for us in book after book ... and now I have sent this book so that you may get understanding of it. For the spell of Pnouthis has the power to persuade the gods and all the goddesses. I will write to you what it has to say on the subject of the acquisition of a demon-assistant.
>
> This is the sacred acquisition of the demon-assistant. It is known that he is a god; he is an aerial spirit which you have seen. If you issue an instruction, he carries out the task at once. He sends dreams, he fetches women, or men without the need for stuff [i.e. a lock of their hair or a piece of their clothing], he kills, he destroys, he rouses winds from the earth, he brings gold, silver, bronze, and gives them to you whenever you have need. He frees chained prisoners, he opens doors, he renders you invisible so that no one at all can see you, he brings fire, he brings water, wine, bread and [whatever] comestible you wish, olive oil, vinegar, except just for fish, and he will bring piles of vegetables of the variety of your choosing, but not pork – make sure you never tell him to bring this. And when you hold a dinner party, just tell him. Think of every attractive place and instruct him to deck one out with speed and expedition. Immediately he will surround you with golden-ceilinged halls, and you will see their walls clad in marble (and you hold these to be partly real and partly mere visions) and expensive wine, suitable for rounding off a splendid dinner. He will quickly fetch demons, and he will dress these servants with sashes for you. He does this quickly. And whenever you instruct him to carry out a task for you, he will do it, and you will see his outstanding work in other departments. He stops ships and lets them go again, he stops a great many bad demons, he stops wild animals in their tracks and he will quickly break the teeth of untamed reptiles, he sends dogs to sleep and removes their barks. He transforms into any shape of animal you want: a flying one, a swimming one, a four-footed one, a

crawling one. He will lift you into the air, and cast you back down into the swollen currents of the ocean, into the waves of the sea-currents. He will quickly freeze rivers and seas so that you can run across them with sure foot, should you wish to do so. In particular he will stop, should you wish it, the sea-coursing foam. And whenever you wish to draw down stars and whenever you wish to render hot things cold and cold things hot, he will light lamps and put them out again. He will make walls shake and set them ablaze. He will not be wanting in any service you design, O blessed initiate into the holy magic, and he will do it for you, this most powerful demon-assistant, the one and only lord of the air. The gods will comply in everything, for there is nothing without him. Do not share this great mystery with anybody else, but keep it hidden, by Helios, considered worthy of it as you have been by the lord god.[9]

The motifs of this recipe-text exhibit striking correspondences with those of Lucian's famous tale of *The Sorcerer's Apprentice* in his *Philopseudes*, which is narrated in its original form by the erstwhile apprentice himself in later life, one Eucrates, at a gathering in his house. He tells how his father had sent him as a young man to Egypt for his education. Whilst sailing up the Nile to Coptus to see the marvellous speaking statue of Memnon, he encountered one of the sacred scribes from Memphis, Pancrates (for whom see Chapter 3). Eucrates gradually ingratiated himself with him and the master began to share his secrets. Eucrates continues the tale:

Eventually he persuaded me to leave all my servants behind in Memphis, and to accompany him, the two of us on our own. For, he explained, we would not want for attendants. This is how we lived thenceforth. Whenever we came to an inn, he would take the wooden bar from the door or the broom or even the pestle, dress it in a cloak, utter some incantation over it and make it walk. It would seem human to everyone else. It would go off and pump water, buy provisions and prepare them, and in all respects be a perfect servant and attendant for us. Then, when he no longer required its services, he would speak another incantation over it and make the broom a broom again or the pestle a pestle again.

I was eager to acquire this power, but I had no way of learning this from him, for he was jealous of it, although openly generous with everything else. But then one day I secretly eavesdropped on the incantation – it consisted of three syllables – by lurking in the dark. He then went off to the market after giving the pestle its instructions.

The next day, whilst he was again looking after some business in the market, I took the pestle and dressed it up in the same way, spoke the syllables over it, and bade it fetch water. When it had filled an amphora and brought it back, 'Stop', I said, 'fetch water no more, but be a pestle again.' But it now refused to obey me, and kept on fetching water, until it had flooded our house by its continual drawing. I did not know what to do, for I was terrified that Pancrates would return and be angry, which is in fact what ensued. I took an axe and chopped the pestle in half. But they, each of the two parts, took up amphoras and began fetching water, and I now had two servants instead of one. Meanwhile Pancrates returned to the scene. He realized what had happened and returned the servants to wood, just as they had been before the incantation, but then he had abandoned me before I realized it, and I do not know where he went after disappearing.[10]

As Eucrates finishes his tale, one of his admiring guests, the Stoic Dinomachus, asks him whether he still knows how to make a man out of pestle. Eucrates professes that he does indeed, but that he cannot demonstrate the magic to him, since he still only knows the first half the spell, and not how to turn the man back into a pestle. If, then, he were to perform the spell, his house would be deluged again. The tale is well known now chiefly from Goethe's adaptation of it in his short ballad of 1797, *Der Zauberlehrling*. Goethe exchanged Lucian's featured long pestle for a broom, more meaningful to his own audience, prompted no doubt by Eucrates' initial suggestion that Pancrates could also animate these. One hundred years later Goethe's ballad inspired Paul Dukas' symphonic scherzo, *L'apprenti sorcier* of 1897, and this in turn gave Disney's Mickey Mouse his finest moment when he acted Goethe's tale out to Dukas' music in Walt Disney's *Fantasia* of 1940.

Pnouthis and Pancrates alike are both Egyptian master magicians, and both are explicitly described as sacred scribes (the word used in both cases is *hierogrammateus*). Pnouthis can be seen to enjoy a master-apprentice relationship with his addressee Ceryx, just as Pancrates does with Eucrates. Pnouthis' demon-assistant checks wild beasts, breaks the teeth of fierce reptiles, and enables one to walk over rivers: these are powers which Pancrates seemingly wraps together in his riding on crocodiles. Pnouthis' demon-assistant also exercises powers of a domestic nature, including, strikingly, those with which Lucian's pestle is endowed, to fetch water and to buy provisions. Pnouthis explicitly exhorts Ceryx to keep his spell secret, and this finds its parallel in Pancrates' insistence on keeping his animation spell secret, which is what motivates the central action of Lucian's tale. Even the famous focal motif of Lucian's tale, the apprentice's failure with his master's spell, is latent in the Pnouthis spell-text. For the prospect of failure is contemplated in Pnouthis' introductory words: 'so that you should not fail in the performance of the rite'.

We may note here that the much-travelled Lucian, by his own account, ended his career, either in the 170s or the 180s, in imperial service in Egypt, probably as an *eisagōgeus*, an official whose role it was to bring cases before a Roman prefect's court, although he would hardly have had to travel to Egypt to hear stories of the Sorcerer's Apprentice type.[11]

Another recipe presented in the form of a letter is found in the fourth-century AD (but probably second-century AD in origin) formulary known as *The Great Magical Papyrus in Paris* (*PGM* IV). Once again we have a letter of instruction from an Egyptian master-magician to a pupil, this time from Nephotes to his fellow Egyptian pupil, the pharaoh Psammetichus. The recipe's principal function, as initially laid out, is to bring about a one-to-one encounter with a god through lecanomancy, that is, through scrying with a bowl. But as the exposition of the recipe continues it broadens out to incorporate necromantic divination also: the use in the bowl of rainwater from the sky will summon gods from heaven, seawater gods from the sea, river-water gods of the land, Osiris and Sarapis, and springwater (i.e. water from underground), the dead. The recipe summarizes the alternative powers summonable as 'god or dead man'. This recipe too seems to exhibit curious links with the introduction to the treatise *On the Power of Plants* attributed to Thessalus of Tralles and discussed in the previous chapter. There we saw how 'Thessalus' tells of his wanderings across Egypt in search of the wisdom that would enable him to make sense of Nechepso's medical book. He eventually secures the promise of revelation from an Egyptian master in the form of a chief priest in Diospolis. The Greek version of the Thessalus text indicates that this will be through the medium of lecanomancy, the Latin version of it (based on a translation of a slightly different Greek original), through the medium of necromancy in a crypt. When the time comes for his supernatural encounter, the priest articulates the possibilities on offer: 'either a ghost of some dead person or a god'.[12]

Epistolary recipes are inevitably influenced by literary considerations, even if not influenced directly by existing narratives of magic. But sometimes the lines of influence between magical recipes and literary texts can be seen to operate more comprehensively in both directions.

Let us consider the case of a literary narrative seemingly influenced by a recipe-type. The *Great Magical Papyrus in Paris* contains a series of four recipes for magical operations with a human skull ascribed to the Thessalian king Pitys. Here is the opening section of the second recipe:

> **Attraction spell of Pitys.** Pitys sends greetings to king Ostanes. Since you repeatedly write to me about the inquiry into skull-cups (*skyphoi*), I thought I should send you this technique. It is to be treasured, and it has the potential to please you greatly ... Take an ass's skin, dry it in the shade and draw upon it the figure that will be revealed and the following text, in a circle: 'AAMASI NOUTHI APHTHECHEMBŌCH ... I conjure you, demon of a dead man, by the strong and implacable god and by his holy names, to stand yourself at my side in the coming night, in the form you used to have, and tell me whether you are able to perform the task in question. Now, now, quickly, quickly!' Then go swiftly to a place where there is a burial, or where something has been disposed of, if you do not have a burial. Spread the hide underneath at sunset. Go back home and he will by all means come to you and stand himself by you on that night. He reports to you the manner of his death and first he will tell you whether he has the strength to do anything or undertake any service for you ... He attracts people, he lays them down on a sickbed, he sends dreams, he restrains and he procures revelations in dreams too. This spell alone can do all these things. Just modify the commonplaces in accordance with your project. Most of the mages, who carried their equipment with them, laid it aside and used him for an assistant. They accomplished the things laid out above with all speed. For the technique is without all those needless extra words, but it completes the things laid out above quickly and with all ease ...[13]

One is, in other words, to take a human skull from a grave or from wherever one can find one, and lay it out on a hide that has been prepared from the skin of an ass and inscribed with a magical figure and a magical formula. This formula invokes the ghost of a dead man, presumably the former owner of the skull, to manifest himself to the practitioner during the night in the form of a dream. The ghost will tell the practitioner how he died. This is in any case ancient ghosts' favourite topic of conversation, unsurprisingly, because the primary *raison d'être* of the ancient ghost was to function as an indicator of the problematic circumstances surrounding a death or burial. The ghost then goes on to explain whether he has the strength to act as an assistant demon or 'familiar' to the practitioner. It is possible that his degree of strength depends on, and is correlated to, his degree of restlessness. If he does have the strength to act as an assistant, then he will be able, apparently, to perform any task or function the mages of yore or their latter-day counterparts might require, but the functions of erotic attraction, the infliction of illness, dream-sending and binding magic are singled out for mention.

The recipe-series goes on to offer, in the third place, intriguing instructions for decommissioning activated skulls that prove themselves to be unsuitable. The mouth of the skull is to be sealed with dirt from Osiris' temple (Osiris being the dead god), or from a tomb. One is also to make a ring from an iron fetter, worked cold, and engrave upon it, *inter alia*, a headless lion with its front paw crushing a skull. The imagery here is all fairly explicit: the skull is to be silenced with the blocking of the mouth, with deadness, and with an amulet-ring with an image expressive of decapitation in general and of the crushing of the skull in particular. But why should one seek to decommission such a skull? Presumably these 'unsuitable' skulls would continue to send their ghosts to interrupt one's sleep with misleading or useless information. The need for an additional spell to bring to an end another one where the magical equipment had seemingly taken on a life of its own and got out of hand brings us back to the territory of the *Sorcerer's Apprentice*.[14]

Now, we must concede from the first that there is quite a high narrative element in this recipe series. We may note that, as with the 'Old Serving Woman of Apollonius of Tyana', there is already a substantial amount of implicit future-narrative in the sequential instructions, as there is with the construction of a logical arc in accordance with which magical equipment is first activated and then decommissioned. But the Pitys spells also demonstrate a high degree of implicit narrative and literary shaping of a more general nature. In the implied narrative we are told of a series of letters exchanged between the Thessalian Pitys and the Persian Ostanes, culminating in the present one produced, in which Pitys as a master-magician advises Ostanes as a pupil of the skull-cup spell. Behind this lurks a further, broader narrative, to which we will turn shortly. More generally, the Pitys series is framed in a self-consciously literary fashion, as can be seen from its epistolary presentation, and its reference to the lore of the great mages of the past.

We have already suggested that the sorts of magical practice prescribed in these recipes may underlie Lucan's fantastical description of Erictho's corpse-reanimation (Chapter 2). But here we may point to a rather closer realization in narrative literature of a recipe-series broadly similar, though not identical, to this one, and a realization which seemingly retains the consciousness of its recipe book origins. The tale is preserved in the *Chronicle* of John Malalas. Malalas wrote in the fifth or sixth century AD, although the tale in question will not have originated with this author, and elements of it at any rate are attested as far back as the late first century BC. The tale is a semi-rationalized recasting of the famous mythical account of Perseus' beheading of the Gorgon Medusa and of his use of her head to petrify his enemies, Polydectes and others. It also concerns Perseus in his role as the founder of the Persian or Median race (the two are here identified), of the Persian religion of Zoroastrianism, and of course of the characteristic Persian activity of magic. Folk-etymology of a tenuous kind also has an important role to play.[15]

> So his father Picus-Zeus taught him to do and perform the sorcery (*manganeia*) of the abominable skull-cup (*skyphos*), teaching him all its mysteries and impious errors. He told him, 'You will conquer all your public enemies by means of it, and so too your personal enemies and every hostile man. All who look into the face itself will be blinded and stilled as if dead and slaughtered by you.' In due course Perseus followed the instructions of his own father, Picus-Zeus, and later, after his father's death, and when he had come to the fullness of manhood, he conceived a desire for the kingship of Assyria, in envy of the children of Ninus, his uncle, the brother of his father. After consulting an oracle he went off to the land of Libya ... On the road a maiden, a local girl, met this same Perseus. She had wild hair and eyes. Stopping her, he asked, 'What is your name?' And she freely told him, 'Medusa'. He got hold of her by her hair and cut off her head with the sickle-headed spear he carried. Perseus took this same head and at once consecrated it with mystic rites, just as he had been instructed by his father Picus when he taught him the error of accursed sorcery. He brandished this head to aid himself against all enemies, personal and public, and used it to subject them and to slay them. He called the head Gorgon because of the efficiency of its service and its effectiveness against his opponents.... [*gorgos* signifies 'terrible', 'vigorous' in Greek]. He taught the Persians the rite of the accursed and godless skull-cup of Medusa (*Mĕdousa*). Because of this instruction he called their land that of the Medes (*Mēdoi*) ... After some time King Cepheus, the father of Andromeda [Perseus' wife], came against him from Ethiopia, and made war upon him. Cepheus was unable to see because of old age. Perseus, hearing that he was making war on him, became very angry and went out against him brandishing the head, and he showed it

to him. Because he was unable to see, Cepheus rode against him on his horse. Perseus did not realise that he could not see, and reasoned that the head of the Gorgon he held was no longer working. So he turned it towards himself and looked at it. He was blinded and frozen like a corpse and killed. After that the son of Perseus and Andromeda ruled the Persians, established by his own grandfather Cepheus, the king of Ethiopia. Cepheus gave an order and the accursed head of the Gorgon was burned.[16]

Here Perseus himself is portrayed as behaving in an arbitrary, amoral and most unsympathetic fashion. We should not hastily ascribe the origin of this kind of portrayal of the great pagan hero to a Christian desire to denigrate the stars of the rival religious system. Rather, it derives from an old pagan tradition of rationalizing or 'euhemerizing' the myth of Perseus, the roots of which tendency can be traced back to Palaephatus in the late fourth century BC.[17]

We can see that the author of this narrative has in mind a recipe series for the creation of a magical skull of a broadly similar type to the Pitys series. This is indicated by four considerations above all. First, there is the narrative's own concentration on the rites of consecration needed to create the magical skull. Secondly, there is the explicitly instructional context: the story is very much one of Perseus putting into action a set of instructions handed down to him from his father Picus-Zeus. Thirdly, there is an intriguing coincidence in mode of discourse between Pitys' recipe and Picus-Zeus' words of instruction. Both men combine the instructional exposition of the spell with explicit, 'hard-sell' protreptic praise for its efficacy. In other words, the Malalas narrative continues to exhibit the impress of the rhetoric that is distinctive to magical instruction in the papyrus recipes. Fourthly, the coda of the Malalas narrative, which pursues the details of the final decommissioning of the Gorgon head, seems a little under-motivated in context. Its presence is surely determined by the convention of recipe-series of the Pitys type to incorporate decommissioning instructions. And in the light of these, decommissioning is aptly used in the case of a piece of magical equipment that has got out of hand, as in this case by destroying its own master and creator. In an admittedly elementary way, the narrative progression reflects the order of the sets of instructions as laid out in the recipe series.

We should also take note of a further broad narrative, or even 'argument', that underpins both the Pitys recipes and the Malalas tale, and this is a narrative about cultural transfer, cultural hegemony and cultural influence. In the Malalas tale, one of the greatest and most iconic of the Greek heroes, for all that he is undercut here, Perseus, is projected as the founder of Persian magic. In other words, the great technology regarded almost as a defining characteristic of Persian culture is derived from Greek culture. The Pitys recipe series gives us the same grand narrative, but with different actors. The Ostanes to whom Pitys writes is certainly to be identified with Ostanes the great Persian mage traditionally regarded as having introduced Persian magical arts into Greece in connection with Xerxes' invasion of 480–79 BC. The broader narrative then tells not merely of a single Thessalian specialist's instruction of a single petulant Persian pupil, but again of the Persians' derivation of the magical technology for which they were famous from Greek culture. Pitys is appropriately derived from the home region of Greek magic, Thessaly. But it is rare for Thessalian magical adepts to be male: Thessaly is the land of female witches. It may be then that Pitys is also subtly projected as an agent of the transfer of original magical technology from women to men. (Pitys' reference to the great mages of the past, a commonplace, as we have seen, of the protreptic rhetoric of magical instruction, remains awkward in context.)[18]

Circles of protection: amulets

It may be thought that ancient magic's wordy and expository recipe books offer more obviously fertile ground for the deployment of narrative or quasi-narrative than do other varieties of magical document, amulets and curse tablets. But in fact both amuletic texts and curse tablets deploy narrative in interesting ways.

Amulets were the most ubiquitous and visible of magical tools in antiquity. In conception, they were a protective or empowering magical bond or loop. The basic Greek words for amulet, *periamma* and *periapton*, literally meant just 'object tied around'. And indeed we hear of amulets that consisted of little more than a loop of tied thread or material. In the *Iliad* Hera borrows from the love-goddess Aphrodite her 'embroidered band' (*kestos himas*). This, context suggests, was a sort of girdle or brassiere that incorporated the powers of love, desire and sweet intimacy, and which could steal away the wits even of sensible men. When, in the *Odyssey*, the young Odysseus' leg is gouged by a boar, the sons of Autolycus bind the wound and speak an incantation over it. In Petronius' *Satyricon* an old woman cures impotence by putting an amulet consisting of no more than a few twisted coloured threads round the patient's neck. Petronius' contemporary, the elder Pliny, speaks of an impotence amulet similarly consisting of knotted threads, which is tied round the groin. In each of these cases, the modern reader may find something to explain the amulet's effectiveness: Aphrodite's embroidered band inspires desire by enhancing the figure. Odysseus' leg binding serves as a bandage. Petronius' amulet promotes erotic asphyxiation. Pliny's serves as splint and stimulus.[19]

Metal rings too could serve as amulets, and their effectiveness could be enhanced and specialized with direct engraving or the insetting of an 'intaglio', a stone, precious or otherwise, engraved with an image or with words. Vast numbers of such intaglios, which were particularly popular in Egypt, survive from the imperial period. The images of copulating couples engraved on intaglios are designed to enhance their wearer's sexual (and other) attractiveness and retain their immediacy. Literary sources give us some idea of how such ring amulets may have been given a special degree of activation by their wearer. Plato tells us of a magical gold ring discovered by the Lydian shepherd Gyges in a giant's tomb. He finds that by turning the ring's bezel and stone to the inside of his hand (perhaps thereby encompassing it and its power with his fist), he can become invisible. He uses its powers to enable him to seduce the king's wife and assassinate him, taking the king's place. So too in the *Philopseudes* Lucian's Eucrates tells us of a ring he acquired from an Arab sorcerer. When he one day found himself confronted by a terrible manifestation of Hecate in the woods, he contrived to protect himself from her and avert her similarly by turning the ring's bezel and stone to the inside of hand. Hecate stamped on the ground with her single snake-foot (she is here conceptualized as an anguipede), opened up a chasm to the underworld and disappeared down it. A now famous Romano-British ring-amulet was stolen or somehow expropriated from the pagan Silvianus by a Senicianus in the fourth century AD. Silvianus did what any pagan would in such circumstances and went to a local temple, that of the Romano-Celtic god Nodens at Lydney Park, and made a lead prayer-for-justice tablet seeking the ring's return, with a curse upon the health of those called Senicianus until the ring should be returned (we will say more of prayers for justice below). Poor Silvianus probably never recovered his ring, but modern archaeologists seem to have done so. The ring in question was found in Silchester, some 30 miles distant from Lydney Park. Its seal is inscribed with the name of the pagan deity Venus, and this would doubtless, like the erotic intaglios described above, have conferred sexual attractiveness on the pagan

Silvianus. But the ring carries an additional Christian inscription on its loop: 'Senicianus, may you live in God!' The Christian Senicianus evidently recustomized the lucky ring for himself and his own religion.[20]

In the imperial period too text-amulets became popular. These were usually inscribed on silver lamellas or papyrus strips which were rolled up, like curse tablets, and then worn in a bronze tube or fabric pouch around the neck. Amulets of this sort can of course afford to be much more verbally expansive than intaglios, and so they are able to tell us much more about themselves and how they were understood to function and the contexts in which they might be used.[21]

One of the most striking text-amulets to survive is a damaged silver lamella from the first or second centuries AD. This Greek text was found in a third-century AD stone coffin in Altenburg-Petronell in Austria, the former Roman Carnuntum. It reads as follows:

> For half-of-the-head. Antaura came up out of the sea, she shouted out like a deer, she cried aloud like an ox. Ephesian Artemis meets her: 'Antaura, where are you taking yourself?' 'Into the half-of-the-head.' 'You certainly will not go into the ...'[22]

Antaura is often casually referred to in scholarship as a 'mermaid'. But for all that she is here said to come from the sea, she is nothing of the sort. The etymology of her name tells us rather that she is a 'hostile wind', an 'ill wind', or even a 'hostile aura' (*anti-*, *aura*), and she is in fact a demoness who inflicts migraine. The 'half-of-the-head' that Antaura threatens to occupy is expressed as *hēmi-kranon* in Greek, a term that ultimately gives us our own English term 'migraine' (*-mikran-*). Sufferers will recognize that the term characterises the complaint well, with migraine pain being strongly concentrated within one half of the head.

Despite being incompletely preserved, this text gives us the most elaborate and distinctive use of a 'historiola' in any ancient magical document. The term 'historiola', Latin for 'little story', is applied, as we saw briefly in Chapter 2, to a short paradigmatic narrative of a supposed past event which is deployed to effect a similar outcome in the future. Thus the narrative of Artemis' successful past aversion of Antaura from entering half of someone's head is used to ensure that Antaura will not enter half of the head of the person protected by the narrative. It remains possible to reconstruct Antaura's final fate in the historiola, for all that the ending is lost, and that too from an unexpected group of sources, namely Byzantine Christian exorcistic spells, which, for all their variations, adhere closely to the phraseology of the Antaura text. Let us consider two examples, the first undated:[23]

> Spell for migraine, to counteract head pain.
> Half-head emerged from the sea shouting and hollering.
> Our Lord Jesus Christ confronted him and said to him:
>> Where are you taking yourself, headache, half-head, head-pain, eye-pain, inflammation, tears, white-spot of the eye, vertigo?
> And the head-pain replied to our Lord Jesus Christ:
>> I am taking myself to settle down in the head of (supply name), the servant of God.
> And our Lord Jesus Christ said to him:
>> Look here, you will not take yourself into my servant, but flee and take yourself off into the uncultivated mountains and mount into the head of a bull, and there feast on meat, drink blood, there destroy eyes, there make the head dizzy, lunge about and twist yourself this way and that. If you do not heed me, I will destroy you there on a mountain of fire, where no dog barks and no cockerel can be heard.
> You who established a boundary in the sea, put an end to the headache and the half-head and the pain in the head, forehead, eyes and marrow of (supply name), the servant of the Lord.[24]

The similarities with the Antaura text are remarkable, even if the demon's name and female identity have been lost. The demon similarly emerges from the sea making a big noise and with the intention of taking himself into the head of the amulet's victim. Similarly he is confronted by a major divine power, who forbids him to proceed. Instead, the divine power commands the demon to go off to the wilderness and there enter the head of a cow.

The second text is a portion of a longer exorcistic spell attributed to St Gregory against the demoness Abra. It derives from a prayer book from the Mt Sinai monastery dated to 1153 AD:

> This Abra came out of the sea.
> The first archangel Michael confronted her and said to her:
>> Where are you going and where are you taking yourself, black, blackening Abra, three-lipped and three-headed?
>> – I am taking myself into the bones of a person, to eat his bones and to devour his flesh.
> The first archangel Michael says to her:
>> You do not have permission, Abra, to eat a person's bones and to devour

his flesh, but the Lord God will pour fire down on you from heaven and scatter you over the rivers and the sea. Get out and withdraw from the body and the bones of the servant of the Lord, (supply name) ...[25]

The coincidences in this text are even more remarkable. Again the demoness comes out of the sea, again she is confronted by a major divine power, here the archangel Michael rather than Christ himself, and again she is refused entry into the body she has chosen. The demoness has lost her specific province of headache-infliction, to be credited instead with a more generalized devouring of the body, but she has intriguingly retained her identity. The name-form 'Abra' would have been pronounced 'Avra' in the Byzantine period, whereas the ancient form 'Antaura' would have been pronounced 'And-avra' at this time. Abra is, in other words, a short version of the ancient name, and retains the simpler meaning of 'wind' (*aura*).

The ending of the Jesus spell (as opposed to the more uniquely Christian ending of the Michael spell) may well preserve the structure of the lost ending of the Antaura spell. In it too Artemis may have diverted the demoness into the wilderness and into the heads of cattle. The spell's initial references to Antaura crying out like a dear and an ox may anticipate her banishment into the heads of precisely those cattle. If the noises characteristically made by such creatures were interpreted as cries of pain induced by Antaura and other demons like her, then that would retrospectively explain why Antaura herself, in giving expression to the pain she embodies, should make a cry that seems to resemble that of a deer or an ox.

How, precisely, was it thought that the Antaura narrative achieved its effect? The surviving text is not explicit about this, and perhaps it never was. There are a number of possibilities, and these are not mutually exclusive. The model of the Christ spell offers one possibility, namely that the narrative veered off into a prayer to Artemis, as a healing power, and asked her to avert the migraine in the way that she had done in the archetypal tale. The underlying logic of such a prayer-type is that the god should be persuaded to bestow a new benefaction in order to retain the credit she still enjoys for the bestowal of a former one. Such a prayer-type, categorized as *da quia dedisti* ('give because you have already given') in Furley's typology, was a very old one indeed, and it is found already in the poetry of Sappho of *c.* 600 BC.[26]

But the Christ spell's diversion into prayer is indeed a little jarring, and it is unsafe to assume that the Antaura spell did anything of this sort. Rather, we can point to two possible ways in which the narrative of Artemis' former defeat of Antaura was regarded as effective in itself. First, it may simply have been felt that the assertion of a pattern of action in itself encouraged the natural world around into aligning itself with it. Or, it may have been felt, a little less nebulously, that an accosting migraine demon would read the narrative and thus be deterred from the attack. Antaura herself might be reminded of and mortified by her former defeat, and so slink off before making any attempt against the wearer. And other migraine demons might be chastened on learning of the example made of her.

The find-circumstances of the amulet may be able to tell us something more of its use. The handwriting style dates it to the second or perhaps the first century AD, but it was found with three other much simpler amulets, consisting of little more than a few magical names, in a stone coffin dating from the third century AD. It may well be, therefore, that the amulet had been used by several generations prior to its burial with its final owner. Since migraine is hereditary, perhaps it had been passed down within a family. Amulets were often customized for a named wearer, as we have seen, and the Christian recipe texts discussed require the patient's name to be inserted at key points. The Antaura amulet is not customized, at any rate in its surviving part, and this lack of customization may have allowed it to travel more easily from relative to relative.[27]

We find another historiola deployed in a spell prescribed in the oldest recipe-collection preserved amongst the Greek Magical Papyri. The damaged first-century BC papyrus as it stands seems to have contained three spells, the first, 'for headache', is almost completely lost; the second is 'the spell of the Syrian woman from Gadara for any inflammation' (mentioned in the previous chapter), and the third runs as follows:[28]

Spell of the Thessalian Philinna against headache
Flee, pain in the head, vanish and flee | under a rock.
Wolves flee, | single-hoofed horses flee |
[dispatched] with blows by ...[29]

Frustratingly, the end of this historiola text too is lost. Nonetheless it seems that here, more simply than in the Antaura text, the headache is exhorted to flee in the general fashion in which wolves and horses do. Whether the headache is also to be transferred into animals of these species is less clear. The papyrus does not specify whether the spell was to be used verbally, or was to be copied out and incorporated in an amulet. Its brevity may suggest the latter, but both possibilities may have been entertained by the author.

This text too, for a similar complaint, also makes use of a historiola narrative, albeit a seemingly etiolated and generalized one. But the spell as a whole is also placed by the recipe book in the context of a minimal, albeit powerful, implied narrative of a rather different sort. We are told nothing more here of Philinna, but her designation as a Thessalian tells us at least that she was a witch from a race of witches. Both the fact in itself that Philinna is credited with the recipe, and the fact that she is referred to in such lapidary fashion, serves to project her as a mistress of magic, an authority amongst her countrywomen. Such ascriptions of spells are common in the wider corpus of the recipes of the Greek Magical Papyrus, although the professionals credited are usually male, as in the cases of Pitys (also Thessalian) and Pnouthis, considered above. Thence it is implied, probably, that the recipe has been handed down across generations, and has spread itself across the Mediterranean before arriving in the Egypt of the late Ptolemies. All these considerations, of course, enhance the prestige and authority of the little spell that follows.[30]

Given this, it is not absolutely necessary to enquire further into the background of Philinna, but further enquiries may reveal an even more elaborate implicit narrative contextualization for the spell. Now, we know of no Philinna famous for magical activities as such, but we do know of one famous Thessalian Philinna, and that is the Larissaean wife of Philip II of Macedon. A case can be made that this was the Philinna the papyrus' composer had in mind. In the traditions that came to flourish around Philip's chaotic, polygamous court, Philinna's fellow wife Olympias, the mother of Alexander the Great, certainly came to be seen as a witch, and it could well be that the notorious rivalry between these two women was projected by the developing Alexander legend as a sort of war of witches. Plutarch spoke of Olympias' use of magic (*mageia*) and spells (*pharmaka*). In the Alexander tradition's most mature form, that of the second-century AD *Alexander Romance*, Olympias, as we have seen, came to be portrayed in circumstances of intimate involvement and collaboration with the pharaoh, astrologer and mage Nectanebo, manipulator of voodoo dolls and erotic magic. Now, Olympias was believed to have made good use of her witchcraft specifically to remove the threat to her son Alexander's succession posed by Philinna's son Arrhidaeus. Plutarch tells us that this Arrhidaeus was 'imperfect in his thinking on account of a bodily disease. This was not something that had befallen him naturally or by accident. Rather, they say that when he had been a child his graceful and noble mien had shone out, but that then he was destroyed by Olympias' drugs or spells (*pharmaka*), and his mind was ruined.' Plutarch elsewhere recounts an anecdote that gives us Olympias in rivalry before Philip with an unnamed Thessalian woman, and here too the Thessalian's use of magic is at issue, for all that she is acquitted of it in this case: 'King Philip conceived a desire for a Thessalian woman, and she was accused of having bewitched him (*katapharmakeuein*). Olympias was accordingly keen to get the woman under her control. When she came into view, she was manifestly beautiful to look at, and conversed with her in a way that was far from ignoble or stupid, "No more", said Olympias, "of these slanders. For you have the charms (*pharmaka*) in yourself."' The healing role in which our papyrus text presents its Philinna sits naturally with Philinna the mother of the blighted son Arrhidaeus. It is tempting to think that the headache spell attributed to her may have been supposed to have been her cure or palliative specifically for the mental problems that Olympias had inflicted upon him, magic used against magic. But at any rate, we see how in the case of this brief recipe an elaborate history of magic and counter-magic may be invoked and brought to the aid of the spell in question by little more than the use of a single name.[31]

We may feel that the amulet was the natural home of the historiola, but they could be used in other contexts too: that of spoken spells and that of curse tablets. As we have seen, Theocritus' Simaetha uses one in the context of a verbal spell: she prays that Delphis may forget his new love as Theseus once forgot Ariadne. The Greek Magical Papyri preserve a recipe that prescribes another spoken spell involving a historiola, in which both Egyptian and Greek precedents are invoked. The fundamental function of the spell is to attract a woman by means of a penis-lotion:

> **Vulva key.** Take a crow's egg, the juice of the crow's foot plant, the bile of an electric ray from the river, work them together with honey and say the spell whenever you work them and anoint your genitals with them. The spoken spell is this: 'I say to you, womb of (insert her name), gape open and receive the seed of (insert your name) and the uncontrolled seed of IARPHE ARPHE (write this). Let (insert her name) love me all her life, as Isis loved Osiris, and let her stay chaste for me as Penelope did for Odysseus. You,

womb, remember me for the entirety of my life, because I am AKARNACHTHAS.' Say these things as you work the substances, and whenever you anoint your genitals, and so have sex with the woman you want. She will love only you, and no one but you will copulate with her.[32]

The historiolas cast the hoped-for relationship with the female victim in terms on the models of enduring love enshrined in Isis' love for Osiris and Penelope's love for Odysseus.

The precedent of Isis is again invoked in a historiola found in a lead erotic attraction curse tablet made in Graeco-Roman Egypt in the second century AD. Here Ammonion seeks to make Theodotis his own and to separate her from other men:

> I bind you, Theodotis, daughter of Eus, to the snake's tail, the crocodile's mouth, the ram's horns, the asp's poison, the cat's whiskers, the god's appendage, so that you may never be able to have sex with another man, not be screwed or be buggered or give oral sex, nor do anything that brings you pleasure with another man, unless I alone, Ammonion, the son of Hermitaris, am the man. For I alone am LAMPSOURĒ OTHIKALAK AIPHNŌSABAŌ STĒSEŌN UELLAPHONTA SANKISTĒ CHPHURIS egg. Accomplish this erotic binding-spell, this one that Isis used, so that Theodotis the daughter of Eus may no longer submit to penetration by a man other than me alone, Ammonion, the son of Hermitaris, dragged in slavery, driven crazy, taking to the air in search of Ammonion, the son of Hermitaris, and that she may apply her thigh to my thigh, her genitals to my genitals, for sex with me for the entire span of her life. These are the images: ...[33]

A series of pictures and ten characters follow. The recognizable pictures depict a god with a sceptre, a snake, a crocodile and a couple kissing. A further picture may represent a penis entering a vagina. Here Ammonion seeks to assert his own power through the tablet by identifying himself with a series of words *voces magicae*, or with the demons whose names he takes them to denote. He then seeks further to enhance the efficacy of his spell by asserting briefly that it was used – and inevitably successfully – by the goddess Isis herself.

We may note also in this text an example of the distinctive recurring narrative vignette of erotic attraction magic in which the distracted victim of the attraction spell is dragged through the streets to hammer at their lover's door. We have seen versions of it also in the spell that Lucian's Hyperborean mage inflicted on Chrysis, bringing her to hammer on Glaucias' door on behalf of his client Glaucias (above), and in the result that Cyprian aspired but failed to achieve with Justina on behalf of his client Aglaidas (Chapter 3). This sort of vignette is amusingly parodied in one of Apuleius' tales of the witch Pamphile. She has decided to draw to herself a young Boeotian to whom she has taken a fancy, and requires some of his 'stuff' for the spell. So she sends her maid and apprentice Photis to collect some of his hair from the floor of the barber's shop. Detected in the process, and roughly thrown out of the shop, the timorous Photis does not want to return home empty-handed. So she finds a pile of goat's hair sheared from some hides as they are being made into wineskins, and takes some of this home instead. That night, when Pamphile deploys the hair in her rite, she brings to her door not the Boeotian but the now inflated wineskins, which dash themselves furiously against it in the attempt to enter.[34]

Curse tablets and binding spells

Let us turn to the use of narrative in curse-tablet texts more generally. These tablets are documents of the ancient practice of 'binding curses', known in Greek as *katadesmoi* and in Latin as *defixiones* (they are often generically referred to under the latter term in Classical scholarship). The curses were most typically scratched on small, thin sheets ('lamellae') of lead which were then folded or rolled up tightly, pierced with nails in a 'sympathetic' gesture of binding or confusion, and entrusted to the dead or to deities with some sort of underworld connection for their enactment. The earliest known examples, made c. 500 BC, derive from Selinus in Sicily, but curse tablets eventually came to flourish in all parts of the Graeco-Roman world until the end of antiquity.[35]

Around 2,000 examples of curse tablets have now been unearthed, the majority of them written in Greek. The earlier ones, and indeed most of them, consist of little more than lists of names, with or without the addition of a speech-act phrase such as 'I bind' or 'I register'. But by the late antique period tablets were often being produced with elaborate, extensive and repetitive texts. These could invoke (ghosts aside) a syncretistic range of gods and demons with names of Greek, Egyptian, Jewish, Near Eastern or indeterminate origin. These later tablets often make appeal too to *voces magicae*, not always easily differentiated from demon names, either by their authors or by us, although it is becoming increasingly apparent that many *voces magicae* were rooted in garbled

Egyptian or Hebrew phrases. The inherent magical power of writing and letters is freely exploited: written lines or individual words or names could be reversed, twisted or confused in various ways, for sympathetic effect upon the victim; tablets were decorated with squares or triangles composed of vowels, or with palindromes, or with the 'Characters', letter-like symbols. And the tablets could be illustrated with appropriate images, such as those of bound corpses.[36]

Once manufactured, the tablets were activated through deposition, usually in a grave, and sometimes they were actually placed in the corpse's right hand. Otherwise they could be deposited in sanctuaries of underworld gods, Demeter in particular, or in springs which could carry the tablet down to the underworld. Sometimes ghosts are asked to carry out the act of restraint themselves, appropriately, since any contact with them could be 'deadening'; sometimes they are asked to act as messengers and to convey the curse-request to the underworld powers; at other times the dead are used in a sympathetic fashion, as paradigms of the ineffectualness the curser wishes to inflict upon his victim. The removal of a tablet from its place of deposition, if it could be found, would deactivate the spell. Otherwise, one could wear a protective amulet or even place a binding spell of one's own on the troubling curse.

Most of the extant curses that do indicate something of their context can be classified into five broad types:

- Litigation curses, to which type the Selinus texts and the bulk of those from Classical Athens belong. Such curses typically seek to bind the tongues of legal opponents in trials.[37]
- Sport and choral curses, designed to restrain opponents in formal competitions. The Roman world notably produced some spectacular examples of curses designed to restrain rival charioteers or their horses.[38]
- Trade curses. Noteworthy here are some Athenian curses restraining rival shopkeepers and rival prostitutes.[39]
- Erotic curses, which could either restrain the powers of attraction of rivals in love, actual or potential ('separation curses'), or could, more creatively, constrain the object of one's desire to surrender to the curse-maker ('attraction curses'). The language used in these curses can be crudely sexual. The majority of surviving erotic tablets were made by men in pursuit of women, but curse texts are

also found made by women in pursuit of men, men in pursuit of men, and, in two cases, women in pursuit of women.[40]

A fifth and more distinctive variety of tablets consists of 'prayers for justice', which need not, but often do, use the explicit language of binding. These tablets, usually addressed to deities, seek revenge or restitution for a wrong. Of particular note is the cache of such third- and fourth-century AD tablets retrieved from the sacred spring of Sulis Minerva at Bath. They typically dedicate to the goddess items already stolen by persons unknown in the confidence that her powers of detection are infinitely greater, and at the same time they retrospectively transform the offence from one of mere theft into one of sacrilege, with concomitantly more terrible divine consequences for the perpetrator.[41]

The so-called 'voodoo dolls' (the Greek term was *kolossoi*) were developed long prior to the tablets, and they were already being deployed in the early archaic period. We can see, in retrospect, that they functioned as figurative equivalents to the tablets upon which we depend to make sense of them. Some 38 finds of individual or groups of voodoo dolls have been made over a geographical spread roughly similar to that of the curse tablets. The dolls express the act of binding or confusion in their configuration: they can be bound hands and feet; they can be shut in tiny coffins; their limbs can be twisted; they can be mutilated, for example by decapitation; and they can be transfixed by nails.[42]

Curse tablets, even longer ones, are for the most part intensely formulaic. For this reason, despite initial appearances, it is usually difficult to detect the personal voice of the curser within them. However, just occasionally some of the longer tablets offer such a high degree of particular detail, narrative or other, about the situation in which they are made, that an urgent personal voice can indeed be heard through them. And in these cases, the voice is of particular interest. For these, intriguingly, are words written by people who do not expect them to be read or heard by any living person. They are still usually written with an intended audience in mind, be it ghosts or underworld deities, and the authors' awareness of this audience must still inform the fashion in which he or she expresses himself or herself. But the absence of any anticipated living human audience seemingly means that these outpourings of the heart are qualified or censored by none of the usual self-consciousness experienced when we interact with others in the society to which we ourselves belong. And so the tablets can, it seems, give us brief flashes of direct access to the unmediated innermost feelings of individuals from the ancient world in a way that it is difficult enough to achieve even in the case of the individuals around us. For this reason, the more distinctive curse tablets are of a social-historical importance and interest that goes far beyond anything fundamental they happen to be able to tell us about the practice of cursing and magic in antiquity.

We will consider three of the more expansive Greek curse tablets to have come down to us from antiquity, beginning with a tablet discovered relatively recently, in its original rolled-up form, in a fourth-century BC tomb in Pella, the capital of Macedonia:

> I register the rite and the marriage of Thetima and Dionysophon, and those of all other women, widows and maidens alike, but especially that of Thetima, and I deposit this spell with Macron and the demons. If I were ever to dig up, unroll and read this tablet again, then may Dionysophon marry, but not before. May he take no woman other than me, and let me grow old beside Dionysophon, and no other woman. I am a suppliant woman before you. Take pity on Phila [?], dear demons ... I have no friends or family and I am all alone. But guard this text for me, so that these things don't come to pass and so that the evil Thetima is destroyed in a fittingly evil fashion ... my ... may I become fortunate and blessed ...[43]

Phila (if that was the woman's name: the text is damaged at the key point) seemingly here addresses her curse to the tomb's occupant, Macron, and, through him, to his fellow demons, no doubt 'demons of the dead', other ghosts. Phila's underlying agenda of attracting Dionysophon to herself and marrying him is clear, for all that the spell is expressed in terms rather of the restraint and prevention of other potentially competing marriages, as is proper in a binding curse, with Thetima evidently seen as the principal threat. The other sorts of marriages Dionysophon might make are expressed and rejected in terms of 'exhaustive dichotomies', 'widows' and 'maidens', in a common trope of the tablets. The restraining idiom used here is also common, namely that of 'registration' or 'indictment', a quasi-legal term, before the underworld powers (the key word is *katagraphō*). It is interesting to learn that the exhumation and unravelling of the tablet will deactivate it, although Phila does not seem to contemplate this as a serious possibility.[44]

The text is a poignant one. Phila's expressive description of her loneliness, or at any rate her isolation, does not appear at all formulaic, and the unusual supplicatory nature of her appeal to the ghosts for pity is touching. It seems most likely that Phila was indeed passionately in love with Dionysophon. However, it remains theoretically possible that her primary goals, despite the vigour of her expression, were ones of social and financial aspiration. Although Thetima and the other women are the tablet's victims, the explicit restraint is, interestingly, not put upon them themselves but upon the abstract entities of their potential marriages. For good measure, the final line seeks Thetima's death too, and this is markedly unusual for the early tablets. The request seemingly serves as a further expression of Phila's desperation.

Secondly, the following litigation curse was written on a lead tablet and deposited in a grave with its corpse in the second or first centuries BC, in either Megara or Arcadia:

> **Side A.** Whenever you, O Pasianax, read this text – but neither will you, O Pasianax, ever read this text, nor will Neophanes ever bring a case against Agasibolos. But just as you, O Pasianax, lie here ineffectual, so too may Neophanes become ineffectual and nothing.
>
> **Side B.** Whenever you, O Pasianax, read this text – but neither will you ever read this, nor will Acestor or Timandridas ever bring a case against Eratomenes. But just as you lie here ineffectual and nothing, so may Acestor and Timandridas be ineffectual and nothing.[45]

The Pasianax addressed is the name of the dead man into whose tomb the curse was placed. He may have been a boy still, if the corpse exploited was one of the untimely dead. The curser may have known Pasianax, or even inserted the curse in the course of the obsequies (compare Erictho's exploitation of invitations to funerals). Otherwise, the curser may simply have read the name from the tombstone. There is no narrative progression in this text as such, but there is a progression of thought that turns back upon itself in a particularly interesting way. Underlying the spell is the paradox that the ghost is viewed in contradictory ways at the same time. On the one hand the ghost is projected as a vigorous and powerful agent with the ability to enact the binding in question in direct fashion, but on the other it is projected as a paradigm of ineffectuality, a 'sympathetic' model to be imposed upon the binding-victim. The text starts out by making appeal to the former notion, but then disingenuously turns back upon itself with a break in syntax to make appeal rather to the latter notion. We can be sure that this misdirection is an artful contrivance, and not merely the result of careless composition, because of the fact that the trope is repeated in identical fashion on both sides of the tablet. In this way the tablet carries the imagery of twistedness, inversion and reversal typically found in the treatment of the tablets themselves into the very syntax of the inscribed text.[46]

Finally, we turn to a lead tablet of the 'prayers for justice' category from Amorgos. The tablet's date is uncertain, but is thought to have been made between the second century BC and the second century AD:

> Lady Demeter, my queen, I am your suppliant. I fall before you as your slave. One Epaphroditus has lured away my slaves. He has taught them evil ways. He has put ideas into their heads, he has given them advice, he has seduced them. He has laughed at me, he has given them wings to waste time in the marketplace. He gave them the idea of running away. He himself bewitched my slave-girl, so that he could take her to wife against my will. For this reason he bewitched her to run away along with the others. Lady Demeter, being the victim of these things, and being on my own, I take refuge with you. May I find you propitious, and grant that I should find justice. Grant that the one that has done such things to me should find no peace in body or mind anywhere, whether still or moving. May he not be served by slaves or slave-girls, by small people or a large person. May he fail to accomplish his aims. May a binding-curse (*katadesmos*) seize hold of his house and hold it fast. May no child cry [?]. May he not lay a happy table. May no dog bark. May no cockerel crow. May he not harvest after he has sown ... May neither the land nor the sea bear fruit for him. May he not have blessed joy, and may he himself perish miserably, and all that is with him. Lady Demeter, I beseech you as the victim of injustices. Help me, goddess, and make a just choice, so as to bring the most terrible things and even harsher terrible things upon those who contrived such things and laughed at us and inflicted grief upon both myself and my wife Epictesis. Queen, heed us in our plight and punish those who are glad to see us in such a condition.[47]

Since the prayer is addressed to Demeter, we may conclude that the tablet was originally deposited in a sanctuary of hers. The precise nature of the circumstances it describes are partly disguised behind the curser's anger and allusiveness. How could Epaphroditus succeed in 'luring away' slaves? Did the curser not have recourse to law? Or does he resort to a curse because the law cannot give him any effective help in an under-policed society? It is noteworthy too that the cursed Epaphroditus is himself accused of having used erotic magic to lure away the slave-girl. In expressing the wish 'May a binding-curse seize hold of his house', the tablet oddly seems to distance the act of binding from itself.

Of all surviving curse tablets, this is the one that contains the strongest and most distinctive narrative element. The protracted narrative in some ways resembles a legal indictment, but is nonetheless vivid and heartfelt. The curser evidently wishes to use it fully to convey to Demeter the extent to which he and his wife have been the victims of a concerted campaign of mocking and hurtful harassment, and it is this (paranoid?) perception on the curser's part, one feels, rather than any single misdemeanour on Epaphroditus' part, that has fired his need for revenge. Here, then, it seems that the author saw the act of narration as itself integral to the hoped-for success of the curse.

Conclusion

This chapter has moved beyond narrative portraits of individual witches, mages and sorcerers to look rather at some of the uses to which narrative is put in the documentary sources for ancient magic, namely in the recipe books of the Greek Magical Papyri, in amulet texts and in curse texts. The recipe books among the Greek Magical Papyri deploy narrative, or elements of it, in a variety of ways. Most obviously, the course of complex spells can be laid out, for lucidity and for the benefit of the recipes' consumers, as a kind of future-narrative. Other recipes locate themselves within past or present narratives to endow themselves with venerability and authority. Sometimes this narrative siting can be achieved in sophisticated ways, for example by dressing a recipe up as a letter. Magical narratives, as this book in its entirety seeks to show, are extremely engaging, but the details of magical procedures, particularly the complex ones of the mature and elaborated magical culture of late antiquity, are less so. The appeal to familiar narrative types, direct or indirect, accordingly lends the recipes a degree of immediacy, meaningfulness and plausibility. Attention to such narratives can help us to bridge the gap between the thought-worlds of the papyri and those of ancient magical storytelling, which otherwise can seem far removed from each other. Text-amulets can make very specific use of paradigmatic mini-narratives, which have come to be known as 'historiolas', the force of which, somehow, is supposed to impact upon future action. Curse tablets, normally terse and formulaic documents, occasionally use narrative almost in a forensic fashion to persuade the ghosts or the powers to whom appeal is made of the rightness or importance of enacting the curse. Such narratives can give a palpable sense of the curse-maker's feelings of frustration, and in so doing may give us uniquely privileged and direct access to the innermost life of individuals who lived two millennia ago.

5

Across the Divide: Love and Sex between the Living and the Dead

Love beyond the grave

We have seen throughout that ghosts were one of the principal motors of ancient magic, and that they were in any case often tightly associated with it. Witches and ghosts were no doubt the twin stars of ancient folktales and, to the extent that these may have differed, the tales of the *aretalogi* discussed in Chapter 2. So in this final chapter we turn to some traditional narratives, and traditional ways of thinking about, ghosts in their own right, and we go beyond the ghost stories to which attention has already been drawn to look in particular at those that clustered around the exotic theme of love, and usually indeed sex, between the living and the dead.[1]

The combination of the motifs of sex and the return from the dead was a potent one in the ancient imagination. The two are brought together strikingly in the tale of Pausanias and Cleonice, which, although attested only rather later, must have been developed in essence already by the end of the fifth century BC. Pausanias was the greatest of the Greeks. It was he who, as Spartan regent, vanquished the mighty Persian invasion force at the battle of Plataea in 479 BC and so ushered in the age we now call Classical. But shortly afterwards, whilst taking the fight to the enemy and commanding the allied Greek forces at Byzantium, power went to his head and he began to behave in autocratic fashion. Plutarch, in the wake of many others, takes up the story. He tells how Pausanias conceived a desire for a local virgin girl in Byzantium, Cleonice by name, the daughter of good parents. He summoned her to his bed, and her fearful parents sent her out to him, under compulsion and in fear. As she arrived at Pausanias' chamber, where he lay already asleep, she asked the guards before the bedroom to remove the light, so that she could retain some vestige of modesty. As she duly made her way towards the bed in the dark, she stumbled into a lampstand. The resulting clatter roused Pausanias, who lashed out with the sword he kept by his side thinking that assassins had come for him, as well they might have. Cleonice fell and died from the blow. Thenceforth her ghost would not permit Pausanias to be at peace, but would harass him in his sleep, declaring in anger the hexameter, 'Go to justice; hubris is a very bad thing for men.' The Greek allies were outraged by the girl's fate and, with the Athenian Cimon as their ringleader, forced Pausanias out of the city. Now hounded to distraction by the ghost, he fled east along the south coast of the Black Sea to the oracle of the dead or *nekuomanteion* at Heracleia Pontica. There he called up the ghost of Cleonice and tried to beg off her anger. Her ghost manifested itself before him and told him that he would quickly be delivered from his troubles when he came to Sparta. But this was a riddle about the death that awaited him there upon his arrival.[2]

Upon his return to Sparta, Pausanias was accused of betraying the Greeks to the Persian enemy he had done so much to defeat, but before he could be arrested he ran for asylum into the temple of Athene Chalkioikos. The Spartans bricked him up in it – the legend has Pausanias' own father or mother righteously laying the first stone – and starved him to death. Such was the revenge of Cleonice's ghost. Thereafter it was the Spartans' own turn to be harassed by Pausanias' restless ghost, until, at the behest of professional ghost-evocators (*psychagōgoi*), imported either from Phigalia or even from Italy (the oracle of the dead at lake Avernus?), they placated it with a dedication of double statues. These perhaps represented a symbolic restitution of Pausanias both in body and in spirit.[3]

Let us note here a recurring theme in ancient Greek ghost stories, and indeed ancient Greek ghost-lore more generally: an angry or restless ghost attacks its living victim in terrifying but, it seems, otherwise uncommunicative fashion. If the victim wishes to know from the ghost how to give it peace, and therefore to hold some kind of rational conversation with it, then he must encounter it in a context in which he himself exercises greater control over it, as here Pausanias summons up Cleonice's ghost in an oracle of the dead.[4]

The Greeks also told stories in which desire between the living and the dead was so strong that sex was actually achieved between the two, whether by necrophilia, or by the dead person returning, somehow, from the underworld, whether as ghost, demon or as revenant. Let us consider first some tales in which the living retain a sexual compulsion for their dead partners.

One of the most intriguing of these was already known to Herodotus, who, writing *c.* 425 BC, recounts the bulk of it for us. It concerns

Periander, the semi-legendary tyrant of Corinth, who supposedly ruled *c.* 627–587 BC, and his wife Melissa. Periander loved his wife obsessively, but she fell victim to the slander of his concubines. Whilst we are not explicitly told the content of the slander, we may safely infer that it impugned her fidelity. And so Periander killed Melissa in a fit of temper, either by kicking her or by throwing a footstool at her whilst she was pregnant. He repented of his actions at once, and burned the concubines alive. Herodotus recounts the finale of the story in engaging fashion. Before dying Melissa had concealed a deposit on behalf of a guest-friend, and Periander now had no way to find out where she had put it, so he sent messengers to the oracle of the dead on the Acheron river in Thesprotia, at the northern limit of his empire, to call up her ghost and ask where she had put the deposit. But on appearance Melissa professed that she was cold and naked, and would not reveal where the deposit was until this was put right. The clothes buried with her had been no use to her because they had not been burned. To prove what she was saying was true, she declared that Periander had thrown his loaves into a cold oven. The token was proof, for Periander had had sex with Melissa's corpse. When the ghost's words were brought back to the tyrant he issued an edict to the effect that all the women of Corinth should go out to the precinct of Hera. So they all came out, as to a festival, in all their finery. But Periander posted his guards in ambush, and stripped them all alike, free and slave. He piled all their clothing up into a pit and burned it for Melissa. After this he sent again to the Acheron oracle to consult Melissa's ghost a second time, and this time she duly told him where she had put the deposit.[5]

Brief as it is, this tale complexly interweaves two deeply traditional types of ghost story. In the first type, a dead person is denied peace because he has not yet received the due rites of burial in perfect form, and so his ghost manifests itself to a living person and makes petition to him to rectify the burial so that he can achieve the rest he craves. Already in the *Iliad*, Patroclus' ghost manifests itself to Achilles in a dream to urge him to complete its due rites of burial promptly rather than tarrying over elaborate preparations, so that it can be at peace. In the *Odyssey* the ghost of Odysseus' dead companion Elpenor manifests itself unbidden before Odysseus as he practises a necromantic rite, to ask him to return to Circe's island and give his body due burial. In Euripides' *Hecabe* the ghost of Hecabe's son Polydorus, who has been murdered, with his corpse thrown into the sea, manifests itself before his mother to ask that she give his body, washed up on the shore, the due rites of burial. Theopompus tells how Pelops' charioteer Cillus died in Lesbos. His ghost then appeared to Pelops in a dream asking him for burial, and Pelops obliged by building him both a tomb and a temple. This story-type was popular in Latin literature too. Perhaps its most amusing manifestation is found in the pseudo-Virgilian *Culex* ('Gnat'). In this delightful poem a shepherd sleeping in a grove is threatened by a huge snake. A public-spirited gnat, observing the scene, bites the shepherd to wake him up so that he can save himself. The shepherd crushes the gnat in an automatic reflex before quickly noticing the snake and killing it with a branch. As he sleeps again the following night the ghost of the gnat manifests itself to him in his dreams and makes an extended and pitiful lament, and this induces the shepherd to hasten back to the grove and construct a cenotaph for the gnat there.[6]

In the second traditional story-type underpinning Herodotus' tale a living person needs by all means to locate an item concealed by a loved one now dead. The ghost of the dead person appears, either spontaneously or summoned in necromancy, to tell their beloved where the object had been hidden. The Judaeo-Christian tradition is particularly rich in examples of this story-type. Augustine tells how a man dies after paying off a debt. The opportunist creditor attempts to dun his son for the money a second time. But the father's ghost appears to the son to locate the receipt for him. A more graphic example is afforded by the *Apophthegms of St Macarius.* This work tells how St Macarius of Egypt (fourth century AD) saved a woman threatened with enslavement. Her husband had agreed to keep a deposit, but had died before he had been able to tell her where he had put it. The owner of the deposit, unable to retrieve it, purposes to take the woman and her children as slaves in lieu. When Macarius learns of this, he summons the widow to him, enquires about her situation, and then asks to be shown to her husband's tomb, and takes his disciples along with him. Once arriving at the tomb, he sends the widow herself home, before calling up the ghost of the dead man and asking him, 'O so-and-so, where did you put the dead man's money?' The ghost replies that he had concealed it in his house, under the leg of the bed. Macarius then instructs the ghost to go back to sleep until the day of the resurrection. Macarius' disciples fall at his feet in fear, but he is careful to advise them that he has not done this for his own sake, but that God has done it for the sake of the orphans. He instructs them to go and tell the widow where the deposit is, which they duly do. She takes the deposit to the creditor, who acknowledges the discharge of the debt and leaves her and her children free. Neither of these tales, we may note, make sense in terms of canonical Christian beliefs, according to which the souls of the dead should be absolutely confined beneath the earth until the Day of Judgment: this is a striking testament to the engaging and enduring power of the story-type. Nor could ghosts leave their confinement according to Jewish orthodoxy either, but the Talmud similarly tells how Zeēraj gave an innkeeper money to keep safe for him, but returned to find her dead. He went to her grave to ask her where it was. Her ghost told him that it was under the door-hinge and asked him to bring her offerings (compare Melissa's demand for clothing).[7]

We find a related tale in Virgil's *Aeneid*. Here Pygmalion, the wicked king of Tyre, kills the wealthy Sychaeus, husband of his sister Dido. The ghost of Sychaeus then manifests itself to Dido in order to locate for her the hidden treasure she will need to flee Tyre and found for herself the new city of Carthage. However, Virgil refines the story-type in an interesting way, for he indicates that the treasure thus located is not the rich Sychaeus' own money but an ancient lost and forgotten treasure buried in the earth. The implication is thus that Sychaeus has been able to locate it by virtue of his new role as a denizen of the underworld, and perhaps also by ghostly powers of insight.[8]

Lucian paid tribute to and gently parodied Herodotus' tale in a charming episode recounted by Eucrates in the *Philopseudes*. Eucrates tells how, after the death of his beloved wife Demaenete, he burned with her all the clothes and all the jewellery in which she delighted in life. On the seventh day after her death he was lying on the couch and trying to come to terms with her death by quietly reading Plato's book on the soul, the *Phaedo*. Whilst he was doing this Demaenete herself came to him and sat next to him. When he saw her, he embraced her, wailed out loud and started to weep. She stopped him crying and reproached him because, even though he had given her everything else, he had failed to burn one of her two golden sandals. She told him it was under the chest, where it had landed when thrown off. This was why he had not been able to find it, and so had burned just the one. As they were still speaking a Maltese dog barked underneath the couch, and Demaenete disappeared at the bark. The sandal was indeed found under the chest and subsequently burned for her.[9]

Here Lucian satirically offers us two ways of reading the story. In the first reading, the ghost actually manifests itself, but then flees prematurely back to Hades at the sound of the 'dog ... underneath'. That is, either the ghost mistakes the lapdog's bark for the call of Cerberus himself, the terrible warden of souls it has temporarily evaded, or Eucrates misconstrues the call of Cerberus, which he has heard to come from below, to be the bark of the lapdog beneath the couch. Or again, perhaps Cerberus acts through the lapdog, as his vicar on earth. In the second reading, Eucrates falls asleep on the couch and dreams on the subject of the book he is reading and so imagines that he sees the soul of Demaenete before him. When the dog barks Demaenete disappears along with the rest of his dream simply because the bark wakes him up. Now, the tribute to Herodotus' tale is explicit in the identification of the dog as a 'Maltese'. In Greek, the term is *Melitaios*, a term strongly evocative of *Melitta*, the familiar alternate form of *Melissa*. But it can be seen that Lucian has realigned and integrated the two constituent story-types with each other in a rather neater way than Herodotus had done, with the lost object itself serving as the cause of the imperfect burial which leaves the ghost restless. By comparison, Herodotus' rectification-of-burial tale somewhat awkwardly interrupts his retrieval-of-lost-object tale. However, the phenomenon of a ghost using the opportunity of being summoned up in necromantic consultation on another matter to complain about imperfect burial can be paralleled. Philostratus, writing in the early third century AD, tells how the first-century AD sage Apollonius of Tyana called up the ghost of Achilles at his barrow on the Trojan plain in order to put some Homeric questions to it. The ghost obliges, but first takes the opportunity to complain that the Thessalians have been neglecting his tomb cult, and to ask Apollonius to prompt them on the matter before it has to visit its anger upon them.[10]

But the most illuminating comparison for the Periander tale is found again in the Jewish tradition. A story attached to Herod the Great is preserved in part by Hebrew and in part by Greek sources. Josephus, writing in Greek, tells how Herod the Great loved his wife Mariamme obsessively. But she is hated for her haughtiness by his mother and her sister, and so they slander her before Herod. They choose the allegation that they know will upset him most, that of adultery. Herod has her killed in a fit of anger, together with her supposed lover, only to repent of his actions immediately. In a state of distraction he continues to speak to her as if still alive. The points of contact with the Periander tale are self-evident: the ruler's obsessive love for his wife; the envy directed towards the wife by rival womenfolk of the court; the slanderous allegation of adultery; the ruler's impulsive and precipitate response, in which the very depth of his love becomes the instrument of his wife's demise; the ruler's immediate repentance; the ruler's attempt to hold conversation with his beloved wife even after her death. It is immediately apparent either that the Herod story is modelled on the Periander story (although there is no clear reason why it should be), or that both tales represent independent manifestations of the same traditional and widespread story-type.[11]

The Hebrew sources add a most intriguing detail: Herod had Mariamme's corpse preserved in honey whilst he continued to have sex with it for seven years. This, then, corresponds strikingly with the Herodotean motif in accordance with which Periander had had sex with Melissa after her death. As it stands, the text of Herodotus gives no indication as to whether Periander had sex with Melissa's fresh (albeit cold) corpse just once or twice in the immediate aftermath of her death, for old time's sake, as it were, or whether he had preserved the corpse, like Herod, and had sex with it over a more extended period. But a telling clue lurks in the name that the tradition has bestowed on Periander's wife, for *melissa/melitta* is none other than the Greek word for 'bee'. Here, surely, we have a trace of the notion that Periander, just like Herod, had preserved his wife in honey. Now this shared motif strongly invites us to conclude that the Herod tale is a cousin to the Periander tale, rather than a descendant of it, for while it is easy to believe that the Greek tradition deferred the motif of pickling in honey into the wife's name, it is difficult to believe that the Jewish tradition would have unfolded the motif of pickling in honey out of Melissa's name alone.[12]

It would certainly have made sense for Periander to pickle Melissa in honey in terms of Greek culture and thought. This seems to have been the Greeks' usual method of embalming human bodies, when they had call to do so, and it seems on occasion to have been associated with the possibility of return to life. The Spartans, for instance, used this method to transport the bodies of their kings home when they died in remote parts, and the *Alexander Romance*, truthfully or otherwise, tells that Alexander the Great's body received the same treatment from Ptolemy as he transported it to Egypt. But the honey-pickling of corpses, or parts thereof, could also be associated, as it was in Melissa's case, with necromancy, and indeed with more general returns from the dead. Aelian records that Cleomenes I, the notorious mad king of Sparta, had sworn before his accession to his friend Archonides that he would include him in all his affairs, should he achieve power. But upon achieving the throne he beheaded Archonides and kept his head in a jar of honey. Before embarking upon any enterprise he would thenceforth lean over the jar and 'discuss' it with the head, thus remaining true to his oath. Although the primary purpose of the tale is to express the insanity and cruelty of Cleomenes, it also seems to hint at necromantic activity. Hyginus, writing in the second century AD, preserves the myth in which Cretan king Minos' son Glaucus disappeared and died after falling into a jar of honey. Minos commissioned the seer Polydius ('Much-seeing') to find him, and he was duly led to the jar by a dream. But then Minos ordered him also to restore the boy to life, which he could not do, and so the king immured him with the boy's corpse in his tomb. A snake penetrated the tomb, and the despairing Polydus killed it, only to see another snake enter and revivify the first one by laying a herb upon it. Polyidus took his cue from the snake, picked up the herb and laid it on the body of Glaucus, and the boy did indeed return to life. (We recall that Apuleius' Zatchlas had similarly laid a herb on the dead Thelyphron to restore him, if only temporarily, to life.) But the honey, it seems, was a sine qua non of Glaucus' restoration, for the popular Greek proverb that remembered the tale stated simply, 'Glaucus drank honey and rose again'.[13]

A gentle reminder of the necrophiliac aspect of the Periander tale may be found in Xenophon of Ephesus' *Ephesiaca* ('Ephesian Tale'), probably composed in the first half of the second century AD. In this the hero Habrocomes lodges in Sicily with an old and poor Spartan fisherman who lives by the sea, Aigialeus ('Of the shore'). Aigialeus tells him that he had once been a rich man, and had fallen in love with a beautiful Spartan girl, Thelxinoe ('Bewitching the mind'). But their love was threatened when Thelxinoe's parents engaged her to another Spartan, Androcles. So they eloped, with Thelxinoe disguised as a young man, by way of Argos and Corinth, and then fled to Sicily, where they made their lives, poor but happy. Thelxinoe had died in old age, but Aigialeus could not bring himself to be parted from her, so instead of burying the body he mummified it in the Egyptian fashion, and he now keeps it in an inner room. He talks to her as if she were still alive, lies beside her and takes his meals with her. As Aigialeus explains to Habrocomes, she looks different to him than she does to his visitor: he sees her still as the beautiful young girl she was when he first set eyes on her at a festival back in Sparta. It may be that the eloping lovers are made to flee through Corinth (hardly an obvious stage between Sparta and Sicily) in tribute to Periander's story, and if so, this is a further indication that the tyrant was indeed held to have preserved his wife's body whilst having sex with it.[14]

The themes of apparitions and bizarre sex recur in another traditional tale associated with Periander. This is recounted most fully by Parthenius, who wrote in the first century BC. He tells that as a young man the tyrant was reasonable and gentle, but that he became maddened and murderous as a result of the trauma of an affair with his own mother, who, as we learn elsewhere was called Crateia. She was seized by a great desire for her son. When she could no longer contain her passion with embraces, she devised a plan. She told him that a certain married woman of exceptional beauty had fallen in love with him, and urged him to assuage the woman's passion. At first he piously refused to corrupt a married woman, but eventually, as his mother continued to pressurize him, assented to an assignation. A night was appointed. His mother told Periander that the woman, for shame, required that there should be no light in the bedroom, and that he should not compel her to converse with him. Periander agreed, and the assignation duly took place on the stated terms, with, of course, his mother as the secret lover. She was careful to leave before daylight. In response to his mother's subsequent enquiry, he professed that he had enjoyed himself very much, and so frequent visits of a similar sort ensued. Eventually, Periander was himself overcome with love for his secret lover and became keen to discover who she was. He begged his mother to persuade the lover to reveal herself to him, but she forbade it, appealing again to the woman's shame. So Periander now devised a plan of his own and had one of his servants conceal a lamp within the chamber. As his mother came in the usual way and was about to lie down beside him, he raised the lamp high. Upon recognizing his mother he leapt at her as if to kill her, but was checked from doing so by a sudden divine apparition. But from this point on he was stricken in heart and mind. He descended into cruelty and slaughtered many of his citizens. His mother, lamenting her lot, killed herself.[15]

This wider nexus of traditions surrounding Periander's exotic sex life was kaleidoscoped and refracted in the traditions that subsequently developed around the Roman emperor Nero (ruled AD 54–68), for reasons that remain ultimately obscure. Nero supposedly kicked his wife Poppaea Sabina to death in a fit of temper during her pregnancy in AD 65, before having her body stuffed and embalmed. We are not told explicitly of any act of necrophilia, although the notion that he preserved the body in this fashion seems to bring us some way towards it. Nero also supposedly had an incestuous relationship with his own mother, Agrippina, before eventually murdering her too, at Baiae in AD 59. And Nero also had recourse to calling up the ghost of a murdered sexual partner, albeit not that of his wife, but that of his mother. After Agrippina's murder, as Suetonius tells us, Nero found himself haunted by her ghost, and chased by the Furies' whips and burning torches. He actually went so far as to bring in mages to perform a rite to call up her ghost so that he could beg off its anger. We may note that just as with Pausanias and Cleonice, Nero is first harried by the ghost in a form with which he cannot communicate, but he then has it ritually evocated so that he may eventually communicate with it. The elder Pliny tells that Nero was in any case obsessed with necromancy, and devoted the entire wealth and power of the Roman empire to the pursuit of it. Even so he was able to achieve nothing, and eventually abandoned it: an elegant proof, notes Pliny, of the impossibility of the practice. Pliny further tells that Nero's instructor was the Armenian mage Tiridates, who came to Rome in AD 66. It is noteworthy that the great Tiridates arrived long after Agrippina's death, but relatively soon after Poppaea's death in AD 65. We may wonder, accordingly, whether Nero's necromantic efforts – or rather the early traditions surrounding them – did not focus as much on the retrieval of Poppaea's ghost as Agrippina's, upon, that is, the retrieval of his wife' ghost, again in line with the template offered by the traditions surrounding Periander.[16]

In the tale of Periander and Melissa the motif of Periander's calling up of the ghost of his dead wife is explained not by his passion but by his need to find the treasure she had concealed in life. Nor indeed, according to Herodotus' tale, is he even present in person when the ghost is summoned up. Rather, he sends a messenger from Corinth all the way up to the oracle of the dead on the Acheron to do it for him. Even so, it is possible that there lurks behind this narrative the notion that Periander had called up the ghost too for erotic purposes parallel to those for which he preserved the corpse. This certainly seems to have been the notion behind the traditions relating to Alexander's rogue treasurer Harpalus, which we mentioned in Chapter 3. The Babylonian mages that offered to call up the ghost of his dead mistress Pythionice for him at the 'birdless' oracle of the dead undoubtedly did so in order that he could, in some way, assuage his sexual desire for her. We can, perhaps, say something of the developmental background of this tale. Despite Athenaeus' contention that the play was written for Alexander's army on the Hydaspes, there are strong reasons for thinking that it was rather written in and for Athens, the city with which Harpalus had built up a special relationship. In particular Harpalus had built on the road to Eleusis a magnificent tomb for Pythionice, which was held to be the most magnificent tomb by far in Athens. Outrage was expressed that the tomb of a mere prostitute should so far excel in magnificence the tombs of the good citizens who had died fighting on behalf of their city. And here surely lies the key. The notion that Harpalus was excessively obsessed with his dead girlfriend will have been back-formed from the fact of this over-the-top tomb he built for her, and it is from this that the comic fantasy of him having her ghost called up for him will have been spun. The supposed temple Harpalus built for Pythionice too is no doubt a reflection of the Athenian tomb itself, transposed to the play's Babylonian setting. The pitiful foundations of her Athenian tomb, incidentally, have been identified, but, alas, they can convey nothing of the structure's original splendour.[17]

So tradition may have told, it seems, that Periander attempted to recover the experience of living and loving with his wife in both body and spirit, by sleeping with her preserved body and by calling her ghost back to him. We hear of other tales in which bereaved lovers went to other extreme lengths to meet their loved ones again in body and soul, whilst stopping just short of actual necrophilia. The surviving accounts of the myth of Protesilaus and Laodameia, a brief passage in the *Iliad* apart, probably all derive from Euripides's lost tragedy *Protesilaus*. After spending only one night with his new bride, Protesilaus became the first Greek to die at Troy, killed as he leapt from the ship to the shore. The gods of the underworld took pity on the bride's desperate love and so sent the ghost of Protesilaus back up to her to spend a limited time with her, variously given as three hours or a single day. Either before or after this, Laodameia had a life-size effigy of Protesilaus made, from wax or from wood, which she kept in her bedroom and which she slept with. The mythographer Hyginus tells that Laodameia's father Acastus, thinking the effigy unhealthy, and being cruel to be kind, had it burned on a funeral pyre. The Byzantine scholar Tzetzes, drawing on other ancient texts now lost to us, links the use of the effigy to the manifestation of the ghost with the rationalizing claim that the tale of the effigy was invented out of the fact that Laodameia saw Protesilaus's ghost in her sleep during the night.[18]

It was no doubt as a result of being called back to sleep with his wife that Protesilaus' ghost continued to intervene vigorously in the world of the living. The final anecdote in Herodotus' *History* tells how in the aftermath of the great Persian invasion of Greece in 480–79 BC Protesilaus' ghost accomplished the downfall of the wicked Persian governor Artayctes, who had plundered the shrine built around his tomb at

Elaios on the Thracian Chersonese, and had defiled it by raping women in it. When Artayctes has finally been captured by the Greeks and awaits his crucifixion, one of his guards cooks some dried fish over a fire, and they begin to leap about and writhe as if still alive. Artayctes realizes that this is a message to him from Protesilaus, to the effect that, though dead, Protesilaus yet remains vigorous enough to exact his revenge on Artayctes. Herodotus projects the Persian war as completing the business of conflict between east and west that first erupted in the Trojan war. Accordingly he exhibits a nice sense of balance and ring-composition in allowing Protesilaus, the first man to die in the Trojan war, to deliver the final victorious blow of the Persian war.[19]

Euripides probably had Protesilaus, and perhaps even his own play of that name, in mind when he wrote his *Alcestis* in 438 BC, his earliest dramatic work to survive. The setting is Thessaly again, this time the city of Pherae. The main arc of the story is well known. Apollo bestows on Admetus the gift of being able to postpone his own death, if he can persuade someone else to die in his place. Admetus has no luck in persuading his elderly parents, but his loyal wife Alcestis does indeed agree to die for him and duly does so. Heracles arrives to find Admetus grief-stricken and repentant, and decides to help out his host by retrieving Alcestis from death. He waits by her tomb as Death personified comes to collect her, wrestles with him and defeats him, and restores Alcestis to a delighted Admetus. Alcestis will in due course be fully restored to life, but at her first reappearance she remains mute and strongly reminiscent of the corpse or ghost she has recently been. Prior to Heracles' arrival, Euripides presents us with the lamenting Admetus declaring his intention to have his carpenters make an image of Alcestis which he can lay out in his bed and embrace, an image presumably made, therefore, of wood. He calls upon her ghost to visit him in his dreams by night, and he expresses the wish that he could sing like Orpheus so that he might descend into the underworld, enchant Hades and Persephone and compel them to release her back to him, as Orpheus had attempted to do to recover his dead wife Eurydice. Here again it seems that the doll is to be used, somehow, to stimulate encounters with the ghost of Alcestis.[20]

We have an anomalous example of a tale in which a ghost is brought back from beyond the grave by or for the sake of maternal rather than erotic love. A rhetorical exercise pseudonymously ascribed to Quintilian, deliberately absurd and composed at some point before the fourth century AD, imagines that it is arguing in court a case of mistreatment brought by a wife against her husband. Their son had died, but then his ghost had returned regularly to visit her in the shape of the beautiful young man he had been in life. The ghost would embrace her and kiss her and spend whole nights with her. The mother derived great comfort from this. But the boy's father saw the ghost as something rather more sinister, as a source of torment for his wife, and perhaps too as an indication of his son's restless state in the afterlife, and so he determined to lay it. He brought in a mage to do the job: those with the ability to raise ghosts are equally adept at putting them back to rest. The mage achieved this by the metaphysical means of a 'barbarian' incantation, as well as by the very physical means of literally binding the ghost into the grave by laying iron bars and knotted chains over it, driving swords down into it (ghosts are ever weak before metal) and then piling stones over it. But the boy's mother now sees this as a form of unjust imprisonment inflicted upon her son, and so brings the case in the terms laid out.[21]

Sometimes the relationship that continued after the death of one partner could be engineered by prior agreement in life. The great Athenian mythographer Pherecydes, whose floruit, according to tradition, was 456 BC, told of Sisyphus' clever mechanism to allow himself to return to live with his wife after death. Sisyphus had already evaded Death (Thanatos) once when targeted by him by ambushing him and chaining him up, so that for a while indeed no human at all could die. But Death was eventually released by Ares and came against him once more. This time Sisyphus forbade his wife to carry out the customary rites of burial for him after his decease, so that Hades eventually sent him back to tell her off about it. But, having arrived back, he declined to tell her off and rather lived with her until old age before, somehow, dying again at that point. For his troubles, Sisyphus was subject to a well-known eternal punishment in the underworld. He was forever fated to push a rock up to the top of a hill, only for it to roll back down to the bottom as he neared the summit. We only know Pherecydes' tale from a summary preserved by a Homeric commentator, and this leaves big questions unanswered: did Pherecydes' Sisyphus return as a ghost, as a revenant, or, somehow or other, as a regular living man? How did he contrive to die a second time?[22]

The notion that a lover's ghost could be brought back by prior agreement seems to underpin Dio Cassius' understanding of the circumstances surrounding the death of the emperor Hadrian's favourite, Antinous, in 130 AD. Whilst the emperor himself put it about that

Antinous had accidentally drowned after falling into the Nile, Dio knew rather that the emperor had been obsessed with divinations and sorceries, and so, on advice, had sacrificed a willing Antinous in order to secure a necromantic divination, and perhaps also to manufacture a tame and familiar demon from his ghost. Antinous was compensated with the founding of the city of Antinoopolis in his name, and by the dedications of countless numbers of statues to him throughout the Roman empire, large numbers of which can still be seen in the world's museums. Dio does not tell us whether Hadrian and Antinous were able to enjoy any kind of love life or effective proximity after the latter's death, but the premise of the sacrifice, or at any rate of the tale about it, is that Antinous should retain his love for Hadrian in his ghostly form and act accordingly. Later Latin sources bring the advisors behind Antinous' death into sharper focus for us, describing them as 'mages'. But these sources' understanding of the nature of Antinous' death is rather that the boy sacrificed himself in an act of ritual *devotio* or self-sacrifice to prolong the emperor's life, somewhat in the way that Alcestis had famously given up her life so that her husband Admetus could live on in her place.[23]

The idea that boys could be sacrificed to produce demon familiars was a widespread one. The Pseudo-Clementine *Recognitions* similarly tells how Simon Magus sacrificed a boy to produce a magical demonic familiar. The horror of his crime was, however, perhaps mitigated by the fact that he had first manufactured the boy for himself out of thin air. Perhaps we may assume that this boy too, insofar as he was endowed with any individual consciousness, was also a willing victim. But we hear (as it seems) of a less willing boy-victim in an engaging narrative recounted by Zacharius the Scholastic in the late fifth century AD. The Greek original of the text is lost, and it survives only in Syriac. Zacharius tells how a group of young legal students in Beirut interested themselves in magic and collected books on the subject. One of their number, John Foulon of Egyptian Thebes, was desperately in love with a chaste woman, and so the group hatched a plan to manufacture an obedient demon that they could then use to cast erotic desire upon the woman and bring her forcibly to him (note this further example of the attraction vignette discussed in Chapter 4). To create this obedient demon they proposed to sacrifice John Foulon's own Ethiopian slave-boy in the circus. They escorted the slave-boy to the circus in the middle of the night, but as they were about to commit the crime God took pity on the slave and made some people pass by the place. The young men took alarm at this and turned to flight, whilst the Ethiopian slave took his own opportunity to escape. In this case, it was obviously anticipated that a friendly familiar could be obtained even from the ghost of a living boy killed against his will.[24]

In these texts the purpose of the boy-sacrifice is to produce a familiar from the boy's ghost that will then deliver prophecies or execute magical operations for his maker and controller, but boys could also supposedly be sacrificed for other magical and divinatory ends. Cicero, writing in 56 BC, claimed that his opponent Vatinius sacrificed boys to the – apparently already existing – ghosts of the dead, for the purposes, apparently, of receiving a divination from them. Such a notion – that boys should be sacrificed to conciliate with their blood other – already-existing-ghosts who will then work for the magician, seems anomalous even within the fantasy world of ancient boy-sacrifice. Horace's hag-witches, Canidia, Sagana, Veia and Folia, as we have seen in Chapter 2, murder a boy they have kidnapped in order to make a love potion from his dried and powdered liver and bone marrow. According to Philostratus, the emperor Domitian accused Apollonius of Tyana of cutting up a boy to make a necromantic divination. In this case it is made clear that the supposed divination consisted of an inspection of the boy's guts, much as one would inspect the liver of a regular sacrifice for divinatory purposes. Perhaps we are to imagine that a mantic impression was left upon the guts by the departing ghost.[25]

New love between the living and the dead

The tales considered so far have concerned the desires of a living person to maintain a relationship of love and sex with their established partner after their death. But the ancient world knew stories also of fresh loving and sexual relationships between individuals who met for the first time only after the death of one of them.

The notion, at any rate, that one can fall in love with a ghost seems to have underpinned Menander's lost New Comedy, *Ghost*, which will have been written *c.* 300 BC. A summary of the play is preserved by Donatus, who compiled a commentary on the plays of Terence in the fourth century AD. According to this, the play told of a young man whose father had recently acquired a new wife. In the past the woman had been seduced and given birth to a baby girl, whom she has had reared in secret. On beginning the marriage she surreptitiously installs the girl, now a young woman, in the house that adjoins that of her new husband. She communicates with her daughter through a ruse. She has dug a hole in the party wall through to her, and disguises the hole as a niche-shrine, which she decorates with garlands and at which she frequently pretends to worship. All the while she is calling her daughter to her and conversing with her. One day her stepson catches sight of what is happening, and mistakes the beautiful girl he sees in or through the shrine for a ghost. He is stricken with terror, but nonetheless contrives, as young men do in these comedies, to fall in love with her. Eventually the whole truth emerges, and the young man's wedding to the girl is arranged with the consent of his father. In New Comedy young men always fall in love at first sight, and so the terror of first seeing the ghost must have given way to love instantaneously. And since the truth of the girl's nature and origin only emerged slowly in the course of the play, we are obliged to believe that the young man persevered with his love for the girl whilst continuing to believe that she was a ghost, with all the comic potential of such a situation.[26]

This love-relationship between the living and the dead seems to have been initiated from the living side, but more often, interestingly, such relationships seem to have been initiated from the dead side. Let us begin with a striking tale from a text we have already met, Philostratus' early third-century AD *Life of Apollonius of Tyana*. The tale in question is set in Corinth, the great home for ghost stories, and concerns the Lycian Menippus, a pupil of the Cynic Demetrius, who has gravitated into Apollonius' circle. He is 25 years old, and has a handsome and toned athletic body. One day he is out walking alone down the road to Cenchreae when he is accosted by a ghost materialized in the form of a beautiful, gentle and rich woman. She clings to his hand and claims that she has been in love with him for a long time. She tells him that she is Phoenician and has been living in one of the suburbs of Corinth. She tells him that he should come to her house that evening. She will be singing a song for him as he arrives, and she will give him wine of a sort he has never drunk before. There he will face no competitor for her love, and they will live together, a beautiful woman with a beautiful man. The young man is enticed, for although philosophically strong and morally restrained in other respects, he cannot resist sex. So he goes to see her that evening and thenceforth pays her constant visits, without any idea, of course, that she is a ghost. Apollonius takes the measure of his new pupil intently, and tells him that he is a beautiful man, pursued by beautiful women, but that he is warming a snake on his bosom, and that it is a snake that is warming him, not a woman fit to marry.

Demetrius asserts to Apollonius that the woman truly does love him, acting as such in all ways, and that he will marry her on the following day, for it is a delightful thing to marry a woman that loves one.

Apollonius is sure to attend the drinking party that precedes the celebration of the marriage, and asks to be introduced to the gentle lady for whose sake all have gathered. Demetrius, blushing, brings her forward. Apollonius asks to which of them belong the fine things with which the room has been decorated, including its gold cups and silver tableware. Menippus tells him that it all belongs to his bride, for all that he owns is the rough philosopher's cloak customarily adopted by the Cynics. Apollonius asks the pair whether they know about the fantastic gardens of Tantalus, which both exist and do not exist at the same time. They reply that they do, whereupon Apollonius asserts that the room's wonderful decorations are of the same kind and wholly insubstantial and illusory. He reveals that the bride is one of the so-called *empousai*, which many consider to be *lamiae* or bogies. These female creatures, he explains, fall in love and crave for sex, but most of all they crave for human flesh, and they use sex to ensnare the men upon whom they wish to feed. The *lamia* pretends to be repulsed by what she has heard, telling Apollonius angrily to shut up and get out. She jeers at the philosophers for always talking rubbish as they do. But then the golden cups and silver tableware are shown to be made of air and everything flies from sight. The wine-pourers and the cooks and all the servants disappear after their unmasking by Apollonius. The ghost now pretends to cry and begs Apollonius not to subject her to torture or compel her to admit what she is. But Apollonius is insistent and will not release her. She admits that she is an *empousa* and that she has been feeding on Menippus' fat with pleasure as a prelude to devouring his body. It is her practice, she confesses, to feed upon beautiful young bodies, since their blood is pure.[27]

In this fascinating tale we find the nearest construction the ancient world has to offer us to the modern vampire: the *lamia-empousa* is some sort of ghost; she devours the living, and she has some sort of serpentine aspect to put alongside the modern vampire's fangs. It might seem in immediate context that the reference to the being as a snake is to be read merely as a passing metaphor expressive of her treachery, but its significance is probably rather greater. The history of Greek ideas about *lamiae*, or about individual creatures named Lamia, is a complex one that stretches back even into the *lamashtu* demons of the ancient Neat East. *Lamiae* were often conceptualized as child-devouring demons, and as deriving, in some form, from an archetypal mythical Lamia, whose own children Hera had killed. But two earlier texts seem to shed particular light on Philostratus' tale here. Nicander, writing probably in the second century BC, tells how the Delphians had once been terrorized by a terrible beast that had dwelled in a cave on Mt Parnassus. This creature was known as Lamia, and also as Sybaris. It would venture forth each day and snatch up flocks and people alike. Apollo told his people that they would be delivered if they sacrificed a citizen lad to it. The lot selected the fair Alcyoneus, but Eurybatus fell in love with him and substituted himself as the sacrifice. He did battle with the monster and destroyed her by hurling her down from the rocks. We have no specific physical description for this Lamia, but a serpentine nature is suggested by her modus operandi which is strongly (though not exclusively) reminiscent of ancient and medieval dragons. However, unlike such dragons, and rather more like Philostratus' *lamia*, the creature's meal of choice is a desirable young male. Writing in the late first century AD, Dio Chrysostom had described the terrible *lamiae* of Libya. For him they are a race of dangerous creatures, rather than ghosts or apparitions. They take the form of beautiful woman in their upper part, but of a serpent in their lower part, which culminates in a serpent head. They then enchant unsuspecting men with their upper part, exposing their breasts, and as the man is mesmerized their concealed snake-end whips round, snatches him up and devours him. These *lamiae* at any rate share with Philostratus' *lamia* a serpentine element, and the practices of concealing their true monstrous nature, of ensnaring men with erotic desire and of devouring them once caught.[28]

The Greeks had complex notions about the creatures to which they gave the name *empousai* too. In general they seem to have been conceived of as obstructing, shape-shifting underworld demons associated with Hecate. But the most enlightening text for this particular *empousa* is Philostratus' own brief description of Apollonius' encounter with another of them, in India. This *empousa* appeared to Apollonius and his travelling companions in the light of a bright moon. It repeatedly changed its form, sometimes disappearing completely. Apollonius and his companions shouted abuse at it, and it ran off shrieking in the fashion of a ghost.[29]

Apollonius deals with the Corinthian *lamia-empousa* with the familiar Judaeo-Christian technique of exorcism, by which a ghost or a demon is neutralized and expelled by being made to confess its true identity, as we have seen in Chapter 3. Philostratus does not, it seems, have a completely settled idea about the inner world of his *lamia*. Much of what Apollonius is made to say about this *lamia* in particular suggests that she is merely a heartless creature of deception and dissimulation. But when he first introduces Menippus to the concept of *lamiae* and *empousai*, he seems to imply that their love – the word used is one that covers sexual desire and passion – is genuine. This suggests rather that the *lamiae* exist in a poignantly tragic condition: they are forever destined to kill and eat the men with whom they fall in love. We may note a certain correspondence between this tale and Homer's tale of Circe, discussed in Chapter 1. Here again we have a beautiful supernatural woman, who welcomes a young man to her house with sweet singing and special variety of drink, who enchants the young man, who will feed him with a view to eating him herself in due course, and who also seems to fall in love with her victim.

Another, seemingly more tender, story of love between a living man and a dead woman, where again the love is initiated by the dead woman, is to be found in the tale of Philinnion in Phlegon of Tralles' collection of *Marvels*. Phlegon compiled his collection *c.* 140 AD, but he almost certainly took the story over from an early Hellenistic source. Unfortunately the first part of Phlegon's narrative is lost, but its outline can be recovered from the fifth-century AD summary of the whole made by Proclus. The events of the tale supposedly took place in Amphipolis during the reign of Philip II, and therefore during the period 357–336 BC. The account of the events is cast in the form of a report by a governor of Amphipolis, named either Hipparchus or Arrhidaeus, to one of Philip's more immediate staff. The girl Philinnion has died immediately after marrying one Craterus, under circumstances that remain unclear. But evidently, her desire for love and sex has been aroused. Just short of six months after her death her bereaved parents, Charito and Demostratus, take in a young man as a guest-friend or lodger, one Machates of Pella, perhaps installing him in their dead daughter's former bedroom. Philinnion then returns from the dead, visits Machates in his room by night and sleeps with him. He has no idea of her dead state. She tells him that she is sleeping with him without her parents' knowledge; it is not clear whether at this point he assumes her to be a daughter of Demostratus' house, or of some other. On their first night Machates gives her an iron ring and a gold-plated cup, whilst Philinnion presents Machates with a gold ring that has been left with her in her tomb.[30]

From this point onwards Phlegon's original narrative survives. The girl is discovered during her second nocturnal visit by one of the household slaves, her former nurse. From the door of Machates' room she sees Philinnion within in the lamplight, sitting beside Machates. She runs to tell the girl's parents that their daughter has rematerialized. They initially berate her as insane, but in due course the nurse is able to drag them to the bedroom door. The girl is now asleep beside Machates, but Charito thinks she can make out her daughter's form, and resolves to confront her in the morning. But when she comes back to the room at that point, the girl has gone. So instead Charito throws herself on Machates' mercy, tells him what she had seen and its significance and begs him to tell her everything. Upset at first, Machates eventually does as she asks, and confesses that her name is Philinnion. He shows her the things the girl has left behind with him, the golden ring she has given him, and a bra she has left the night before. Charito recognizes these tokens as belonging to her daughter, clasps them to her breast and falls to the ground in shock. Machates promises that if the girl comes to visit him again he will show her to them. He is intrigued but does not really believe that his lover is dead. He conjectures rather that the dead girl's tomb has been robbed, and that the grave-robbers have sold her clothes and jewellery on to his lover's father. Night comes on and the hour at which Philinnion is accustomed to visit Machates. She duly appears and sits beside him on the bed. Wishing to know the truth of it all, and whether he really is sleeping with a dead woman, Machates secretly sends the slaves to fetch Charito and Demostratus, who arrive forthwith. As they now see her properly for the first time they are at first speechless and terrified, but then shout out aloud and embrace their daughter. But Philinnion remonstrates with her parents for begrudging her spending three days with her father's guest. She has been causing no one any trouble. But because of their interference she must now return to her appointed place, for it had been by the will of the gods that she had come. This said, she dies at once, and her body is stretched out for all to see. Her mother and father throw themselves upon her, and the house is once again filled with uproar and lamentation over her death. Henceforth, there is to be no return from the dead for Philinnion. The rumour of what has happened quickly spreads through the city and comes to the governor. He keeps the crowds back from the house for that night, and holds a public meeting in the theatre the next day to discuss the affair. There it is resolved to open Philinnion's tomb to see whether her body remains on its bier. On entering the vault the governor and his men find the bodies or the bones of all Philinnion's dead relatives in place, but her own bier is empty, save for the iron ring and the gold-plated cup that Machates had given her on their first night. Amazed and terrified, they proceed on to Demostratus' house and find that Philinnion's body is indeed lying there. They return to the assembly to report, and meet with uproar. The experienced seer Hyllus bids them burn the girl's body outside the city limits and bury her there, and to propitiate Chthonic Hermes and the Eumenides. He tells the governor, privately, about the prophetic implications of the episode for his king, and bids him make lavish sacrifices to Hermes, Zeus of Guest-friends and Ares. His instructions are duly carried out. But Machates himself commits suicide from despair.[31]

Philinnion was evidently tangible enough to make love to the living Machates – far more tangible, therefore, than the wraiths of Homer's *Nekuia*, in which, when Odysseus tries in vain to embrace the ghost of his mother, his arms simply pass right through her, whilst the ghost of Agamemnon tries in vain to embrace him in turn. It is clear that Philinnion's manifestation exploits her actual corpse. She should accordingly be considered a 'revenant'. An even more tangible revenant is described in the second tale of Phlegon's *Marvels*. Here, in another tale with an early Hellenistic setting, Polycritus, a commander of the Aetolian league, dies after three nights of marriage with his Locrian wife and leaves her pregnant. When the child is born, it is a hermaphrodite. The woman's relatives bring it to an assembly to discuss the implications of this portent, and what is to be done with the child. The seers suggest that it be burned outside the city limits. But before action can be taken, the ghost of Polycritus manifests itself, garbed in black. It speaks to the citizens in measured tones and asks them to give it the child. The citizens continue to argue amongst themselves about whether the child should be handed over, whereupon the ghost seizes it, tears it apart limb from limb, and devours it. The people throw stones at the ghost to drive it away, but these can do it no harm. The ghost leaves only the child's head uneaten, before disappearing instantaneously. The child's head, lying on the ground where it has been deposited by its father's ghost, then proceeds to utter prophecies of doom for the Aetolians.[32]

Philinnion's claims prior to her second death seem to imply that, if she had not been spied upon by her parents, she may in time have been fully and permanently restored to life, but the mechanism by which this might have been achieved must remain obscure to us. The principle invoked may be that by which Orpheus lost the chance to restore his dead wife Eurydice to life as he walked her out of the underworld: he did this, as is well known, by succumbing to the temptation to gaze upon her too soon.[33]

Phlegon's tale was to become the model for Goethe's *Bride of Corinth*, which transforms the sympathetic Philinnion into a rather less sympathetic deceitful vampire who is frustrated in her attempt to devour the guest. This sinister reading may at first appear to be a travesty of Phlegon's story, but it may be less inappropriate than it initially appears. We can see that it bears a general similarity to Philostratus's tale of Apollonius's exposure of the *lamia*-bride in Corinth. Here again we have a bold female ghost who comes across a young man she finds desirable and pushes herself upon him, developing a loving relationship. And the Philinnion tale – in a sense going further than the Apollonius tale – does indeed result in the actual death of the living beloved, albeit from a broken heart rather than by being devoured. But the tale makes sense according to a different logic too: the logic that says that contact with the dead in itself transmits the contagion of death. Philinnion's love for Machates was surely genuine and passionate but, even so, Machates may have been destined for death by that love, just as surely as Menippus was destined for death by the love of his *lamia*. The *lamia* seemingly possessed this grim knowledge, but it is less clear whether the ghost of Philinnion did. Her hopes of making her union with Machates permanent seem to have focused on the prospect of her own return to the world of the living rather than upon his coming to join her in the world of the dead.[34]

An example of a male ghost attempting to take a female lover among the living may be found in the *Ephesiaca* of Xenophon of Ephesus, probably written in the first half of the second century AD. The novel's heroine Anthia feigns an epileptic attack to avoid the fate of a slave prostitute, and she then explains how she supposedly contracted the disease. As a girl she had wandered away from a night-festival and found herself by the tomb of a man who had recently died. A fearful figure, with a voice yet more terrible, leaped up from the tomb and tried to hold on to her. When daylight came he let her go, but struck her on the chest and declared that he had cast a disease into her. Presumably this was a gesture of frustration on the ghost's part when he found himself unable to take her back to the underworld with him as his bride.[35]

The mechanism of possession allowed the less tangible variety of ghost to get closer to the object of its affections than any living lover could. A distinctive example of this is afforded by another episode in Philostratus' *Life of Apollonius*. The episode, like the story of Antinous, offers a relatively rare example of homosexual love between the living and the dead. It takes place during Apollonius' trip to India, when a group of suppliants make appeal to Apollonius for deliverance from their sundry ills. Among the suppliants is a woman who pleads on behalf of her son. He is sixteen years old, and has been possessed for two years. The demon that possesses him is, she says, a dissembler and a liar. She explains that her son is very attractive, and that the demon is in love with him, and so it will not allow him to keep within his own senses, or go to school or archery class, or even to stay at home, but it drives him out into the desert. Nor does it leave the boy his own voice, but speaks through him with its voice, the deep, hollow voice of a man. The expression in the boy's eyes too belongs to the demon, and is not his own, and he no longer recognizes his own mother. But the demon had already been made to reveal itself when she had threatened to bring the boy before Apollonius (she had, in other words, used the name of a powerful sorcerer against it), and it had explained at that point that it was the ghost of a man who had died in war. When he died he had been in love with his wife, but he had then been dismayed to find his wife insult their marriage bed my marrying another man on the third day after his death. As a result of this he had come to hate love for women, and so transferred his affections to boys, and to this boy in particular. The ghost had then claimed that, if the mother did not slander him before Apollonius, it would bestow many good and fine qualities on the boy. But nothing had come of this, and the demon was now in sole control of her house. Apollonius enquires whether the boy is at hand. The mother says that he is not: she has not been able to make him come, despite much effort. The demon threatens that he will throw the boy down from a cliff-top or into a deep pit if she brings him before Apollonius. Apollonius reassures the woman and draws a letter from his robe and gives it to her. This is addressed to the demon and contains terrifying exorcistic threats. We are not explicitly told the outcome of the letter, but we may infer that it was successful. As deriving from a man killed in war, the possessing ghost belongs to one of the familiar categories of restless ghost, that of the 'dead by violence' or *biaiothanatoi*. One of the most curious aspects of this episode is the fact that the ghost has already confessed its identity, yet somehow contrives to possess its victim still. Normally, as we have already seen, the act of compelling the possessing ghost or demon to confess its identity is *ipso facto* an act of expulsion. The undertakings the ghost has given to the boy's mother, to the effect that it will bestow fine qualities upon the boy, though fraudulent, are not completely absurd. The education and improvement of a boy's soul is presented as the ideal goal of a pederastic relationship in Plato's *Symposium*.[36]

The theme of a ghost possessing a person for whom it feels love and erotic desire anticipates Ansky's famous Yiddish play of 1914, *The Dybbuk*, which was fashioned from folkloric material he had gathered amongst the Hasidic Jewish communities of Eastern Europe. In this play, Nisn and Sender make a pact that the former's son Hannan should marry the latter's daughter Leah (Leah'le). But Nisn dies and Hannan, an impoverished scholar of the Talmud and the Kabbalah, comes to manhood knowing nothing of the pact. He falls in love with Leah, but the rich Sender rejects Hannan's suit and resolves to find a rich husband for her instead. Hannan drops dead on the day Sender announces the engagement. As Leah visits the cemetery before her wedding, to invite her mother's spirit to it, she is possessed by the spirit of Hannan, the 'Dybbuk', and so refuses her new husband at the wedding, whilst Hannan affirms through her, with his own voice, that he has returned to the bride destined for him and that he will not leave her. After a lengthy exorcism, in the course of which the spirit of Nisn has returned to tell its story too, the spirit of Hannan is eventually driven from Leah's body. But she dies before the rabbis can proceed with her intended marriage, to be united with Hannan in the afterlife. Whilst the act of loving possession is itself heterosexual, a homosexual frisson remains in the prospective marriage between two men.

Conclusion

This chapter has looked, by way of coda, at a theme that flourished alongside and often in intimate connection with that of magic in ancient folktales and popular traditions, namely that of ghosts. Here we have pursued the more particular and somewhat pathological theme of love and sex – heterosexual and homosexual – between the living and the dead, a theme which was evidently highly popular in the ancient world. One series of tales is preserved in which lovers in life continue a relationship, or seek to do so, after death, sometimes even by previous arrangement, and sometimes even with a partner willingly going to death in order to achieve the result. Another series of quite striking tales is preserved in which fresh relationships are established between living and dead people not previously known to each other. Such tales do not end happily.

Notes

Introduction

1. I thank my editor, Mr Michael Greenwood, for suggesting the title.
2. Hippocrates, *On the Sacred Disease* 1.10–46 = *MWG* no. 13. Plato, *Republic* 364b-e = *MWG* no. 14. Pliny, *Natural History* 30.1–20 = *MWG* no. 45. Apuleius, *Apology* esp. 35–7 = *MWG* no. 299. Tertullian, *De anima* 56–7 = *MWG* no. 112. See Dickie 2007 for an interesting argument that ancient sorcerers openly combined supposedly genuine magic with attention-grabbing conjuring tricks.

Chapter 1

1. For discussions of Circe, see Meuli 1921: 97–114, Wildhaber 1951, Touchefeu-Meynier, 1961, Beck 1965, Segal 1968, Paetz 1970, Page 1973: 49–69, Dyck 1981, Crane 1988, Heubeck and Hoekstra 1989: 50–74, Moret 1991, Canciani 1992, Yarnall 1994, Brilliant 1995 (and Cohen 1995 more generally), Marinatos 1995, 2000, West 1997: 405–12, Karsai 2000, de Jong 2001: 255–70, Martin 2005: 45–54, Carastro 2006: 151–9.
2. Homer *Odyssey* 10.133–574 = (in part) *MWG* no. 72. The Cyclopes episode: 9.105–564. The Laestrygonian episode: 10.80–132.
3. Homer *Odyssey* 11 *passim* = (in part) *MWG* no. 144.
4. Homer *Odyssey* 12.1–153.
5. On the formulaic nature of the Homeric poems: Lord 1960, Kirk 1963, Hainsworth 1968, Foley 1988, all building on the papers collected in Parry 1971. For the era in which Proto-Indo-European culture flourished, see Mallory and Adams 2006: 460–3. For the Proto-Indo-European poetic phrase see above all Nagy 1974 and also Watkins 1995: 12–13, 173–8, 415, Mallory and Adams 2006: 117–19, West 2007: 406–10. Greek *kleos aphthiton*: Homer *Iliad* 9.413. Sanskrit *srávas áksitam*: Rig Veda 1.9.7bc.
6. Nausicaa: Homer *Odyssey* 6.25–299. Helen: 4.219–29 = *MWG* no 74. Penelope: 2.85–118 (shroud), 23.177–206 (bed).
7. Calypso: Homer *Odyssey* 1.13–15, 5.5–264, 7.251–66. Odysseus himself draws an explicit parallel between Calypso and Circe at 9.27–33. Sirens: 12.39–45,

181–200. Laestrygonian girl: 10.104–24. Scylla and Charybdis: 12.73–123, 226–59, 429–43. Charybdis as a nickname for a prostitute: Anaxilas *Neottis* F22 K–A = Athenaeus 558a–c. For the Sirens, see now Carastro 2006: 101–40.

8. For traditional tales in the Homeric and Hesiodic poems shared with the Near East, see Page 1973, Walcot 1966, Penglase 1994 and West 1997 especially 276–437.

9. For Circe's relationship with Mistress of Animals figures in the Near East and the Greek world, see Crane 1988: 61–85, Yarnall, 1994: 26–52 and Marinatos 2000 especially 32–45. Ishtar: *Gilgamesh* tablet 6, at Dalley 1989: 77–9. Circe also exhibits a broad correspondence with *Gilgamesh*'s 'alewife' Siduri, who dispenses drinks and directs the hero across the waters of death to a forest of the dead in order to converse with the dead Utnapishtim: tablet 10, at Dalley 1989: 99–102; see West 1997: 404–12. Aphrodite and Anchises: *Homeric Hymn to Aphrodite* 45–7, 53–5, 68–83 (animals fawn), 161–7, 180–90 (Anchises' disability). The paraplegic Anchises: Virgil, *Aeneid* 2.707, etc.

10. For the folktale background to the Circe episode see Bolte and Polívka 1913–23: ii, 69, Radermacher 1915: 4–9, Carpenter 1946: 136–56, Germain 1954: 130–50, Wildhaber 1951, Page 1973: 49–69, Heubeck and Hoekstra 1989: 50–2. Witch motifs in folk literature: Thompson 1955–8: iii, 285–310, nos G200–99; much of ii is also relevant, comprising sections D and E on 'magic' and the 'the dead' respectively. Tale-series in which a witch transforms men into animals: G263 Thompson. The Corsican tale: Ortoli 1883: 31–2, summarized at Page 1973: 58. The story of Bedr Basim and Queen Lab in the *Arabian Nights* (Night 510 in the Lane 1839–41 translation; the tale is not included in the Haddawy selection), in which the witch transforms her lovers into animals once she has tired of them (cf. Ishtar), is often cited as if it is an independent tale that may accordingly shed light on the genesis of Circe, but it is quite possible that this tale, like the Sinbad tales (for which see below) itself ultimately derives from the *Odyssey*. 'Circe' as 'Hawk': Deroy 1985: 185–6 (though the author advances a contrary view), Yarnall 1994: 26–52, West 1997: 408, Marinatos 2000: 32–45. Witches as raptors in folktale: G211 Thompson, with Scobie 1978 (and note his words on the Sirens at 76).

11. Homer *Odyssey* 10.234-40 (into pigs), 276 (*polypharmakos*) and 391-6 (back into men).

12. Homer, *Odyssey* 10.212–19.

13. Circe's transformations in ancient art: see *LIMC* Kirke *passim* and Frontisi-Ducroux 2003: 61–93. The ass, lion and bull vases: *LIMC* Kirke nos 5,

5bis, 124. Apollonius of Rhodes, *Argonautica* 4.659–82. *Island of Dr Moreau*: Wells 1896, succeeded by many film adaptations. Apollodorus, *Epitome* 7.14–18.

14. That pigs constitute the principal meat source of the Odyssean world is suggested at Homer, *Odyssey* 14.72–82, where the swineherd Eumaeus feeds Odysseus on his pigs and complains about the depredations on his herd by the wicked suitors. Comparison of Circe tale with that of the Laestrygones: Carpenter 1946: 137. For the dating of the Sinbad tales see Irwin 1994: 122. *Third Voyage of Sinbad*: translation at Haddawy 1995: 18–20. Other motifs from the *Odyssey*'s Cyclopes episode are displaced into other *Voyages*. The motif of the lulling of the monster to sleep is displaced into Sinbad's encounter with the rather un-Odyssean 'Old man of the Sea' in the *Fifth Voyage*, at Haddawy 1995: 34–6. The motif of clinging to the underside of a sheep is displaced into the *Second Voyage*, at Haddawy 1995: 14–15. *Fourth Voyage of Sinbad*: Haddawy 1995: 25–6. The Lotus Eaters: Homer, *Odyssey* 9.83–104.

15. Homer, *Odyssey* 10.156–84 (stag), 10.375–99 (Odysseus refuses to eat), 10.468, 477, 12.19, 30 (meat in Circe's house).

16. Homer, *Odyssey* 10.395.

17. Homer, *Odyssey* 10.569–74.

18. Hermes' instructions to Odysseus: Homer, *Odyssey* 10.299–301. Meroe and Socrates: Apuleius, *Metamorphoses* 1.7 = *MWG* no. 104. Odysseus and Calypso: Homer, *Odyssey* 5.152–5 = *MWG* no. 73. Sirens: Homer, *Odyssey* 12.37–54 and 165–200. Songs of Calypso and Circe: Homer, *Odyssey* 5.61–2, 10.221. Xenophon, *Memorabilia* 2.6.10–13 = *MWG* no. 75. Women's erotic magic against men as feminizing in effect: Faraone 1999.

19. Circe's necromantic instructions: Homer, *Odyssey* 10.488–5.50 = (in part) *MWG* no. 144. The Sibyl: Virgil, *Aeneid* 6. Erictho: Lucan, *Pharsalia* 6.588–830 = *MWG* no. 155; see Chapter 2. Thrinacia: compare Tiresias' words at Homer, *Odyssey* 11.105–13 with Circe's at 12.137–41. For Circe as a mistress of necromancy, see Ogden 2001: 139–41.

20. The *mōly*: Homer, *Odyssey* 10.287–306. Medea as a plant-cropper: see the discussion below of Sophocles' *Rhizotomoi* or *Root-cutters*. *Mōly* as garlic: Theophrastus, *Historia Plantarum* 9.15.7. *Mōly* as oral antidote: Apollodorus, *Epitome* 7.16. Plants in ring-amulets: *Cyranides* 1.13.16–29 = Waegeman 1987 *nu* = *MWG* no. 266; *Cyranides* 1.4.45–51 = Waegeman 1987 *epsilon* = *MWG* no. 253.

21. Ovid, *Metamorphoses* 14.1–74 (Scylla) and 320–416 (Picus). Apollodorus, *Epitome* 7.15. Polites: Strabo C255 (for the Hero's identity) and Pausanias 6.6.7–11 = *MWG* no. 140.

22. Dickie 2001: 23 (the Homeric Circe not a sorceress), 5, 15, 34–5, 128, 135 etc. (the identity between ancient and modern concepts of magic), 20–1, 26 (the concept of magic invented in the fifth century BC), 6, 23 (magic not a category that informed the thinking behind the *Odyssey*). Dickie's notion that the concept of magic was invented in the fifth century BC is shared with Graf 1997: 30–5, but otherwise the two scholars have little in common, and Dickie does a good job of exposing and demolishing Graf's ivory-tower notion that the concept of magic was cooked up in the select circles of doctors and philosophers (cf. 339 n. 6, where Graf's views on the development of the concept of magic at Rome are also rejected). The case laid out here is anticipated in my review, Ogden 2002b, of Dickie's generally excellent book.
23. Listed at Dickie 2001: 33. For discussions of male magical practitioners of various sorts in the fifth and fourth centuries BC, see Bernand 1991, Burkert 1962, 1983b, 1992: 55–73, Graf 1994, 1997: 20–60, 89–117, Kingsley 1994, 1995, de Jong 1997: 76–121, Bremmer 1999, Johnston 1999: 82–123, Luck 1999: 102–10, 2006: 93–102, Motte 2000, Dickie 2001: 47–78, Ogden 2001: 95–115, 2002a: 9–60, Bordoy 2002, Llamosas 2002, Carastro 2006: 17–61, 189–216.
24. Herodotus 7.191 = *MWG* no. 41. Pherecrates F186 K–A. Aristophanes, *Clouds* 746–57 = *MWG* no. 214. Hippocrates, *On the Sacred Disease* 1.29–31 = *MWG* no. 13.
25. Euripides, *Suppliants* 1110–13; for the date, Collard 1975: i, 8–14.
26. Gorgias, *Encomium of Helen* 10 = *MWG* no. 12; for the date, cf. MacDowell 1982: 9. Euripides, *Iphigenia in Tauris* 1337–8; for the date, Lesky 1972: 405. Hippocrates, *On the Sacred Disease* 1.10–12 = *MWG* no. 13.
27. Euripides, *Bacchae* 234, 258–62. Heraclitus of Ephesus DK 12b F14 = F87 Marcovich = Clement of Alexandria *Protrepticus* 22 = *MWG* no. 10.
28. Euripides, *Orestes* 1494b–7b.
29. Homer, *Odyssey* 11.6–8, 15–19 and 12.149.
30. Odysseus' double life: Homer, *Odyssey* 12.22. Calypso offers Odysseus immortality: 5.135–6; Circe rejuvenates Odysseus' companions: 10.395.
31. The command to go to the sty: Homer, *Odyssey* 10.320 = *MWG* no. 72. Prayer to the dead: 10.526 = *MWG* no. 72.
32. Homer, *Odyssey* 10.512 = *MWG* no. 72. See Ogden 2001: 125–7.
33. Homer, *Odyssey* 10.571–4 = *MWG* no. 72.
34. Herodotus 7.43 = *MWG* no. 41; see the discussion at Ogden 2001: 130. Persepolis Tablets: PF 758; cf. Briant 2002: 246. The Persian elders with Atossa: Aeschylus, *Persians* 598–708 = *MWG* no. 36; see the discussion at Headlam 1902, Eitrem 1928, Lawson 1934, Broadhead 1960: 302–9, Haldane

1972, Jouan 1981 and, with further bibliography, Ogden 2001: 129–30. Mage Arabos (*Magos Arabos*): Aeschylus, *Persians* 317; alternatively, we may have here an 'Arab called Magos' or a corrupt text; cf. Broadhead 1960 *ad loc.* and Bremmer 1999: 3. Aeschylus, *Choephoroe* 822. Here we may note that we can unfortunately learn nothing of the actual functions of the Persian magi from the two surviving fragments of Xanthus of Lydia that bear upon them, and derive from that part of Xanthus' *Lydiaka* that actually acquired the name *Magika*, *FGH* 765 FF31–2 = *MWG* no. 3. These mention only that there was a 6,000-year succession of mages between the first, Zoroaster (i.e. Zarathustra) and Xerxes' 480 BC invasion of Greece, and that they practised the customs of incest and wife-swapping. If one accepts Dionysius of Halicarnassus *On Thucydides* 5 = Xanthus *FGH* 765 T4, Xanthus wrote just before the Peloponnesian war, which suggests a floruit of *c.* 440; see Kingsley 1995, who suggests that Xanthus' reference to Empedocles (Diogenes Laertius 8.63 = F33) may have been made in connection with his discussion of the mages.

35. Herodotus 1.107, 120, 128 = *MWG* no. 39 (dream interpretation), 7.113–14 = *MWG* no. 41 (white horses). Sophocles, *Oedipus Tyrannus* 380–403 = *MWG* no. 11. The dating of the play is insecure, but metrical criteria suggest that it should be subsequent to 415 BC: Dawe 2006 on lines 1515–30. Sophocles died in 406 BC.

36. *Phoronis* F2 West. Pherecydes *FGH* 3 F7 = F47 Fowler. Herodotus 4.107; at 2.33 he refers to a race of *goētes* in connection with the Nasamones, but without further definition. Hellanicus *FGH* 4 F89. At some point in his long career, which endured at least from 439 to 388 BC, the comic playwright Aristomenes wrote a comedy entitled *Sorcerers* (*Goetes*), but we can learn nothing of the titular characters' activities from the six surviving fragments of the play, FF6–10 K–A.

37. Homer, *Odyssey* 10.514–40 = *MWG* no. 144.

38. Homer, *Odyssey* 10.156–88, 212–13, 233–43, 316–20 = *MWG* no. 144.

39. Homer, *Odyssey* 10.299–301, 342–5. It could be, however, that erotic magic is implicitly associated with Aristophanes' Thesssalian witch: she draws down the moon, and in the mature magical tradition at any rate, this activity was to become primarily associated with the performance of erotic magic: e.g. Theocritus, *Idylls* 2 = *MWG* no. 89, Horace, *Satires* 1.8 = *MWG* no. 91, Lucian, *Philopseudes* 13–15 = *MWG* no. 244; see Ogden, 2002a: 236–40, with cross-references.

40. Circe as 'goddess': Homer, *Odyssey* 10.136, etc. Aphrodite's *kestos himas*: Homer, *Iliad* 14.197–222; for this cf. Bonner 1949 and Faraone 1999: 97–110.

41. 'Either goddess or woman': Homer, *Odyssey* 10.228. Polydamna: 4.228.

42. This narrative is extracted from (in chronological order) Euripides, *Medea*; Apollonius of Rhodes, *Argonautica* 3–4, especially 3.475–80, 528–33, 1026–62, 1191–1224, 1246–67, 4.123–66, 445–81, 1636–93 = *MWG* no. 68; Diodorus 4.45–56 = (in part) *MWG* no. 66; Ovid, *Metamorphoses* 7.98–424, of which 159–351 = *MWG* no. 69; Seneca, *Medea*, Valerius Flaccus, *Argonautica* 5–8 Apollodorus, *Bibliotheca* 1.9.23–8 = (in part) *MWG* no. 70 and *Epitome* 1.5–7 Hyginus, *Fabulae* 26. For general discussion of Medea see Lesky 1931, Page 1938, Belloni 1981, Parry 1992, Schmidt 1992, Halm-Tisserant 1993, Moreau 1994, Fowler 1995, Corti 1998 (not confined to Classical material), Mastronarde 2002, Martin 2005: 129–42, Griffiths 2006. Of the three collections of articles on Medea that appeared at the end of the millennium, Clauss and Johnston 1997, Gentili and Perusino 2000 and Moreau and Turpin 2000: ii, 245–333, Gentili and Perusino has the most to offer.
43. Homer, *Iliad* 11.739–41; cf. Hainsworth 1993 *ad loc*.
44. *LIMC* Medeia 2 and 1, respectively. Discussion at Schmidt 1992 and Isler-Kerényi 2000.
45. Mimnermus F11 West. If the mysterious female helper is not after all Medea, it may be a goddess.
46. Hesiod, *Theogony* 956–62, 992–1002; cf. West 1966 *ad loc*. and Gantz 1993: 372. Eumelus F17, F20, F23 West. Eumelus' traditional mid-eighth-century dating is certainly too early: see the (inconclusive) discussion in West 2002. Creophylus: Scholiast Euripides, *Medea* 273. Creophylus is probably a fictional construct, but in any case Davies 1988 and West 2003 reject the ascription of this fragment to *The Siege of Oechalia*, whether by Creophylus or no; cf. Gantz 1993: 369–70. *Nostoi* F6 West. *Naupactia* FF5–9 West.
47. Pots: *LIMC* Peliades 4–10, Pelias 10–19 (cf. also Pelias 20–1, Iason 58–62); see Gantz 1993: 366–7. Simonides F548 *PGM*/Campbell, with T6 *PGM*/Campbell for his lifespan.
48. Pot: *LIMC* Iason 62. Pindar, *Pythians* 4.213–19 = *MWG* no. 224 (*iynx*), 220–3 (ointment of invincibility), 250 (Medea kills Pelias). Medea and spells of erotic attraction: the nearest we come is perhaps Apollonius of Rhodes, *Argonautica* 4.57–65. Pherecydes *FGH* 3 F60 = F105 Fowler, FF74a + 74b = F113 Fowler. Euripides, *Peliades* FF610–16 *TrGF*. Aeschylus, *Nurses of Dionysus* (*Trophoi*) F246a *TrGF*. Medea poisons Theseus on pots: Gantz 1993: 255. Aegeus plays: Sophocles, *Aegeus* FF19–25a *TrGF*; Euripides, *Aegeus* FF1–13 *TrGF*; cf. Gantz 1993: 372.
49. *LIMC* Talos i 6. A comparable scene, superbly rendered, is to be found on

LIMC Talos i 4, a red-figure crater of *c.* 400 BC. Apollodorus, *Bibliotheca* 1.9.26; cf. Gantz 1993: 365.

50. Euripides, *Medea* 716–18 (infertility), 774–89 and 1136–1230 (incendiary wedding dress). For an elaborate account of Medea's magical preparations for the destruction of Glauce with the wedding dress, see Seneca, *Medea* 670–843 (where the victim is called rather Creusa). Neophron, *Medea* FF1–3 *TrGF*: cf. Gantz 1993: 370–1. The motif of the burning robe may have been borrowed from the myth of Deianeira, for which see Seneca, *Hercules Oetaeus* and Hyginus, *Fabulae* 33–6. For tales with a similar theme of a supposed love potion that damages the man to whom it has been given, see Antiphon 1.14–20 =*MWG* no. 77, [Aristotle], *Magna Moralia* 1188b =*MWG* no. 78, Plutarch, *Moralia* 139a = *MWG* no. 80, Suetonius, *Caligula* 50 =*MWG* no. 81.
51. *LIMC* Iason 37–42; cf. Gantz 1993: 360.
52. Sophocles, *Colchides* FF336–49 *TrGF*, *Skythai* FF546–52 *TrGF*. Sophocles, *Rhizotomoi* F534–6 *TrGF* = *MWG* no. 67. It is common for Medea and other witches to perform their rites with their clothing untied (e.g. Ovid, *Heroides* 6.83–94 = *MWG* no. 98), but Sophocles takes the notion to an extreme degree here. For the melting of wax dolls in the context of oath-taking ceremonies, see the Cyrenean Foundation Decree, Meiggs and Lewis 1988 no. 5, lines 40–51 = *MWG* no. 236. For the melting of dolls in the context of erotic magic, see the following chapter.
53. Medea, Medeios, Circe and Perse: Hesiod, *Theogony* 956–62, 992–1002. Herodotus 7.62 = *MWG* no. 40. Circe and Perseis: Homer, *Odyssey* 10.139 = *MWG* no. 72. Mages originate among the Medes: Herodotus 1.101 = *MWG* no. 39. Medea and the Medes: Herodotus 7.62 = *MWG* no. 40. Sophocles and the Chaldaeans: *Tympanistai* F638 *TrGF*.

Chapter 2

1. Theocritus, *Idylls* 2 (*Pharmakeutria*) = *MWG* no. 89. For discussion see Schweizer 1937, Gow 1952, Dover 1969, Segal 1973, Faraone 1995a, Andrews 1996, Graf 1997: 176–90, Pralon 2000, Fernández 2002. The closest identifiable antecedent to Theocritus' poem is a fragmentary mime of Sophron, composed at some point in the fifth century BC (Page 1942 no. 73 = *MWG* no. 88), and probably to be identified with his poem *Women Who Claim that they Drive out the Goddess* (sc. Hecate), referred to at Athenaeus, *Deipnosophistae* 480b.
2. For the *iynx* see Tavenner 1933, Gow 1934 (the standard article), Tupet

1976: 50–5, Vermeule 1979: 199, Pirenne-Delforge 1993, Johnston 1995 and *MWG* nos 224–9.
3. For Hippomanes, sometimes conceptualized, as here, as a plant, and at other times as a growth on the forehead of a newborn foal, a mare's secretion, or stallion's semen, see Stadler 1913, Tupet 1986: 2653–7 and *MWG* nos 230–2.
4. Agamede: Homer, *Iliad* 11.739–40. Medea and Perimede are subsequently brought together at Propertius 2.4.7–8, and note also the chorus at Petronius, *Satyricon* 52, *madeia perimadeia*. Gow 1952 and Dover 1969 on 2.15–16 hold that Theocritus misremembered Agamede's name. One of Theocritus' ancient commentators tells us that Perimede should be identified rather with the *Odyssey*'s Polydamna.
5. Transference of magical expertise between genders: but the notion is repeated in Virgil's adaptation of this poem, *Eclogues* 8. 95–9 = *MWG* no. 90 (for which see below), in which Simaetha's counterpart claims instruction from the Egyptian sorcerer Moeris. For the transfer of magical expertise within gender, cf. Ovid, *Fasti* 2.572–83 =*MWG* no. 103, where an old witch instructs young girls in cursing; more on this below. Medea and the *iynx*: Pindar, *Pythians* 4.213–19 = *MWG* no. 224; cf. Chapter 1.
6. Faraone (whose handling of literary texts is naive) 1999: 153–4 contends that the varieties of attraction-magic Simaetha uses are typically associated either with men or with 'structurally male' courtesans. But even according to Faraone's own understanding of ancient erotic magic, the context in which Simaetha makes her spells, namely the attempt to retain an existing lover and her use of separation magic to detach Delphis from any new lover, are characteristic rather of women. Dickie 2001: 99–104 wishes to recruit Simaetha for his substantial (and in general sound) thesis of a strong association between witchcraft and prostitution in the ancient world.
7. Virgil, *Eclogues* 8.64–109 = *MWG* no. 90. For discussion see Richter 1970, Tupet 1976: 223–32, Coleman 1977: 227–55, Faraone 1989.
8. Fragments of the *Twelve Tables* Ernout 1957b: 119. Cresimus: Piso F33 Peter, at Pliny, *Natural History* 18.41–3; for *excantatio cultorum* cf. Tupet 1976: 181–7, 1986: 2610–17. Cato, *De agri cultura* 160 = *MWG* no. 258; cf. Tavenner 1916: 70–6. For the Indo-European parallels, Mallory and Adams 2006: 116–17, West 2007: 336–9. Homer, *Odyssey* 19.449–58 = *MWG* no. 256.
9. For thumbnail sketches of bawd-witches in Augustan Latin poetry, see: Tibullus 1.5.39–59 = *MWG* no. 100 (*c.* 27 BC), Propertius 4.5.1–18 and 63–78 = *MWG* no. 101 (Acanthis, *c.* 16 BC), Ovid, *Amores* 1.8.1–20 and 105–14 =

MWG no. 102 (Dipsas, *c.* 16 BC), *Fasti* 2.572–83 = *MWG* no. 103 (*c.* 8 AD). See also the thumbnail sketches of witches (not specifically of bawds) at: Tibullus, *Elegies* 1.2.42–66 = *MWG* no. 97 (*c.* 27 BC), Ovid, *Amores* 3.7.27–36, 73–84 = *MWG* no. 99 (*c.* 16 BC), *Heroides* 6.83–94 = *MWG* no. 98 (Medea, before 2 BC), *Remedia Amoris* 249–88 (1 BC–2 AD). For discussion of the witch-figure in Latin, particularly Augustan, poetry, see above all Tupet 1976 and 1986, and also Fahz 1904, Tavenner 1916, Eitrem 1941, Luck 1962, 1999, Caro Baroja 1964, Xella 1976, Myers 1996, Novara 2000, Dickie 2001: 162–201, Muro 2002.

10. The three passing references to Canidia's poison: respectively, Horace, *Satires* 2.1.48, *Epodes* 3.7–8 and *Satires* 2.8.95. For Canidia see above all Watson 2003: 135–6, 174–250, 266–86; see also Manning 1970, Ingallina 1974, Tupet 1976: 284–329, Watson 1993: 20, Freudenburg 1995, Mankin 1995: 108–36, 272–93, 299–301.

11. Horace, *Satires* 1.8 = *MWG* no. 91. Priapus statues and their culture: Parker 1988, O'Connor 1989. Culling of herbs naked or unbound by moonlight: Sophocles, *Rhizotomoi* F534 = *MWG* no. 67. Doll-pairs in erotic-attraction magic: see Virgil, *Eclogues* 8.80 = *MWG* no. 90 ('as this clay grows hard and as this wax melts. . . .') and especially *PGM* IV. 296–466 = *MWG* no. 239. We find an odd combination of necromantic divination and erotic magic also in the spell attributed to the Hyperborean mage at Lucian *Philopseudes* 13–15 = *MWG* no. 244, for which see Chapter 4.

12. Horace, *Epodes* 5 = *MWG* no. 92. Odysseus as cannibal: see Chapter 1. Dido's curse on Aeneas: Virgil, *Aeneid* 4.504–21, 607–65; cf. Eitrem 1933, Delcourt 1939, Kraggerud 1999. Folia's sex drive: line 41, *masculae libidinis*; cf. Horace, *Epistles* 1.19.28, *mascula Sappho*, and, more generally, Martial 7.67 and 70.

13. The epitaph: *CIL* vi 19747 = Bücheler 1895–7: ii no. 987 = *MWG* no. 93. Livilla's execution for poisoning Drusus: Suetonius, *Tiberius* 62, etc.

14. Horace, *Epodes* 17 = *MWG* no. 94. For the physical effects of the binding spell, we should compare Porphyry's third-century AD description of the effects of a binding spell on Plotinus (*Life of Plotinus* 10 = *MWG* no. 184). His body felt drawn tight, as if by purse-strings, and his limbs were crushed together. Heracles and Deianeira: Sophocles, *Trachiniae* esp. 531–87, 672–707, 750–93, Diodorus 4.36 and 38 = *MWG* no. 76, Ovid, *Metamorphoses* 9.98–238. For the animation of voodoo dolls, cf. Lucian *Philopseudes* 13–15 = *MWG* no. 244, and Chapter 4 below. Slander-magic: see, e.g., *DT* 155 = *MWG* no. 173, *PGM* VII.593–619 = *MWG* no. 211, LXII.76–106 = *MWG* no. 234. Slander between magical practitioners: see, e.g., Hadrian of

Tyre at Polemon, *Declamationes,* pp. 44–5 Hinck = *MWG* no. 295 and Libanius, *Declamationes* 41.22, 26–7, 41 = *MWG* no. 300.

15. Pseudo-Acro on Horace, *Satires* 1.8.24 (= *MWG* no. 95), *Epodes* 3.8 and 5.1; Porphyrio on *Satires* 1.8.13, *Epodes* 3.7 and 5.43 (note the last in particular for the extrapolation of Naples as Canidia's home).
16. Gyllis: Herodas, *Mimes* 1; cf. Dickie 2001: 102–3. The old Syrian: Lucian, *Dialogues of the Courtesans* 288–9 = *MWG* no. 52. We may note that the necromantic witch of Endor of 1 Samuel 28.3–25 (who is not, however, explicitly said to be old) entered Greek literature in the earlier third century BC when the Septuagint was translated at the behest of either the first or the second Ptolemy.
17. For Erictho, see Bourgery 1928, Ahl 1969, 1976: 130–49, Schotes 1969: 50–99, Fauth 1975, Baldini-Moscadi 1976, Volpilhac 1978, Martindale 1980, Gordon 1987, Masters 1992: 179–215, Tupet 1988, Viansino 1995 *ad loc.*, Korenjak 1996, Graf 1997: 190–204, Ogden 2001 esp. 144–5, 202–8, 2002c. For further items, see Ogden 2002a: 309.
18. Lucan, *Pharsalia* 6.413–568 = *MWG* no. 96, and, for the cave and Erictho's Fury-like appearance, 6.642–56 = *MWG* no. 155. Avernus: see, e.g., Strabo C244–6 = *MWG* no. 153. Tainaron: see, e.g., Plutarch, *Moralia* 560ef = *MWG* no. 152. Manipulators of the dead as themselves resembling the dead: cf. Aristophanes, *Birds* 1553–64 = *MWG* no. 26 (Socrates calls up his philosophical partner Chaerephon as if a ghost), Lucian, *Philopseudes* 29–31 = (in part) *MWG* no. 115 (Arignotus and the ghost he confronts are alike long-haired and squalid). Abortionists: but abortion could itself be the province of magic, as we see from *PGM* LXII.76–106 = *MWG* no. 234, a third-century AD abortifacient spell, and the inscription at Petzl 1994 no. 59 = *MWG* no. 233. Pamphile's workshop: Apuleius, *Metamorphoses* 3.17 = *MWG* no. 107.
19. Lucan, *Pharsalia* 6.569–87 = *MWG* no. 96. Spells to avert war: see, e.g., [Callisthenes], *Alexander Romance* 1.1–3 = *MWG* no. 55.
20. Lucan, *Pharsalia* 6.588–830 = *MWG* no. 155. For divinations from decapitated skulls, see Apuleius, *Apology* 34 = *MWG* no. 158, Philostratus, *Heroicus* 28 = *MWG* no. 159, Hippolytus, *Refutations* 4.41 = *MWG* no. 160, *PGM* IV.2006–2240 = *MWG* nos 161 and 273; see the discussion at Ogden 2001: 202–16. With the bizarre list of magical ingredients, compare the fourth-century list among the Greek magical papyri, *PGM* XII.401–44 = *MWG* no. 156. This list provides banal and everyday equivalents for a string of seemingly exotic and impossible magical ingredients. Second spell: see Ogden 2001: 176–7. For Demogorgon see Statius, *Thebaid* 4.500–18 and *Adnotationes super Lucanum* at 6.746.

21. The reason for thinking that reanimation scenes of this sort were well established in the literary tradition when Lucan wrote is Ovid's broadly similar description of Medea's *rejuvenation* of Aeson (*Metamorphoses* 7.159–351 = *MWG* no. 69). This in itself is untypical of the broader tradition of rejuvenation narratives, in which the client is typically hacked apart limb from limb and boiled up together with the requisite magical ingredients in a cauldron. So it seems most likely that Ovid has here reshaped an already traditional variety of reanimation narrative and made it serve the purposes rather of a rejuvenation spell. For reanimation narratives subsequent to Lucan, see Apuleius, *Metamorphoses* 2.28–30 = *MWG* no. 105 (discussed below) and Heliodorus 6.12–15 = *MWG* no. 157 (for which see Chapter 3).
22. Luck 2006: 212 (originally 1985). Shelley 1818, esp. chapters 2 (ghosts), 4 (graves etc.), 5 (the monster awakens), 24 (pyre); Frankenstein destroys the bride-monster before she reaches the point of reanimation (chapter 20). Lucan seems to have contributed more to the nuts and bolts of Shelley's narrative, even if the big idea behind it was derived rather from Ovid's description of the gods' creation of Prometheus in his *Metamorphoses* (1.76–88), as suggested by the novel's subtitle, *The Modern Prometheus* and by the monster's Promethean discovery of fire (chapter 11).
23. On the *Satyricon* in general see Harrison 1999, Courtney 2001, Jensson 2004.
24. Petronius, *Satyricon* 61 = *MWG* no. 141. For ancient werewolves see especially Schuster 1930 and Buxton 1987, and also Smith 1894, Cook 1914–40: i 63–99, Eckels 1937, Villeneuve 1963, Tupet 1976: 73–8, 1986: 2647–52, Gernet 1981: 125–39, Burkert 1983a: 83–134, Mainoldi 1984, Jost 1985: 258–67, Hughes 1991: 97–106.
25. Hero of Temesa: Pausanias 6.6.7–11 = *MWG* no.140, with Strabo C255. See the *MWG* commentary for the difficulties with the Pausanian text. Neuri: Herodotus 4.105 = *MWG* no.139.
26. Arcadian werewolf lore: Pliny, *Natural History* 8.80–2 = *MWG* no. 143. The thief and the innkeeper: Aesop 419 Perry.
27. Petronius, *Satyricon* 63 = *MWG* no. 106. Note folk-literature motif no. G252 Thompson, in which a *witch* is wounded whilst assuming animal form; she is recognized when she reverts to human shape but exhibits the corresponding wound.
28. Lucian, *Philopseudes* 18–20; cf. Ogden 2005.
29. Lucian, *Philopseudes*; for this text see Müller 1932, Schwartz 1951, Ebner *et al.* 2001, Ogden 2007a. All the stories referred to here, except for that of

Cleodemus' premature descent, are discussed elsewhere in this book. For Cleodemus' tone, see particularly Lucian, *Philopseudes* 7, 13.
30. Suetonius, *Augustus* 74; Juvenal, *Satires* 15.16. The scholiast to Juvenal amplifies the term with *falsidicus, mendax, artificiosus*. Porphyrio on Horace, *Satires* 1.1.120 recalls that Plotius Crispinus wrote poems of such prolixity (*garrule*) that people called him an *aretalogus*. The basic collection of aretalogical inscriptions is that of Longo 1969. The term *aretalogia* is first found at LXX Ecclesiasticus 36.17 (Jesus Sirach's second-century BC translation of the Hebrew). For Asclepius inscriptions see also Edelstein and Edelstein 1945. Confession inscriptions are collected by Strubbe 1997. For aretalogy in general see further Reitzenstein 1906, Weinreich 1909, Kiefer 1929, Scobie 1983: 11–16, Totti 1985, Beck 1996.
31. For Apuleius' *Apology* see especially Hunink 1997, and also Abt 1908, Butler and Owen 1914, Hijmans 1994, Fantham 1995, Graf 1997: 61–88, Méthy 2000. Selections from the *Apology* are reproduced at *MWG* nos 134, 158, 226, 242 and especially 299.
32. For Apuleius' *Metamorphoses* see Fick 1985, Griffiths 1975, Harrison 2000, Hijmans and van der Pardt 1978, Hijmans *et al.* 1977–95, Hoevels 1979, Molt 1938, Sandy 1997, Scobie 1969, 1975, 1978, 1983, Tavenner 1916: 40–5, van der Paardt 1971. For an edition of the text of the *Ass*, printed in parallel with Apuleius' *Metamorphoses*, see van Thiel 1972: ii. For 'Lucius of Patras', see Photius, *Bibliotheca* cod. 129 (at ii pp. 103–4 Henry). For the view that 'Lucius of Patras' is our Lucian and the author of the *MLD*, see Perry 1967: 211–82 and Bowie 1994: 444. Anderson 1976: 34–67 contends that *both* the *MLD and* the *Ass* were written by Lucian. At the opposite end of the range Caster 1937: 325–6, Harrison 1996: 500–2 and Mason 1999 think *neither* of the Greek texts were written by Lucian. The character of Lycinus appears in Lucian's *Dance, Dispades, Hesiod, Eunuch, Hermotimus, In Defence of Portraits, Lapiths, Lexiphanes, Portraits* and *Ship*, and also in the probably spurious *Cynic* and the definitely spurious *Loves*.
33. Lucian, *Ass* 4–5, 11–13. For the folktale or folkloric context of Apuleius' witch-stories, see Scobie 1978, 1983; cf. Hoevels 1979 for the folktale background context of Apuleius' tale of Cupid and Psyche.
34. Apuleius, *Metamorphoses* 1.5–19 = *MWG* no. 104.
35. Euripides' *Medea*: Apuleius, *Metamorphoses* 1.10. Meroe's literary allusions: 1.12.
36. Pamphile and Photis: Apuleius, *Metamorphoses* 3.15–25. Isis: 11.30.
37. Cicero, *On Divination* 1.57, Aelian F82 Domingo-Forasté; cf. Felton 1999: 20–1, 29–34, Ogden 2001: 234–5.

38. For the principal varieties of binding magic, see Gager 1992, Ogden 1999a, 2002a: 210–19; further discussion in Chapter 4.
39. Apuleius, *Metamorphoses* 2.21–30 = *MWG* no. 105. For the details of the dinner party itself, see 2.19.
40. Thelyphron begins his tale: Apuleius, *Metamorphoses* 2.20. For the projection of Thelyphron as a story-teller, see Anderson 2000: 56–8.
41. Apuleius, *Metamorphoses* 9.29–31 = *MWG* no. 114. Giovanni Boccaccio, *Decameron* Day 5 Tale 10 (composed in Florence in 1349–51).
42. Levi 1947: 255–8.
43. Levi 1947: 21–2.
44. Levi 1947: 16–17, 228–9.
45. Levi 1947: 99–107 (Giulia Venere, with 103 for the principle that free and easy women are witches), 244 (Maria).
46. Levi 1947: 152.
47. Levi 1947: 197. The notion that remote lovers are connected by celestial bodies is crisply expressed in the Meredith Willson song 'I See the Moon', famous in the UK from the Stargazers' 1954 version: 'I see the moon, the moon sees me,/ Down through the leaves of the old oak tree./ Back where my heart is longing to be,/ Please let the light that shines on me/ Shine on the one I love.'
48. Levi 1947: 69–73 (the eunuch gravedigger), 112 (the werewolf at the door), 142–8 (spirts of dead children).
49. Levi's linking of Lucanian magical practices to those of the Classical past: 1947: 225–7. For Levi as a fictive 'creator of reality', see Bronzini 1996: 9–140, de Donato 1998, Grigniani 1998, Carducci 1999: 139–74. Formal anthropological investigations inspired by Levi and broadly reproducing his portrait of rustic Italian society: see Gallini 2003. Moss and Cappannari 1960 might be cited s an example of this. This article, detailing work carried out in the Abruzzi-Molise highlands in 1955–6 paints a strongly Levian picture; the Levian agenda acknowledged at p.102. Other literary travellers in southern Italy had observed similar phenomena before Levi, e.g. Douglas 1915, especially 56–7, 176 (I thank my colleague Dr Elena Isayev for drawing this superb book to my attention).
50. Ovid, *Fasti* 2.571–82 = *MWG* no. 103; cf. Gager 1992: 251–2.

Chapter 3

1. Herodotus 1.101, 107–8, 120, 128 (= *MWG* no. 39), 7.43, 113–14 (= *MWG* no. 41), 7.62 (= *MWG* no. 40). Xanthus of Lydia *FGH* 765 F31–2 = *MWG* no. 37.

2. For the *Philopseudes* see Müller 1932, Herzig 1940, Schwartz 1951, Albini 1993, Ogden 2007a (with further bibliography).
3. The historical mages, Media and Zurvan: Handley-Schachler 1992: 39–69b, 367; I thank Dr Maria Brosius for this reference. For the historical mages of the Persian empire see also Benveniste 1938, Bickerman and Tadmor 1978, Burkert 1983b, 1992, Briant 2002: 94–6, 130–4, 244–6, 266–8. Herodotus on the Medes and Medea: 1.101 = *MWG* no. 39 (mages as Medes), 7.62 = *MWG* no. 40 (Medea and Medes). The historical Chaldaeans: Lipinski 2000: 416–22; see also Leick 2003: 56–61. For historical Mesopotamian magic and divination see Meier 1937, Contenau 1940, Finkel 1983–4, Galter 1993, Bottéro 1987–1990, 2000, Tropper 1989, Scurlock 1995. Herodotus on the Chaldaeans: 1.181–3 (priests), 3.155 (a gate in Babylon named for them), 7.63 (associated with Assyrians/Syrians in Xerxes' army). Sophocles on the Colchian-Chaldaean-Syrian: *Tympanistai*, F638 *TrGF*. For the projections of mages and Chaldaeans in Graeco-Roman literature, see above all Kingsley 1995 and de Jong 1997, and also Bidez and Cumont 1938, Bernand 1991, Bremmer 1999, Boulogne 2000.
4. Athenaeus 595e–596a, incorporating Python, *Agen TrGF* 91 F1 = *MWG* no. 42. Exegesis of the *Agen* fragment: Snell 1964, Ogden forthcoming a. Avernus and its birdlessness: Strabo C244–6. Imperial identifications of Persians and Chaldaeans: Strabo C763 = *MWG* no. 44, Lucan, *Pharsalia* 6.449 = *MWG* no. 96, Diogenes Laertius 8.3 = *MWG* no. 2.
5. Lucian, *Menippus*, esp. 2, 6–10, 21–2 = *MWG* no. 148. See Ogden 2001 index s.v. Menippus.
6. For the oracle of Trophonius see Bonnechère 2003.
7. Iamblichus, *Babyloniaca* at Photius, *Bibliotheca* 74b = *MWG* no. 50.
8. Lucian, *Philopseudes* 12–13 = *MWG* no. 49; cf. Ogden 2007a: 65–104.
9. New Testament parallels: Matthew 9.6–7; so too Mark 2.9 and 11–12, Luke 5.24–5 and John 5.8–9. The earliest version of the tale of St George and the Dragon: *Miracula Sancti Georgii*, pt. 12 (*Codex Romanus Angelicus* 46), reproduced at Aufhauser 1911: 52–69. The canonical version of the story is that of Jacobus de Voragine's thirteenth-century *Golden Legend* (58), reproduced at Aufhauser 1911: 202–6, with translation in Ryan 1993.
10. Thomas: *Acts of Thomas* 30–3 at Lipsius and Bonnet 1891–1903: ii.2, pp.147–50. Philip: *Acts of Philip* 94–147 at Lipsius and Bonnet 1891–1903: ii.2, pp. 36–89. The text also tells how Philip and his team go on to the city of Hierapolis-Ophioryme ('Snake-attack'), where he confronts the Echidna or Viper that the locals have been worshipping. Hilarion: Jerome, *Life of St Hilarion the Hermit* 39 at *PL* 23, 49. Donatus: Sozomen, *Ecclesiastical History* 7.26.1–4 at Bidez and Hansen 1960: 341 and *PG* 67.2, 1497–

1500. The same tale is recycled more briefly and without any additional content in the sixth- or seventh-century Isidore of Seville's *Chronicle* 107 (*draconem ingentem*), at Mommsen 1894: 470 and *PL* 83, 1051.
11. Pliny, *Natural history* esp. books 20–32. For the significance of Bolus of Mendes see Dickie 1999 and 2001: 117–22.
12. Pliny, *Natural History* 28.92–106 = *MWG* no. 47. For further cures of the magi see, e.g., 28.226 (epilepsy and madness cured by the drinking of asses' urine), 232 (dropsy cured by drinking boar's urine), 30.21 (earache cured with the head of a rabid dog), 83 (pain soothed by an amulet made from a tick taken from a dog's left ear), 91 (epilepsy averted with an amulet made from the tail of the dragon-snake, wrapped in a gazelle-skin and tied on with deer-sinews), 98 (quartan ague cured by an amulet made from a wasp caught with the left hand, or from the heart of a viper, or from the muzzle and ear-tips of a mouse, wrapped in a red rag), 102 (fever dispelled by slugs or newts kept in a box under the head).
13. Pliny, *Natural History* 30.1–20 = *MWG* no. 45. For Pliny on the mages see Ernout 1957a, Beagon 1992: 102–13, Graf 1997: 49–56 and Diouf 2000.
14. Cornelius Hispalus: Valerius Maximus 1.3.3 = *MWG* no. 283. Agrippa: Dio Cassius 49.43.5 = *MWG* no. 286. Tiberius: Tacitus, *Annals* 2.27–32 = *MWG* no. 291. Claudius: Tacitus, *Annals* 12.52. Vitellius: Suetonius, *Vitellius* 14 = *MWG* no. 294. Constantius II: *Theodosian Code* 9.16.4. For magic and Roman law, see above all Pharr 1932, and also Massoneau 1934, Xella 1976, Ward 1981, Phillips 1991, Clerc 1995, Graf 1997: 36–60, Kippenberg 1997, Gordon 1999: 243–66.
15. Dio Cassius 52.36.1–2 = *MWG* no. 286.
16. Arnouphis: *Suda* s.v. *Arnouphis* and Dio Cassius 72.8.4; cf. Guey 1948, Dickie 2001: 206 and Ogden 2007a: 248. For the Chaldaean oracles see des Places 1971, Lewy 1978, Majercik 1989. Faustina: Scriptores Historiae Augustae *Marcus Aurelius* 19 = *MWG* no. 203.
17. Theocritus 2.182 = *MWG* no. 89. Aristotle F32 Rose (Diogenes Laertius 2.45). Does this story have anything to do with the tradition that Plato was visited by a Chaldaean on the eve of his death (Philip of Opus as recycled by Philodemus, *History of the Academy* iii at pp. 133–4 Dorandi = *P.Herc.* 1021)? Tarmoendas: Pliny, *Natural History* 30.1–20 = *MWG* no. 45.
18. *Cyranides* lines 12–15 (p. 14 Kaimakis) and lines 40–68 (pp. 16–17 Kaimakis); for a translation of the relevant part see Ogden 2007a: 261–2 n.18.
19. For the text see Radermacher 1927; for a translation of the central portion, see Ogden 2007a: 105–8. See Delehaye 1921 and Krestan and Hermann 1957. In the mid-fifth century AD Eudocia, empress of Theodosius II, worked the text up into the first book of her three-book hexameter account of the

life of Cyprian of Antioch (the subsequent books being based respectively upon Cyprian's confessions and martyrology). This work can be found at *PG* 85, 831–64 and Ludwich 1897. The beginning is lost, the surviving text taking up with Aglaidas' attempted rape of Justina, but the whole is summarized at Photius, *Bibliotheca* cod. 184.
20. *PGM* IV.3007–86 = *MWG* no. 131.
21. Hilarion: Jerome, *Life of St Hilarion the Hermit* 21 = *PL* 23, 38–9. Macarius: Palladius, *Lausiac History* 17.6–9 = *PG* 34.1044–9; cf. *Historia Monachorum* 21.17, composed *c.* 400 AD; for the theory, see Frankfurter 2001.
22. Jacobus de Voragine, *Golden Legend* no. 142 (Cyprian) and no. 131 (Theophilus: the tale is entitled 'The nativity of the blessed virgin Mary'). For the impact of the Cyprian tradition on the Faust legend, Radermacher 1927. The same reduction of lover and sorcerer into a single character is already to be found in the 379 AD version of the tale by Gregory of Nazianz, *Oration* 24, *PG* 35, 1169–93, especially 1177–9. Cyprian's Christian magic: Heidelberg Kopt. no. 684, translated at Meyer and Smith 1994 no. 73.
23. Lucian, *Dialogues of Courtesans* 288–9 = *MWG* no. 52.
24. Homer, *Odyssey* 4.219–39 = *MWG* no. 74. For historical Egyptian magic Borghouts 1978, Roccati and Siliotti 1987, Pinch 1994, Ritner 1993, Szpakowska 2006. For the projection of Egyptian sorcerers in Graeco-Roman literature see de Salviat 1987, Dickie 1999, 2001: 203–5, 229–31.
25. Virgil, *Eclogues* 8.95–9 = *MWG* no. 90. The pharaoh Moeris: Herodotus 2.13 etc. The choice of name was also perhaps inspired by Simaetha's phrase *nai Moiras* ('by the Fates!'), towards the end of his model poem, line 160.
26. Ps.-Callisthenes *Alexander Romance* 1.1–14 = *MWG* no. 55. For the *Alexander Romance* see Merkelbach 1954 and Jasnow 1997. For the projection of Nectanebo in the *Romance* see Aufrère 2000.
27. [Callisthenes] *Alexander Romance* 1.4 = *MWG* no. 55.
28. The classic study of the Anticythera mechanism has long been Price 1974. The series of new X-ray tomography-based studies finds consummation in Freeth *et al.* 2006, with intervening bibliography. For astrology in the Graeco-Roman world see Bouché-Leclercq 1899, Olivieri, *et al.* 1898–1936, Barton 1994, Gordon 1997, Denzey 2003 (an interesting piece), Luck 2006: 285–370, Beck 2007.
29. Apuleius, *Metamorphoses* 2.28–30 = *MWG* no. 105. Lucian, *Philopseudes* 33–6 = *MWG* no. 54.
30. [Thessalus of Tralles] *De virtutibus herbarum* 1–28 Friedrich (pp. 43–53). For the ending, preserved only in the Latin version, see p. 271 Friedrich.

For a full formal translation of the prologue, see now Ogden 2006a: 124–5 = Ogden 2007a: 233–5, superseding *MWG* no. 53. For discussion of this text see Festugière 1939, J.Z. Smith 1978: 172–89 and (with care) Moyer 2003.

31. [Clement of Rome] *Homilies* 1.5 and *Recognitions* 1.5.
32. See Bidez and Cumont 1938: ii 317–18. For Bolus of Mendes see Dickie 1999 and 2001: 117–22 and, for his date, Fraser 1972: i, 440.
33. [Democritus], *Physica et Mystica* 3 = ii p.42 Berthelot (Bidez and Cumont 1938: ii 317–18). Cf. Synesius, *Against Dioscorus on the book of Democritus* at Berthelot 1888: ii, 57 and Bidez and Cumont 1938: ii, 312–13.
34. Heliodorus *Aethiopica* 3.16 = *MWG* no. 56. On Heliodorus generally see Morgan 1996.
35. Heliodorus, *Aethiopica* 6.12–15 = *MWG* no. 157.
36. Virgil, *Aeneid* 4.478–98.
37. For discussions of ancient exorcism, see Oesterreich 1930, Bonner 1943, 1944, Smith 1965, Thraede 1967, Kotansky 1995, Edwards 1989, Cotter 1999: 75–130, Janowitz 2001: 27–46, Ogden 2002a: 166–71, Trzcionka 2007: 142–60.
38. Eleazar: Josephus, *Jewish Antiquities* 8.42–9 = *MWG* no. 127. *Eighth Book of Moses*: *PGM* XIII.242–4 = *MWG* no. 132.
39. Legion at Gerasa: Mark 5.1–20 = *MWG* no. 128 and Luke 8.26–39. For other exorcisms by Jesus, see Matthew 4.23–5, 12.22–4, 15.29–31, 17.14–18, Mark 9.17–29, Luke 4.31–41 and 9.37–43. Antaura: Kotansky 1994 no. 13 = *MWG* no. 260. The Biblical scapegoat: Leviticus 16.
40. Paul and Silas: Acts 16.16–24 = *MWG* no. 129. The prophetic demon is described as being of the *pythōn* variety, for which see *Suda* s.v. *engastrimuthos* = *MWG* no. 34. Discussion at Klauck 2003: 63–73.
41. *PGM* IV.3007–86 = *MWG* no. 131; Acts 19.13–17 = *MWG* no. 130.
42. Lucian, *Philopseudes* 16 = *MWG* no. 51.
43. Midas: Lucian, *Philopseudes* 11–13 = *MWG* no. 49. *Suda* s.v. *Loukianos*.
44. Herodotus 2.104, 7.89; Ovid, *Ars Amatoria* 1.416.
45. Origen, *Contra Celsum* 1.68 = *MWG* no.63. For discussion of the tradition that projected Jesus as a mage, see M. Smith 1978, Aune 1980: 1523–49, Cotter 1999, Martin 2005: 119–26.
46. *PGM* XX.5–11. On this text see Faraone 1995b.
47. Diogenes Laertius 8.3 = *MWG* no. 2; cf., more generally, *MWG* nos 1–10, with commentaries.
48. Lucian, *Philopseudes* 30–1 = *MWG* no. 115.
49. Plautus, *Mostellaria* 446–531 = *MWG* no. 116. Philemon, *Phasma* at vii p. 272 K–A. Pliny, *Letters* 7.27.5–1. Constantius of Lyon, *Life of St Germanus* 2.10. Gregory the Great, *Dialogues* 3.4.1–3. Translations of all these texts

may be found at Ogden 2007a: 205–10. For discussion of this traditional tale see Nardi 1960, Römer 1987, Felton 1999, Stramaglia 1999: 133–69 (the latter two particularly good) and Ogden 2007a: 205–24.

50. Lucian, *Alexander/False Prophet*. The following partial summary pays particular attention to sections 9–18 and 26 = MWG no. 64. The terms applied to Alexander: *goēteia* (etc.): 1, 5, 6, 25, 60; *manganeia* (etc.): 1, 6, 17, 43, 54; *mageia* (etc.): 5, 6, 21, 25. For discussion of this text and the historical Alexander see above all Robert 1980: 393–421, 1981 and also Weinreich 1921, Cumont 1922, Caster 1938, Eitrem 1947: 73–86, Lane Fox 1986: 241–50, Battaglia 1988, Victor 1997.

51. Asclepius' migrations between cult sites in the form of a snake: *IG* ii^2 4960 (Zea to Eleusis; beginning of fourth century BC); *IG* iv^2.1 122.33 (Epidaurus to Halieis; later fourth century BC); Pausanias 2.10.3 (Epidaurus to Sicyon) and 3.23.6–7 (Epidaurus to Epidaurus Limera). The sources for his transition to Rome from Epidaurus, supposedly in 292 BC, are particularly rich: Livy 29.11.1 and *Periocha* 11; Ovid, *Metamorphoses* 15.622–744; Valerius Maximus 1.8.2; Pliny, *Natural History* 29.72; Arnobius, *Against the Gentiles* 7.44–8; Augustine, *City of God* 3.17; Claudian, *On the Consulship of Stilicho* 3.171–3; anon., *De viris illustribus* 22.1–3; *Latin Anthology* 1.2.719e.1–7; Q. Serenus Salmonicus, *Liber medicinalis* prooemium 1–10. All these texts are collected at Edelstein and Edelstein 1945 i nos 423.33, 614–15, 694–5, 720, 748, 757, 846–54, 859; see also ii pp. 228–31.

52. Hippolytus, *Refutations* 4.4 = MWG no. 160; cf. Ganschinietz 1913, Ogden 2001: 210–11.

53. Lucian, *Alexander* 25, 38, 44, 47 and 53–4; cf. 51, where the unnamed Syrian who similarly tricks Alexander may also be a self-reference by Lucian, who hailed from Syrian Samosata. Galen, *Commentary on [Hippocrates] Epidemics* 2.6.9. See Strohmaier 1976: 118–19 for a translation of the Arabic text into German, and cf. Macleod 1979 and Hall 1981: 4–6, 436–40.

54. For the coins, marbles and bronzes, see *LIMC* Glykon, Robert 1980: 396–401 and the plates to the rear of Victor 1997. Coin with Glycon and Ionopolis: Waddington Collection 142, reproduced at Robert 1980: 400–2, with discussion superseding Bordenache 1964. Miletos: *IGRom* iv.1498; cf. Robert 1980: 405–8, Battaglia 1988: 279, Victor 1997: 12–13. Alexander the Great: Plutarch, *Alexander* 2. Augustus: Suetonius, *Augustus* 94 = Asclepiades of Mendes *FGH* 617 F2. The seduction of wives: Lucian, *Alexander* 42. Assuming the fine marble Glycon in Constanza (*LIMC* Glykon 1) to be a life-size cult statue, Battaglia 1988: 283 calculates that the marvellous snake was 4.6 metres long!

55. For Philostratus' text see above all Bowie 1978, with extensive

bibliography; subsequent bibliography at Whitmarsh 2001: 229–30; note in particular Anderson 1986, 1994, Dzielska 1986 and Swain 1996: 381–96.

56. Moiragenes: Origen, *Contra Celsum* 6.41; cf. Bowie 1978: 1673–4 and, for Moiragenes' date, 1678. Lucian, *Alexander* 5. Dio Cassius 78.18.4. 'Old Serving Woman': *PGM* XIa 1–40.
57. Philostratus, *Life of Apollonius* 1.2 (the need for the *Life*, and Apollonius' wisdom, mages, Egyptians, Brahmins; cf. 7.39), 1.18–41 (Babylon and Susa), 5.12 (prophecies).
58. Philostratus, *Life of Apollonius* 4.18 (Eleusis), 8.19 (Trophonius), 8.30 (Dictynna). On these points see further Ogden 2007b.
59. Philostratus, *Life of Apollonius* 3.38–9 = *MWG* no. 57 (pederastic ghost) and 4.20 (playboy).
60. Philostratus, *Life of Apollonius* 4.10 = *MWG* no. 58 (plague demon), 4.25 = *MWG* no. 60 (Lamia). Apollonius teleports again after making his successful defence before Domitian at 8.12.
61. Philostratus, *Life of Apollonius* 4.45 = *MWG* no. 61. Lazarus: John 11.1–44.
62. Philostratus, *Life of Apollonius* 4.11 and 16 = *MWG* no. 59. Philostratus has much more to say about the restless ghosts of the Trojan war warriors on the plain of Troy in his *Heroicus*.
63. Eusebius, *Against Hierocles*, esp. 2 and 27 = *MWG* no. 62.

Chapter 4

1. The Greek Magical Papyri are to be found, in Greek original with German translation, in Preisendanz and Henrichs 1973–4. A complete English translation of these texts and supplementary documents is to be found in Betz 1992, but the under-annotated nature of this volume means that many of the texts are likely to remain baffling to readers. See the helpful discussions of Brashear 1992 and 1995. Dieleman 2005 especially 254–84 has useful discussion of some of the literary packaging of the recipes of the Greek Magical Papyri. The oldest text in the *PGM* collection, the 'curse of Artemisie' (*PGM* XL), dates from the fourth century BC and is actually one of the oldest papyri of any sort written in Greek. Definitely from the Theban library are *PGM* IV, V, Va and XII–XIV. Probably from it are *PGM* I–III, VII, LXI. Alchemical texts were also present. Paul has his converts burn their magical books at Acts 19.19 = *MWG* no. 293.
2. Recipe books from the first century BC: *PGM* CXVII and CXXII. *The Great Magical Papyrus in Paris*: *PGM* IV.
3. *PGM* IV 296–434 = *MWG* no. 239; the curse text is *Suppl.Mag.* no. 47 =

MWG no. 240. The opening paragraphs of this chapter owe much to Ogden 2006c.
4. *PGM* XIa 1–40.The Egyptian goddess Nephthys is 'the house-warden goddess'. She is the sister of Isis and, more germanely here, the wife of Seth-Typhon.
5. For demon-assistants see Ciraolo 1995. Perseus and the Graeae: Pindar, *Pythian* 12.6–26, Aeschylus, *Phorcides* FF261–2 *TrGF*, Apollodorus, *Bibliotheca* 2.4.1–5. Gorgons: see the images collected in *LIMC* s.v. *Gorgones*. Perseus as the founder of the Persian race: Aeschylus, *Persians* 79–80, Herodotus 7.61. For discussion of the magical traditions connected with Perseus, see Ogden 2008: 110–12.
6. *PGM* XII.14–95. The role that dream-sending could play in erotic seduction is most graphically illustrated by the tale of Nectanebo's seduction of Olympias at *Alexander Romance* 1.5 = *MWG* no. 55, discussed in Chapter 3. In contrast to the Hyperborean's technique, the Eros-doll is here to be made as one of a male-female pair (as often in the papyri), together with a Psyche doll, although his mate Psyche is soon forgotten in the recipe. The paradigmatic myth of Eros and Psyche is most famously recounted at Apuleius, *Metamorphoses* books 4–6.
7. Lucian, *Philopseudes* 14 = *MWG* no. 244. For detailed discussion of this text, see Radermacher 1927, Ogden 2007a: 105–30.
8. *Cyprian and Justina* 8.
9. Selections from *PGM* I 42–55 and 96–195. For this text see the commentaries of Hopfner 1921–4: ii no. 135, Preisendanz and Henrichs (*PGM*) and O'Neill (*GMPT*) ad loc. For the epistolary motif in *PGM* recipes, see Dieleman 2005: 269–70.
10. Lucian *Philopseudes* 34–6 = *MWG* no. 54. For detailed discussion of this text, see Ogden 2006a, 2007a: 231–70; cf. also Ogden 2007b. For a treatment of this tale as a folktale, see Anderson 2000: 103–11.
11. Lucian in Egypt: Lucian, *Apology* 12. Hall 1981: 41–3 rightly notes that none of the other references to Egypt in Lucian's oeuvre need depend upon a personal visit.
12. *PGM* IV.154–285. [Thessalus of Tralles], *De virtutibus herbarum* 1–28 Friedrich (pp. 43–53). See Chapter 3 for notes on translations and discussions of this text.
13. *PGM* IV. 2006–87 = *MWG* no. 161. For discussion of the Pitys spells see Ogden 2001: 202–16. Pitys is defined as 'Thessalian' at *PGM* IV 2140. But he also bears some sort of relationship with the fabled Egyptian prophet Bitos or Bitys, who supposedly discovered some Hermetic texts in a sanctuary at Sais and translated them for the pharaoh Ammon: Iamblichus, *On the*

Mysteries 8.5, 10.7, Zosimus, *On Apparatus and Furnaces*, Greek fragments 230–5 Jackson.

14. *PGM* 2125–39 = *MWG* no. 162.
15. Malalas' material here was to be recycled by John of Antioch F1.8, F6.10, F6.18 = *FGH* iv, pp. 539–44 (sixth century AD), [Lucian] *Philopatris* 9 (tenth century AD) and George Cedrenus 1.30–41 (eleventh century AD). Elements of the story are already apparent in the late first-century BC Diodorus, 6.5. For a more canonical account of Perseus' adventures, see, e.g., [Apollodorus], *Bibliotheca* 2.4.1–5, 2.7.3
16. John Malalas, pp. 35–9 Dindorf (selections).
17. Palaephatus, *De incredibilibus FGH* 44 F3. See Ogden 2008: 121–6.
18. For Ostanes see, e.g., Pliny, *Natural History* 8–11 = *MWG* no. 45, Apuleius, *Apology* 27 = *MWG* no. 299, [Democritus], *Physica et Mystica* ii p. 42 Berthlot = *MWG* no. 46.
19. Aphrodite's *kestos himas*: Homer, *Iliad* 14.197–222 = *MWG* no. 248; cf. Bonner 1949, Brenk 1977, Waegeman 1987: 195–221, Faraone 1999: 97–110. Odysseus' wound: Homer, *Odyssey* 19.449–58 = *MWG* no. 256; cf. Renehan 1992. Petronius, *Satyricon* 131 = *MWG* no. 254. Pliny, *Natural History* 28.48.
20. For magical intaglios see above all Bonner 1950 and Delatte and Derchain 1964; cf. also Smith 1979, Schwartz 1981, Waegeman 1987, Lancelloti 2000. Erotic imperial intaglios: see, e.g., Delatte and Derchain nos 324, 329 = *MWG* nos 249, 250 (with illustrations) respectively. Ring of Gyges: Plato, *Republic* 359d–60b = *MWG* no. 274. Eucrates' ring: Lucian, *Philopseudes* 17 = *MWG* no. 275. Does the sorcerer owe his Arab designation to the Mage seemingly named Arabos (*Magos Arabos*) of Aeschylus, *Persians* 317 (for which see Chapter 1)? Silvianus' prayer for justice: *DT* 106 = *RIB* 306 = *MWG* no. 187. The Silchester ring: Goodchild 1953 = *MWG* no. 187.
21. For text-amulets see above all Kotansky 1994; cf. also Tavenner 1916, Gager 1992: 218–42, Kotansky 1991, 1995, Ogden 2002a: 261–74.
22. Kotansky 1994 no. 13 = *MWG* no. 260. Much of what follows is indebted to Kotansky's superb edition and commentary at pp. 58–71. Note, further to the points made here, Kotansky's sophisticated comparison of the imagery of this amuletic text with that of the biblical narratives of the demons-of-Gerasa episode, Luke 8.26–39 and Mark 5.1–20 = *MWG* no. 128. See also Barb 1966.
23. For historiolas see Frankfurter 1995 (though much of this piece is needlessly obfuscatory). The Antaura text might also be described as a *Legendenzauber* or 'Legend-spell': for the term see West 2007: 336–9.
24. Text at Kotansky 1994: 61.
25. Text at Kotansky 1994: 63.

26. Furley 2007: 124–7. Sappho F1 Page/Voigt.
27. Cf. Kotansky 1994: 59. The three other amulets from the same coffin are edited by Kotansky as nos 14–16.
28. For the dating see Koenen 1962: 168, Henrichs 1970: 205 n.1 (with a picture of the text at plate xi), and Brashear 1995: 3413. In fact the papyrus is the second oldest in the entire *PGM* corpus, being second only to *PGM* XL, the fourth-century BC prayer-for-justice text in which Artemisie seeks recompense for her daughter's deprivation of burial.
29. *PGM* XX.13–19 = *MWG* no. 261.
30. Prestige: cf. Dickie 1994: 120.
31. The argument made here is laid out more fully at Ogden forthcoming 6. The connection between the Philinna of the Papyrus and Philip's wife Philinna was first made by Dickie 1994, especially 121–2, but the notion, critical to his argument, that she was a prostitute depends upon an unsustainably literalist reading of the sources: see Ogden 1999b: 17–27 and *passim*. Olympias as a witch in the tradition: Plutarch, *Alexander* 2. Olympias and Nectanebo: [Callisthenes], *Alexander Romance* 1.4–7, 12 = *MWG* no. 55. Olympias corrupts Arrhidaeus with her drugs: Plutarch, *Alexander* 77, cf. Justin 14.5.2. Philip, Olympias and the bewitching Thessalian: Plutarch, *Advice to Bride and Groom* 23, 141b–c. Further sources for Arrhidaeus' mental condition: Diodorus 18.2.2 (Hieronymus of Cardia?), Plutarch, *Alexander* 10.2, *On the Fortune of Alexander* 337d–e, Appian, *Syrian Wars* 52, Heidelberg Epitome *FGH* 155 F1, Justin 13.2.11, Porphyry *FGH* 260 F3.2; for discussion of these see Carney 2001.
32. *PGM* XXXVI.283–94 = *MWG* no. 212.
33. *Suppl. Mag.* no. 38 = *MWG* no. 206.
34. Ammonion and Theodotis: *Suppl.Mag.* 38 = *MWG* no. 206; there is another fine attraction-vignette at *PGM* XVIIa. Apuleius, *Metamorphoses* 3.16–18 = *MWG* no. 107.
35. For the principal standard corpora of curse tablets see Wünsch 1897 (*DTA*), 1898, Audollent (*DT*), Besnier 1920, Kagarow 1929, Ziebarth 1934, Solin 1968, Tomlin 1988, Lopez Jimeno 1991, 1999, Daniel and Maltomini 1990–2 (*Suppl.Mag.*), Bettarini 2005. Note also the important supplementary lists published by Jordan 1985a, 2000. Gager 1992 offers a useful selection of curse tablets in translation; cf. also Ogden 2002a: 210–36. For further discussions, see Preisendanz 1972, Jordan 1985b, Versnel 1985, 1991, Bravo 1987, Bernand 1991: 107–29, Faraone 1991b, Graf 1997: 118–74, Voutiras 1998, Ogden 1999a, Dickie 2000, Lopez Jimeno 2002, Carastro 2006: 163–88. The opening paragraphs of this section remodel Ogden 2006b.

36. Brashear 1995 explores the possibilities of original or lost meaning behind some of the *voces magicae* in the Greek Magical Papyri.
37. E.g. Lopez Jimeno 1991 no. 3 = *MWG* no. 168, Jordan 1999 no. 1 = *MWG* no. 169. Note also Cicero, *Brutus* 217 = *MWG* no. 172. See Gager 1992: 116–50.
38. E.g. Wünsch 1898 no. 16 = *DT* no. 155 = *MWG* no. 173. Note also Augustine, *Confessions* 4.2 = *MWG* no. 175. See Gager 1992: 42–77.
39. E.g. *DTA* no. 87a = *MWG* no. 176, *DT* no. 52 = Jordan 1999 no. 2 = *MWG* no. 177. See Gager 1992: 151–74.
40. E.g., for separation, *DTA* no. 78 = *MWG* no. 198, *DT* 95 = Ziebarth 1934 no. 23 = *MWG* no. 199, *DT* no. 86 = Ziebarth 1934 no. 22 = *MWG* no. 200; for attraction, Jordan 1999 no. 3 = *MWG* no. 205, *Suppl.Mag.* no. 38 = *MWG* no. 206, *Suppl.Mag.* no. 45 = *MWG* no. 207. The rare lesbian attraction curses are *Suppl.Mag.* no. 42 = *MWG* no. 210 and *PGM* XXXII, both from Roman Egypt. See Gager 1992: 78–115.
41. E.g. *Tab.Sulis* no. 62 = *MWG* no. 185, *DT* no. 106 = *MWG* no. 187, *DT* no. 41 = *MWG* no. 191. For 'prayers for justice' see above all Tomlin 1988; see also Versnel 1991, Ogden 1999a: 39–44.
42. For voodoo dolls see the catalogue at Faraone 1991a and also Bonner 1932, Trumpf 1958, Reiner 1987, Faraone 1989, Gager 1992, Graf 1992, Dickie 1996, Ogden 1999a: 71–9, 2002a: 245–60.
43. Voutiras 1998: 8 = *MWG* no. 197.
44. For deactivation of a curse by exhumation, cf. *PGM* XL = *MWG* no. 190, 'The curse of Artemisie'.
45. Voutiras 1998: 65–6 = *MWG* no. 170. Voutiras' texts supersedes that of *DT* nos 43–4.
46. We can find a more elaborate example of the 'sympathetic' use of the ineffectual nature of a corpse in a third- or second-century BC lead separation curse tablet from Boeotia, Ziebarth 1934 no. 23 (superseding *DT* 95) = *MWG* 199: 'Just as you, Theonnastos, have no power in your hands, feet or body to do, organize, love ... so too may Zoilos stay powerless to have sex with Antheira and may Antheira stay powerless to have sex with Zoilos in the same way ...'. Voutiras 1999 has suggested that Pasianax, which literally means 'Lord to all', is not the real name of the dead man but the epithet of a powerful underworld demon with which his ghost is identified. This is hard to accept.
47. Homolle 1901 = *MWG* no. 188.

Chapter 5

1. On ancient ghosts in general see above all Rohde 1925, and also Harrison 1922, Otto 1923, Preisendanz 1935, Hickman 1938, Zintzen 1976, Clark 1978, Winkler 1980, Russell 1981, Bremmer 1983, 2002, Ogden 2001, 2002a: 146–209, Felton 2007. More elementary, but not wholly negligible are Collison-Morley 1912 and Dingwall 1930. For haunted-house stories see Nardi 1960, Felton 1999, Stramaglia 1999: 133–69, Ogden 2007a: 205–24. For ghostly restlessness see Wide 1909, Cumont 1945, 1949, Nock 1950, Waszink 1954, Vrugt-Lentz 1960 and, with care, Johnston 1999.
2. Plutarch, *Cimon* 6 = *MWG* no. 151; see also Plutarch, *Moralia* 555c (*Slow vengeance*), Pausanias 3.17 = *MWG* no. 28, Aristodemus *FGH* 104 F8. We can tell that this tale, or something very similar to it, had developed by the end of the fifth century because the tale at Thucydides 1.132–4 = (in part) *MWG* no. 29, composed by that time, presupposes the existence of the tale of Cleonice or a close equivalent; the case is set out at Ogden 2002d. For the oracle of the dead at Heraclea Pontica, see Ogden 2001: 17–34 (with further references).
3. Thucydides 1.134 = *MWG* no. 29, Plutarch, *Moralia* 560ef = *MWG* no. 152, Scholiast Euripides, *Alcestis* 1127–8, incorporating Plutarch, *Homeric Studies* F1 Bernadakis = *MWG* no. 27, Pausanias 3.17 = *MWG* no. 28
4. See the sacred law from Selinus at Jameson, Jordan and Kotansky 1993, col. B = *MWG* no. 123 and Solmsen and Fraenkel 1966 no. 28 B 27–39 = *MWG* no. 124, both with their *MWG* commentaries.
5. Herodotus 5.92 = *MWG* no. 150. The earlier part of the story must be recovered from a number of sources: Herodotus 3.50–3 (killing of Melissa); Nicolaus of Damascus *FGH* 90 F58 (Periander's erotic attachment to Melissa); Diogenes Laertius 1.94, 96, 100 (concubines, unintentional killing). Herodotus is still sometimes foolishly misread as stating that the deposit had been hidden by Periander himself, who, we must then suppose, had inexplicably forgotten where he had put it. This misapprehension should not have survived the case framed by Stern 1989. The token that the ghost supplies does not, logically, prove the truth of what she is saying, but it does prove that the ghost is indeed that of Melissa. For the Acheron oracle of the dead, see Ogden 2001: 43–60 (with further references). If this tale has any basis in history, it may be rooted in a campaign by the tyrant against the luxury and ostentation of the Corinthian aristocracy around him, as reported by Nicolaus of Damascus *FGH* 90 F58: hence the burning of the women's fine clothes.
6. Patroclus: Homer, *Iliad* 23.65–76. Elpenor: Homer, *Odyssey* 11.61–79.

Polydorus: Euripides, *Hecabe* 47–79. Cillus: Theopompus *FGH* 115 F350. The gnat: [Virgil] *Culex*.
7. Augustine, *De cura gerunda pro mortuis* 13; cf. Russell 1981. *Apophthegmata Sancti Macarii, PG* 34.244–5. Talmud Berachot 18b; cf. Ganschinietz 1929.
8. Virgil, *Aeneid* 1.353–9.
9. Lucian, *Philopseudes* 27. Discussion at Ogden 2004, 2007a: 195–204.
10. Philostratus, *Life of Apollonius* 4.16 = *MWG* no. 59.
11. Josephus, *Jewish War* 1.436–44, *Jewish Antiquities* 15.202–52. For the historical Mariamme, see Schalit 1969: 566–88.
12. *Talmud Baba Batra* 3b, *Kiddouschin* 70b, Sifra on *Deuteronomy* 22.22; cf. Reinach 1907, Nenci 1994 on 5.92, Ogden 2001: 57–60.
13. The principle of embalming in honey: Lucretius 3.889. Spartan kings: Xenophon, *Hellenica* 5.3.9 (Agesipolis), Diodorus 15.93, Plutarch, *Agesilaus* 50 and Nepos, *Agesilaus* 8.7 (Agesilaus); cf. Richer 1994: 71. Alexander the Great: [Callisthenes], *Alexander Romance* 3.34. Cleomenes: Aelian, *Varia Historia* 12.8; Devereux 1995: 111–13 has no basis for assigning this tale rather to Cleomenes III. Glaucus and Polyidus: Hyginus, *Fabula* 136 (the tale); Apostolius 5.48 *CPG* (proverb); as often, snakes serve in this tale as the embodiments, avatars or agents of a healing deity.
14. Xenophon of Ephesus, *Ephesiaca* 5.1. The episode is discussed by Susanetti 1999: 145–55.
15. Parthenius, *Erotica Pathemata* 17. For text, translation and commentary upon this text as a whole see Lightfoot 1999. Cf. Plutarch *Banquet of the Seven Sages* 146d and Diogenes Laertius 1.96 (Crateia).
16. Nero's killing of Poppaea: Pliny, *Natural History* 12.83, Tacitus, *Annals* 16.6. Nero, Agrippina and the mages: Suetonius, *Nero* 13, 34–5, 46 = (in part) *MWG* no. 34, Tacitus, *Annals* 14.2–10 and Dio Cassius 61.11–14, 62.28. Tiridates: Pliny, *Natural History* 30.14–18. For discussion of Poppaea and her death, see Ameling 1986, Holzrattner 1995: 128–32.
17. For Harpalus and Pythionice see Athenaeus 567f, 586c–d, 594d–96b, and 605d (incorporating Python *Agen TrGF* 91 F1 = *MWG* no. 42), Diodorus 17.108.5–6, Pausanias 1.37.5 and Plutarch, *Phocion* 22. The argument enunciated here is laid out more fully in Ogden 2007a. For Pythionice's Athenian tomb see Scholl 1994: 254–61, with a picture of the remains and a reconstruction at 259.
18. Homer, *Iliad* 2.695–702 with Eustathius ad loc., Propertius 1.17.9–10, Ovid, *Heroides* 13, especially 151–66 (wax image), Apollodorus, *Epitome* 3.29.30, Pausanias 4.2.7 (citing *Cypria* F18 Davies), Lucian, *Dialogues of the Dead* 28, Hyginus 103–4 (a bronze image, but how could one burn this? – the *aereum* of the manuscripts may be a corruption of *cereum*, 'waxen'),

Servius on Virgil, *Aeneid* 6.447, Scholiast Aristides vol. iii, pp. 671–2 Dindorf (important for Euripides' play), Tzetzes, *Chiliads* 2.736–759–84 (wooden image). We can glean little of interest from the actual extant fragments of Euripides's play, FF647–57 *TrGF*. See Gantz 1993: 592–3.

19. Herodotus 7.33, 9.116, 120. See Pausanias 1.34 for a general comparison of Protesilaus to the oracular healing gods Amphiaraus and Trophonius. For Philostratus, who wrote his *Heroicus* in the early third century AD, Protesilaus remained a vigorous ghost, stalking the Trojan plain.

20. Euripides, *Alcestis* 348–68 (the image), 1143–6 (Alcestis returns mute). The earliest stages of development of the myth of Orpheus and Eurydice escape us. We are familiar with the version in which Orpheus' attempt to retrieve the ghost of his dear wife Eurydice from the underworld is unsuccessful (e.g. Virgil, *Georgics* 4.453–525, Ovid, *Metamorphoses* 10.1–63, etc.), but it remains possible that in an earlier version the attempt had been successful, and there may be traces of this at Euripides, *Alcestis* 357–62, 962–71, Isocrates 11.8, Plato, *Protagoras* 315a, *Symposium* 179d.

21. [Quintilian] *Declamationes Maiores* 10 esp. 1, 7, 8–9, 15–16, 19 = *MWG* no. 125.

22. Pherecydes *FGH* 3 F78 = F119 Fowler.

23. Dio Cassius 69.11 = *MWG* no. 241. Later Latin sources: Aurelius Victor, *Book on the Caesars* 14 (composed after 360 BC), *SHA* Hadrian 14 (perhaps written in the later fourth century). For further speculation on the identity of the mages who advised Hadrian, see Ogden 2007a: 248–52. For Alcestis, see Euripides, *Alcestis*.

24. Ps.-Clement, *Recognitions* 13 = *MWG* no. 65. For Simon Magus see Edwards 1997, Heintz 1997, Bremmer 1998, 2000, Klauck 2003: 13–23. Zacharius Scholasticus, *Life of Severus of Antioch*, PO 2, pp. 57–9 = *MWG* no. 138; on this narrative see Dickie 2001: 263–4, 314–15.

25. Cicero, *In Vatinium* 14 = *MWG* no. 137; Horace, *Epodes* 5 = *MWG* no. 92; Philostratus, *Life of Apollonius* 7.11 = *MWG* no. 136. Mantic impression on the guts: Ogden 2001: 199. See Watson 2003: 175–7 for the theme of boy-sacrifice in ancient literature.

26. Donatus on Terence, *Eunuch* 9.3 = *MWG* no. 118.

27. Philostratus, *Life of Apollonius* 4.25 = *MWG* no. 60. Discussion at Stramaglia 1999: 266–79. The gardens of Tantalus: Homer, *Odyssey* 11.582–92. For other Corinthian ghost stories, compare, for example, the tale of Periander and Melissa above, and Lucian's tale of Arignotus and the haunted house, discussed in Chapter 3.

28. Nicander, *Heteroioumena*, as recycled at Antoninus Liberalis, *Metamorphoses* 8. Dio Chrysostom, *Orations* 5. For Lamia and *lamiae* in general

see further Heraclitus, *De Incredibilibus* 34, Diodorus 20.41.3–6, Scholiast Aristophanes, *Peace* 758, *Suda* s.v. *Lamia*. General discussion at Johnston 1999: 161–202 (with care). For Lamia and *lamashtu* demons see Burkert 1987: 26–33, 1992: 82–7. For the affinities of *lamiae* with dragons, see Ogden 2008: 96

29. Philostratus, *Life of Apollonius* 2.4.
30. Proclus, *Commentary on Plato's Republic,* pp. 115–16 Kroll. Philip reigned 359–336 and took Amphipolis in 357. The famous Craterus, the future Diadoch, will have been of marriageable age in the latter half of Philip's reign, since it is estimated that he was born c. 370: see Heckel 1992: 109, 2006: 94. It may be worth noting that after Philip's (and indeed Alexander's) death this Craterus married Phila, daughter of Antipater in 322/1, but he (rather than she) was then killed within two years: Memnon *FGH* 434 F1.4.4, Diodorus 18.18.7, Plutarch, *Demetrius* 14.2; see Heckel 1992: 130–3, 2006: 208. However, it is less likely that the original author of the tale as we have it was attempting to integrate actual historical figures into it, Philip aside, than that he was attempting to bestow a verisimilitudinous colour upon it by choosing well-known names from the Macedonian onomasticon. One of Philip's own wives was the Thessalian Philinna (for whom see Chapter 4), of whose name Philinnion is a diminutive form, whilst another of his wives was sister to Machatas, a prince of Elimea in Upper Macedon (Athenaeus 557c = Satyrus F21 Kumaniecki).
31. Phlegon of Tralles, *Mirabilia* 1 = *MWG* no. 119. For interesting commentaries on this text, see Hansen 1996, Stramaglia 1999: 217–57.
32. Homer, *Odyssey* 11.206–22 (Odysseus' mother) and 392–4 (Agamemnon); see Ogden 2001: 220. Phlegon of Tralles, *Mirabilia* 2, with Hansen 1996 ad loc.
33. Virgil, *Georgics* 4.453–525, Ovid, *Metamorphoses* 10.1–63.
34. For Goethe's *Bride of Corinth* (*Die Braut von Korinth*, 1797) see Hansen 1996: 70–1, 201–7. The notion that mere contact with the dead can itself be deadly: see Plautus, *Mostellaria* 446–531 = *MWG* no. 116, Apuleius, *Metamorphoses* 9.29–31 = *MWG* no. 114, Heliodorus 6.12–15 = *MWG* no. 157.
35. Xenophon of Ephesus, *Ephesiaca* 5.7.7–8. The episode is discussed by Puigalli 1986 and Susanetti 1999: 157–66.
36. Philostratus, *Life of Apollonius* 3.38 =*MWG* no. 57.

Bibliography

Abbreviations

CIL	*Corpus Inscriptionum Latinarum*
CPG	Leutsch and Schneidewin 1839–51
DK	Diels and Krantz 1961
DT	Audollent 1904
DTA	Wünsch 1897
FGH	Jacoby 1923–
GMPT	Betz 1992
IG	*Inscriptiones Graecae* 1903–
IGRom	Cagnat *et al.* 1906–27
K-A	Kassel and Austin 1983–
LIMC	*Lexicon Iconographicum Mythologiae Classicae* 1981–
MWG	Ogden 2002a
PG	Migne 1857–66
PGM	Preisendanz and Henrichs 1973–4
PL	Migne 1841–64
PO	*Patrologia Orientalis* 1903–
RE	Pauly *et al.* 1894–1972
RIB	Collingwood *et al.* 1965–
SHA	*Scriptores Historiae Augustae*
Suppl.Mag.	Daniel and Maltomini 1990–2
Tab.Sul.	Tomlin 1988
TrGF	Snell *et al.* 1971–2004

Abt, A. 1908. *Die Apologie des Apuleius von Madaura und die antike Zauberei.* RGVV iv. 2. Giessen. Reprint, 1967.
Ahl, F.M. 1969. 'Appius Claudius and Sextus Pompey in Lucan' *Classica et Mediaevalia* 30, 331–46.
—— 1976. *Lucan. An Introduction.* Ithaca, NY.
Albini, F., ed. 1993. *Luciano. L'amante della menzogna.* Venice.
Ameling, W. 1986. 'Tyrannen und schwangere Frauen' *Historia* 35, 507–8.
Anderson, G. 1976. *Studies in Lucian's Comic Fiction.* Leiden.

―― 1986. *Philostratus. Biography and Belles-lettres in the Third Century AD.* Beckenham.

―― 1994. *Sage, Saint and Sophist. Holy Men and their Associates in the Early Roman Empire.* London.

―― 2000. *Fairytale in the Ancient World.* London.

Andrews, N.E. 1996. 'Narrative and Allusion in Theocritus *Idyll* 2' in Harder, M.A., Regtuit, R.F. and Walker, G.C., eds *Theocritus.* Groningen, 21–53.

Audollent, A. 1904. *Defixionum Tabellae.* Paris. [*DT*].

Aufhauser, J.B. 1911. *Das Drachenwunder des heiligen Georg in der griechischen und lateinischen Überlieferung.* Byzantisches Archiv 5. Leipzig.

Aufrère, S.H. 2000. 'Quelques aspects du dernier Nectanébo et les échos de la magie égyptienne dans le *Roman d'Alexandre*' in Moreau and Turpin 2000, i, 95–118.

Aune, D.E. 1980. 'Magic in early Christianity' *Aufstieg und Niedergang der römischen Welt* ii. 23.2, 1507–57.

Baldini-Moscadi, L. 1976. 'Osservazioni sull' episodio magico del VI libro della *Farsaglia* di Lucano' *Studi italiani di filologia classica* 48, 140–99.

Barb, A.A. 1966. 'Antaura the Mermaid and the Devil's Grandmother' *Journal of the Warburg and Courtauld Institutes* 29, 1–23.

Barton, T. 1994. *Ancient Astrology.* London.

Battaglia, G.B. 1988. 'Glykon' *LIMC* iv. 1, 279–83.

Beagon, M. 1992. *Roman Nature.* Oxford.

Beck, G. 1965. 'Beobachtungen zur Kirkeepisode in der *Odyssee*' *Philologus* 109, 1–29.

Beck, R. 1996. 'Mystery Religions, Aretology and the Ancient Novel' in Schmeling 1996, 131–50.

―― 2007. *A Brief History of Ancient Astrology.* Oxford.

Belloni, L. 1981. 'Medea πολυφᾱρμακος' *Civiltà classica e cristiana* 2, 117–33.

Benveniste, E. 1938. *Les mages dans l'ancien Iran.* Paris.

Bernand, A. 1991. *Sorciers grecs.* Paris.

Besnier, M. 1920 'Récents travaux sur les *defixionum tabellae latines* 1904–1914' *Revue de philologie* 44, 5–30.

Bettarini, L. 2005. *Corpus delle defixiones di Selinunte.* Turin.

Betz, H.D. ed. 1992. *The Greek Magical Papyri in Translation, Including the Demotic Spells.* 2nd edn, Chicago: University of Chicago. [*GMPT*]

Bickerman, E. and Tadmor, H. 1978. 'Darius I, Pseudo-Smerdis and the Magi' *Athenaeum* 56, 239–61.

Bidez, J. and Cumont, F. 1938. *Les mages hellénisés.* 2 vols, Paris.

Bidez, J. and Hansen, G.C., eds 1960. *Sozomenus. Kirchengeschichte.* Berlin.

Bolte, J. and Polívka, G. 1913–32. *Anmerkungen zu den Kinder- und Hausmärchen der Brüder Grimm.* 5 vols, Leipzig.

Bompaire, J. 1958. *Lucien écrivain: imitation et création.* Bibliothèque des écoles françaises d'Athènes et de Rome 190. Paris.

Bonnechère, P. 2003. *Trophonios de Lébadée. Cultes et mythes d'une cité béotienne au miroir de la mentalité antique.* Leiden.

Bonner, C.A. 1932. 'Witchcraft in the Lecture Room of Libanius' *Transactions of the American Philological Association* 63, 34–44.

—— 1943. 'The Technique of Exorcism' *Harvard Theological Review*, 39–43.

—— 1944. 'The Violence of Departing Demons' *Harvard Theological Review*, 334–6.

—— 1949. '*Kestos himas* and the Saltire of Aphrodite' *American Journal of Philology*, 70, 1–6.

—— 1950. *Studies in Magical Amulets, chiefly Graeco-Egyptian.* Ann Arbor, MI.

Bordenache, G. 1964. 'Contributi per un storia dei culti e dell'arte nella Tomi d'età Romana' *Studii Classice* 6, 157–63.

Bordoy, F.C. 2002. 'La crítica platónica de la magia' in Peláez 2002, 191–202.

Borghouts, J.F. 1978. *Ancient Egyptian Magical Texts.* Nisaba 9. Leiden.

Bottéro, J. 1987–90. 'Magie A. In Mesoptamien' in *Reallexicon für Assyriologie* 7, 200–34.

—— 2000. 'Magie, exorcisme et religion en Mésopotamie' in Moreau and Turpin 2000, i, 63–76.

Bouché-Leclercq, A. 1899. *L'Astrologie grecque.* Paris.

Boulogne, J. 2000. 'Plutarque et les mages' in Moreau and Turpin 2000, ii, 59–78.

Bourgery, A. 1928. 'Lucain et la magie' *Revue des études latines* 6, 299–313.

Bowie, E.L. 1978, 'Apollonius of Tyana: Tradition and Reality' *Aufstieg und Niedergang der römischen Welt* ii.16.2, 1652–99.

—— 1994. 'The Readership of the Greek Novels in the Ancient World' in Tatum, J., ed., *The Search for the Ancient Novel.* Baltimore, MD, 435–59.

Brashear, William M. 1992. 'Magical Papyri: Magic in Bookform' in Ganz, P., ed., *Das Buch als magisches und als Repräsentationsobjekt.* Wiesbaden, 25–59.

—— 1995. 'The Greek Magical Papyri: an introduction and survey with an annotated bibliography' *Aufstieg und Niedergang der römischen Welt* ii.18.5, 3380–4.

Bravo, B. 1987. 'Une tablette magique d'Olbia pontique, les morts, les héros et les démons' in *Poikilia: études offerts à Jean-Pierre Vernant.* Paris, 185–218.

Bremmer, J.N. 1983. *The Early Greek Concept of the Soul.* Princeton, NJ.

—— 1998. ed. *The Apocryphal Acts of Peter.* Leuven.

—— 1999. 'The Birth of the Term Magic' *Zeitschrift für Papyrologie und Epigraphik* 126, 1–12.

—— 2000. 'La confrontation entre l'apôtre Pierre et Simon le magicien' in Moreau *et al.* 2000, i, 219–34.

—— 2002. *The Rise and Fall of the Afterlife.* London.

Brenk, F.E. 1977. 'Aphrodite's Girdle: No Way to Treat a Lady' *Classical Bulletin* 54, 17–20.

Briant, P. 2002. *From Cyrus to Alexander. A History of the Persian Empire.*

Winona Lake, IN. Translation of *Histoire de l'Empire Perse. De Cyrus à Alexandre*. Paris, 1996.
Brilliant, R. 1995. 'Kirke's Men: Swine and Sweethearts' in Cohen 1995, 165–74.
Broadhead, H.D. 1960. *The Persae of Aeschylus* edited with an Introduction and Commentary. Cambridge.
Bronzini, G.B. 1996. *Il viaggio antropologico di Carlo Levi*. Bari.
Bücheler, F. ed. 1895–7. *Carmina latina epigraphica*. Leipzig.
Burkert, W. 1962. 'Goes. Zum griechischen Schamanismus' *Rheinisches Museum für Philologie* 105, 36–55.
—— 1983a. *Homo necans*. Berkeley, CA.
—— 1983b. 'Itinerant Diviners and Magicians. A Neglected Element in Cultural Contacts' in Hägg, R., ed., *The Greek Renaissance of the Eighth Century BC: Tradition and Innovation*. Stockholm, 115–19.
—— 1987. 'Oriental and Greek Mythology: The Meeting of Parallels' in Bremmer, J., ed. *Interpretations of Greek Mythology*. London, 10–40.
—— 1992. *The Orientalizing Revolution. Near-Eastern Influence on Greek Culture in the Early Archaic Age*. Cambridge, MA. Translation of *Die orientalisierende Epoche in der griechischen Religion und Literatur*. Heidelberg, 1984.
Butler, H.E. and Owen, A.S. 1914. *Apulei apologia sive Pro se se magia liber*. Oxford.
Buxton, R.W.B. 1987. 'Wolves and Werewolves in Greek Thought' in Bremmer, J., ed., *Interpretations of Greek Mythology*. London, 60–79.
Cagnat, R. et al. eds 1906–27. *Inscriptiones Graecae ad res Romanas pertinentes*. 3 vols. Paris.
Canciani, F. 1992. 'Kirke' *LIMC* vi. 1, 48–58.
Carastro, M. 2006. *La cité des mages*. Grenoble.
Carducci, N. 1999. *Storia intellettuale di Carlo Levi*. Lecce.
Carney, E.D. 2001. 'The Trouble with Philip Arrhidaeus' *Ancient History Bulletin* 15.2, 63–89.
Caro Baroja, J. 1964. *The World of Witches*. Chicago. Translation of *Las brujas y su mondo: con varias ilustraciones*. Madrid, 1961.
Carpenter, R. 1946. *Folktales, Fiction and Saga in the Homeric Epics*. Sather Classical Lecture 1948. Berkeley, CA.
Caster, M. 1937. *Lucien et la pensée religieuse de son temps*. Paris; repr. New York, 1987.
—— 1938. *Études sur Alexandre ou le faux prophète de Lucien*. Paris.
Ciraolo, L.J. 1995. 'Supernatural Assistants in the Greek Magical Papyri' in Meyer and Mirecki 1995, 279–96.
Clark, R.J. 1978. *Catabasis: Vergil and the Wisdom Tradition*. Amsterdam.
Clauss, J.J. and Johnston, S.I., eds 1997. *Medea*. Princeton, NJ.
Clerc, J.-B. 1995. *Homines magici. Étude sur la sorcellerie et la magie dans la société romaine impériale*. Berne.

Cohen, B. ed. 1995. *The Distaff Side. Repesenting the Female in Homer's* Odyssey. New York.
Coleman, R. 1977. *Vergil. Eclogues.* Cambridge.
Collard, C. 1975. *Euripides. Supplices.* 2 vols. Groningen.
Collingwood, R.G., Wright, R.P. et al. 1965–. *The Roman Inscriptions of Britain.* Sundry volumes. Oxford.
Collison-Morley, L. 1912. *Greek and Roman Ghost Stories.* Oxford.
Contenau, G. 1940. *La divination chez les Assyriens et Babyloniens.* Paris.
Cook, A.B. 1914–40. *Zeus: A Study in Ancient Religion.* 3 vols. Cambridge.
Corti, L. 1998. *The Myth of Medea and the Murder of Children.* Westport, CT.
Cotter, W. 1999. *Miracles in Greco-Roman Antiquity. A Sourcebook for the Study of New Testament Miracle Stories.* London.
Courtney, E. 2001. *A Companion to Petronius.* Oxford.
Crane, G. 1988. *Calypso. Background and Connections in the Odyssey.* Beiträge zur klassischen Philologie. Frankfurt am Main.
Cumont, F. 1922. 'Alexandre d'Abonotique et le néopythagoreanisme' *Revue de l'histoire des religions* 83, 202–10.
―――― 1945. 'Virgile et les morts prématures' *Publication de l'ENS, section des lettres* 2, 123–52.
―――― 1949. *Lux perpetua.* Paris.
Dalley, S. 1989. trans. *Myths from Mesopotamia.* Oxford.
Daniel, Robert W., and Maltomini, Franco, eds 1990–2. *Supplementum Magicum.* Papyrologica Coloniensia vol. xvi.1 and xvi.2. 2 vols. Cologne. [*Suppl.Mag.*]
Davies, M. 1988. *Epicorum Graecorum Fragmenta.* Göttingen.
―――― 1989. *The Epic Cycle.* Bristol.
Dawe, R.D. ed. 2006. *Sophocles. Oedipus Rex.* 2nd edn. Cambridge.
de Donato, G. 1998. *Le parole del reale. Ricerche sulla prose di Carlo Levi.* Bari.
de Jong, A. 1997. *Traditions of the Magi. Zoroastrianism in Greek and Latin literature.* Leiden.
de Jong, I.J.F. 2001. *A Narratological Commentary on the* Odyssey. Cambridge.
de Salviat, F. 1987. 'Le figura del mago egizio nella tradizione letteraria greco-romana' in Roccati, A. and Siliotti, A., eds, 1987. *La magia in Egitto ai tempi dei Faraoni.* Modena, 343–65.
Delatte, A. and Derchain, P. 1964. *Les intailles magiques gréco-égyptiennes.* Paris.
Delcourt, M. 1939. 'Le suicide par vengeance dans la Grèce ancienne' *Revue de l'histoire des religions* 119, 154–71.
Delehaye, H. 1921. 'Cyprien d'Antioche et Cyprien de Carthage' *Analecta Bollandiana* 39, 314–32.
Denzey, N. 2003. 'A New Star on the Horizon: Astral Christologies and Stellar Debates in Early Christian Discourse' in Noegel, S., Walker, J. and Wheeler, B., eds, *Magic in History: Prayer, Magic, and the Stars in the Ancient and Late Antique World.* University Park, TX, 207–22.

Deroy, L. 1985. 'Le nom de Circé et les "portulans" de la Grèce archaïque' *Études classiques* 53, 185–91.
des Places, E. 1971. *Oracles chaldaiques*. Paris.
Devereux, G. 1995. *Cléomène le roi fou. Étude d'histoire ethnopsychonanalytique*. Paris.
Dickie, M.W. 1994. 'The Identity of Philinna in the Philinna Papyrus (*PGM*2 XX.15; *SH* 900.15)' *Zeitschrift für Papyrologie und Epigraphik* 100, 119–22.
—— 1996. 'What is a *kolossos* and how were *kolossoi* made in the Hellenistic period?' *Greek, Roman and Byzantine Studies* 37, 237–57.
—— 1999. 'The learned magician and the collection and transmission of magical lore' in Jordan *et al.* 1999, 163–94.
—— 2000. 'Who Practiced Love-magic in Classical Antiquity and in the Late Roman world?' *Classical Quarterly* 50, 563–83.
—— 2001. *Magic and Magicians in the Greco-Roman World*. London.
—— 2007. 'Magic in Classical and Hellenistic Greece' in Ogden, D., ed., *A Companion to Greek Religion*. Oxford, 357–70.
Dieleman, J. 2005. *Priests, Tongues and Rites. The London-Leiden Magical Manuscripts and Translation in Egyptian Ritual (100–200 CE)*. Leiden.
Diels, H. and Kranz, W. 1961. *Die Fragmente der Vorsokratiker*. 3 vols, 10th edn, Berlin.
Dingwall, E. 1930. *Ghosts and Spirits in the Ancient World*. London.
Diouf, E. 2000. 'Magie et droit chez Pline l'Ancien' in Moreau *et al.* 2000, iii. 71–84.
Dorandi, T. 1991. *Filodemo. Storia dei filosofi. Platone e l'Academia*. Naples.
Douglas, N. 1915. *Old Calabria*. London.
Dover, K.J. 1969. *Theocritus: Select Poems* edited with an introduction and commentary. London.
Dyck, A.R. 1981. 'The Witch's Bed but not her Breakfast' *Rheinisches Museum für Philologie* 124, 196–8.
Dzielska, M. 1986. *Apollonius of Tyana in Legend and History*. Rome.
Ebner, M., Gzella, H., Nesselrath, H.-G. and Ribbat, E. 2001. *Lukian. Die Lügenfreunde*. Scripta antiquitatis posterioris ad ethicam religionemque pertinentia (SAPERE) iii. Darmstadt.
Eckels, R.P. 1937. 'Greek Wolf-Lore'. Dissertation, Philadelphia.
Edelstein, E.J., and Edelstein, L. 1945. *Asclepius. Collection and Interpretation of the Testimonies*. 2 vols. Baltimore, MD.
Edwards, M.J. 1989. 'Three Exorcisms in the *New Testament* World' *Eranos* 87, 117–26.
—— 1997. 'Simon Magus, the bad Samaritan' in Edwards, M. and Swain, S., eds *Portraits*. Oxford, 69–91.
Eitrem, S. 1928. 'The Necromancy in the *Persae* of Aeschylus' *Symbolae Osloenses* 6, 1–16.
—— 1933. 'Das Ende Didos in Vergils *Aeneis*' *Festskrift H. Koht*. Oslo. 29–41.

—— 1941. 'La magie comme motif littéraire chez les grecs et les romains' *Symbolae Osloenses* 21, 39–83.
—— 1947. *Orakel und Mysterien am Ausgang der Antike.*
Ernout, A. 1957a. 'La magie chez Pline l'Ancien' *Latomus* 16, 628–42.
—— 1957b. *Recueil de texts latins archaïques.* 2nd edn. Paris.
Fabricius, J.A. 1719. *Codex apocryphus novi testamenti.* 2nd edn. Hamburg.
Fahz, L. 1904. *De poetarum romanorum doctrina magica* RGVV ii.3. Giessen.
Fantham, E. 1995. 'Aemilia Pudentilla or a Wealthy Widow's Choice' in Hawley, R. and Levick, B., eds, *Women in Antiquity: New Assessments.* London, 220–32.
Faraone, C.A. 1989. 'Clay Hardens and Wax Melts. Magical Role-reversal in Virgil's Eighth *Eclogue*' *Classical Philology* 84, 294–300.
—— 1991a. 'Binding and Burying the Forces of Evil: The Defensive use of "Voodoo" Dolls in Ancient Greece' *Classical Antiquity* 10, 165–205.
—— 1991b. 'The Agonistic Context of Early Greek Binding Spells' in Faraone, C.A. and Obbink, D., eds, *Magika hiera: Ancient Greek Magic and Religion.* New York, 3–32.
—— 1995a. 'The "Performative Future" in Three Hellenistic Incantations and Theocritus' *Second Idyll*' *Classical Philology* 90, 1–15.
—— 1995b. 'The *mystodokos* and the Dark-eyed Maidens: Multicultural Influences on a Late Hellenistic Incantation' in Meyer and Mirecki 1995, 297–33.
—— 1999. *Ancient Greek Love Magic.* Cambridge, MA.
Faraone, C.A. and Obbink, D., eds 1991. *Magika Hiera: Ancient Greek Magic and Religion.* New York.
Fauth, W. 1975. 'Die Bedeutung der Nekromantie-Szene in Lucans *Pharsalia*' *Rheinisches Museum für Philologie* 118, 325–44.
Felton, D. 1999. *Haunted Greece and Rome.* Austin, TX.
—— 2007. 'The Dead' in Ogden, D., ed. *A Companion to Greek Religion.* London, 86–99.
Fernández, Á.F. 2002. 'Dos prácticas de encantamiento amoroso: El *PGM* IV (296–404) y el *Idilio II* de Teócrito' in Peláez 2002, 91–102.
Festugière, A.J. 1939. 'L'expérience religieuse du médecin Thessalos' *Revue biblique* 48, 45–77. Reprinted in his *Hermétisme et mystique païenne.* Paris, 1967, 141–80.
Fick, N. 1985. 'La magie dans les métamorphoses d'Apulée' *Revue des études latines* 63, 132–47.
Finkel, I.C. 1983–4. 'Necromancy in Ancient Mesopotamia' *Archiv für Orientforschung* 29–30, 1–17.
Flint, V., Gordon, R.L., Luck., G. and Ogden, D. 1999. *The Athlone History of Magic and Witchcraft in Europe* ii. London.
Foley, J.M. 1988. *The Theory of Oral Composition.* Bloomington, IN.
Fowler, R.L. 1995. 'Greek Magic, Greek Religion' *Illinois Classical Studies* 20, 1–

22. Reprinted in Buxton, R.G., ed., *Oxford Readings in Greek Religion*. Oxford, 2000, 317–43.

Frankfurter, D. 1995. 'Narrating Power: The Theory and Practice of the Magical Historiola in Ritual Spells' in Meyer and Mirecki 1995, 457–76.

—— 2001. 'The Perils of Love: Magic and Countermagic in Coptic Egypt' *Journal of the History of Sexuality* 10, 480–500.

Fraser, P.M. 1972. *Ptolemaic Alexandria*. 3 vols. Oxford.

Freeth, T., *et al.* 2006. 'Decoding the Ancient Greek Astronomical Calculator Known as the Antikythera Mechanism' *Nature* 444, 587–91.

Freudenburg, K. 1995. 'Canidia at the Feast of Nasidienus (Hor. S. 2.8.95)' *Transactions of the American Philological Association* 125, 207–19.

Friedrich, H.-V., ed. 1968. *Thessalos von Tralles. Griechisch und lateinisch*. Meisenheim am Glan.

Frontisi-Ducroux, F. 2003. *L'homme-cerf et la femme-araignée*. Paris.

Furley, W.D. 2007. 'Prayers and Hymns' in Ogden, D., ed., *A Companion to Greek Religion*. Oxford, 117–131.

Gager, J.G. 1992. *Curse Tablets and Binding Spells from the Ancient World*. New York.

Gallini, C. 2003. 'Interpretazioni etnologiche di *Cristo si è fermato a Eboli*' in de Donato, G., ed., *Verso I sud del mondo. Carlo Levi a cento anni della nascita*. Rome, 77–82.

Galter, H. ed. 1993. *Die Rolle der Astronomie in den Kulturen Mesopotamiens*. Graz.

Ganschinietz/Ganszyniec, R. 1913. *Hippolytos' Capitel gegen die Magier*, Refut. Haer. IV, 28–42. Texte und Untersuchungen zur Geschichte der altchristlichen Literatur Bd. 39 Heft 2 (Dritte Reihe 9 Bd. Heft 2). Leipzig.

—— 1929. 'De antiquorum psychagogia' *Eos* 32, 557–8.

Gantz, T. 1993. *Early Greek Myth. A Guide to the Literary and Artistic Sources*. Baltimore, MD.

Gentili, B. and Perusino, F., eds 2000. *Medea nella letteratura e nell' arte*. Venice.

Germain, G. 1954. *Genèse de l'Odyssée*. Paris.

Gernet, L. 1981. *The Anthropology of Ancient Greece*. Baltimore, MD.

Giannini, P. 2000. 'Medea nell'epica e nella poesia lirica arcaica e tardo-arcaica' in Gentili and Perusino 2000, 13–28.

Giordano, M., 1999. *La parola efficace. Maledizioni, giuramenti e benedizioni nella Grecia arcaica*. Biblioteca di Quaderni Urbinati di cultura classica 7. Pisa.

Goodchild, R.G. 1953. 'The Ring and the Curse' *Antiquity* 27, 100–2.

Gordon, R. 1987. 'Lucan's Erictho' in Whitby, M., Hardie, P. and Whitby, M., eds, *Homo Viator. Classical Essays for John Bramble*. Bristol, 231–41.

—— 1997. '*Quaedam veritatis umbrae*: Hellenistic Magic and Astrology' in

Engberg-Pedersen, R.T. and Hannested, L., eds, *Conventional Values of the Hellensitic World*. Odense. 128–52.

—— 1999. 'Imagining Greek and Roman Magic' in Flint *et al.* 1999, 159–275.

Gow, A.S.F. 1934. "ΙΥΓΞ 'ΡΟ'ΜΒΟΣ, rhombus, turbo' *Journal of Hellenic Studies* 54, 1–13.

—— 1952. *Theocritus* edited with an introduction, translation and commentary. 2 vols, Cambridge.

Graf, F. 1992. 'An Oracle against Pestilence from a Western Anatolian Town' *Zeitschrift für Papyrologie und Epigraphik* 92, 267–79.

—— 1994 'The Magician's Initiation', *Helios* 21.2, 161–77.

—— 1997. *Magic in the Ancient World*. Cambridge, MA. Translation of *La magie dans l'antiquité gréco-romaine*. Paris, 1994. Note also the German edition, *Gottesnähe und Schadenzauber : die Magie in der griechisch-römischen Antike*. Munich, 1996: a revised version (unlike the English translation) of the French original.

Griffiths, E. 2006. *Medea*. London.

Griffiths, J.G., 1975. *Apuleius of Madauros. The Isis Book* (Met. Book xi). Leiden.

Grignani, M.A. ed. 1998. *Carlo Levi. L'invenzione della verità. Testi e intertesti per* Cristo si è fermato a Eboli. Turin.

Guey, J. 1948. 'Encore la "pluie miraculeuse"' *Revue de philologie* 22, 18–62.

Haddawy, H. trans. 1995. *The Arabian Nights* ii. *Sinbad and Other Popular Stories*. London.

Hainsworth, J.B. 1968. *The Flexibility of the Homeric Formula*. Oxford.

—— 1993. *The Iliad. A Commentary* iii. *Books 9–12*. Cambridge.

Haldane, J.A. 1972. ' "Barbaric cries" (Aesch. *Pers.* 633–79)' *Classical Quarterly* 22, 42–50.

Hall, J. 1981. *Lucian's Satire*. New York.

Halm-Tisserant, M. 1993. *Cannibalisme et immortalité*. Paris.

Handley-Schachler, M. 1992. 'Achaemenid Religion, 521–465 BC,' dissertation, Oxford University.

Hansen, W.H. 1996. *Phlegon of Tralles' Book of Marvels*. Exeter.

Harrison, J.E. 1922. *Prolegomena to the Study of Greek Religion*. Cambridge.

Harrison, S.J. 1996. 'Apuleius' *Metamorphoses*' in Schmeling, G., ed., *The Novel in the Ancient World*. Leiden. 491–516.

—— 1999. ed. *Oxford Readings in the Ancient Novel*. Oxford.

—— 2000. *Apuleius. A Latin Sophist*. Oxford.

Headlam, W. 1902. 'Ghost-raising, Magic and the Underworld' *Classical Review* 16, 52–61.

Heckel, W. 1992. *The Marshals of Alexander's Empire*. London.

—— 2006. *Who's Who in the Age of Alexander the Great*. Oxford.

Heintz, F. 1997. *Simon 'Le magicien': Actes 8, 5–25 et l'accusation de magie contre les prophètes thaumaturges dans l'antiquité*. Paris.

Henrichs, A. 1970. 'Zum Text einiger Zauberpapyri' *Zeitschrift für Papyrologie und Epigraphik* 6, 204–9.

Herzig, O. 1940. 'Lukian als Quelle für die antike Zauberei', dissertation, Tübingen 1933.

Heubeck, A. and Hoekstra, A. 1989. *A Commentary on Homer's* Odyssey ii. Oxford.

Hickman, R. 1938. *Ghostly Etiquette on the Classical Stage*. Iowa Studies in Classical Philology 7. Cedar Rapids, IA.

Hijmans, B.L.,Jr 1994. 'Apuleius Orator: "Pro se de magia" and "Florida"' *Aufstieg und Niedergang der römischen Welt* II.34.2, 1708–84.

Hijmans, B.L., Jr and van der Paardt, R.T., eds 1978. *Aspects of Apuleius' Golden Ass*. Groningen.

Hijmans, B.L., Jr et al. eds 1977–95. *Apuleius Madaurensis. Metamorphoses*. 4 vols, Groningen.

Hoevels, F.E. 1979. *Märchen und Magie in den Metamorphosen des Apuleius von Madaura*. Amsterdam.

Holztrattner, F. 1995. *Poppaea Neronis potens: Studien zu Poppaea Sabina*. Graz.

Homolle, T. 1901. 'Inscriptions d'Amorgos' *Bulletin de correspondance hellénique* 25, 412–56.

Hopfner, T. 1921–4. *Griechisch-ägyptischer Offenbarungszauber. Studien zur Paläographie und Papyruskunde*. 2 vols. Frankfurt.

—— 1922–5. *Fontes historiae religionis aegyptiacae*. 5 vols. Bonn.

Hughes, D.D. 1991. *Human Sacrifice in Ancient Greece*. London.

Hunink, V. 1997. *Apuleius of Madauros. Pro se de magia*. 2 vols edited with a commentary. Amsterdam.

Ingallina, S. 1974. *Orazio e la magia*. Palermo.

Inscriptiones Graecae 1903–. Multiple series, volumes, parts. Berlin.

Irwin, R. 1994. *The Arabian Nights: A Companion*. London.

Isler-Kerényi, C. 2000. 'Immagini di Medea' in Gentili and Perusino 2000, 117–38.

Jacoby, F. 1923–. *Die Fragmente der griechischen Historiker*. Multiple volumes and parts, Leiden.

Jameson, M.H., Jordan, D.R. and Kotansky, R.D. 1993. *A Lex Sacra from Selinus* GRBS supplement. Durham, NC.

Janowitz, N. 2001. *Magic in the Roman World. Pagans, Jews and Christians*. London.

Jasnow, R. 1997. 'The Greek Alexander Romance and Demotic literature' *Journal of Near-Eastern Studies* 56, 95–103.

Jensson, G. 2004. *The Recollections of Encolpius. The* Satyrica *of Petronius as Milesian Fiction*. Ancient Narrative Supplement 2. Groningen.

Johnston, S.I. 1995. 'The Song of the *iynx*: Magic and Rhetoric in *Pythian* 4' *Transactions of the American Philological Association* 125, 177–206.

—— 1999. *Restless dead*. Berkeley, CA.

Jordan, D.R. 1985a. 'A Survey of Greek Defixiones not Included in the Special Corpora' *Greek, Roman and Byzantine Studies* 26, 151–97.
—— 1985b. 'Defixiones from a Well near the Southwest Corner of the Athenian Agora' *Hesperia* 54, 205–55.
—— 1999. 'Three Curse Tablets' in Jordan *et al.* 1999, 115–24.
—— 2000. 'New Greek Curse Tablets (1985–2000) *Greek, Roman and Byzantine Studies* 41, 5–46.
Jordan, D.R., Montgomery, H. and Thomassen, E., eds 1999. *The World of Ancient Magic*. Papers from the Norwegian Institute at Athens 4. Bergen.
Jost, M. 1985. *Sanctuaires et cultes d'Arcadie*. Paris.
Jouan, F. 1981. 'L'évocation des morts dans la tragédie grecque' *Revue de l'histoire des religions* 198, 403–21.
Kagarow, E.G. 1929. *Griechische Fluchtafeln*. Eus Supplement 4. Leopoli.
Kaimakis, D. ed. 1976. *Die Kyraniden*. Meisenheim am Glan.
Karsai, G. 'La magie dans l'*Odyssée*: Circé' in Moreau and Turpin 2000, ii, 185–98.
Kassel, R. and Austin, C. 1983–. *Poetae Comici Graeci. Fragmenta*. 7 vols. Berlin.
Kiefer, A. 1929. *Aretalogische Studien*. Leipzig.
Kingsley, P. 1994. 'Greeks, Shamans and Magi' *Studia Iranica* 23, 187–98.
—— 1995. 'Meetings with Magi: Iranian Themes among the Greeks, from Xanthus of Lydia to Plato's Academy' *Journal of the Royal Asiatic Society* 5, 171–209.
Kippenberg, H.G. 1997. 'Magic in Roman Civil Discourse: Why Rituals Could be Illegal' in Schäfer, P. and Kippenberg, H.G., eds, *Envisioning Magic: A Princeton Seminar and Symposium*. Studies in the History of Religions 75. Leiden.
Kirk, G.S. 1963. *The Songs of Homer*. Cambridge.
Klauck, H.-J. 2003. *Magic and Paganism in Early Christianity*. London. Tranlation of *Magie und Heidentum in der Apostelgeschichte des Lukas*. Stuttgart, 1996.
Koenen, L. 1962. 'Der brennende Horusknabe: Zu einem Zauberspruch des Philinna-Papyrus' *Chronique d' Égypte* 37, 167–74.
Korenjak, M. 1996. *Die Erictshozene in Lukans* Pharsalia: *Einleitung, Text, Übersetzung, Kommentar*. Frankfurt am Main.
Kotansky, R. 1991. 'Incantations and Prayers for Salvation on Inscribed Greek Amulets' in Faraone and Obbink 1991, 107–37.
—— 1994. *The Greek Magical Amulets. The Inscribed Gold, Silver, Copper and Bronze Lamellae*. Part 1: *Published Texts of Known Provenance*. Papyrologica Coloniensia xxii.1. Opladen.
—— 1995. 'Greek Exorcistic Amulets' in Meyer and Mirecki 1995, 243–78.
Kraggerud, E. 1999. 'Samson Eitrem and the Death of Dido: A Literary Reappraisal of a Magical Scene' in Jordan 1999, 103–12.

Krestan, L. and Hermann, A. 1957. 'Cyprianus ii' *Reallexikon für Antike und Christentum* 3, 467–77.

Lancellotti, M.G. 2000. 'Problèmes méthodologiques dans la constitution d'un corpus des gemmes magiques' in Moreau *et al.* 2000, ii, 153–66.

Lane, E.W. trans. 1839–41. *The Thousand and One Nights, Commonly Called in English 'The Arabian Nights Entertainments'*. London.

Lane Fox, R. 1986. *Pagans and Christians*. London.

Lawson, J.C. 1934. 'The Evocation of Darius (Aesch. *Persae* 607–93)' *Classical Quarterly* 28, 79–89.

Leick, G. 2003. *The Babylonians. An Introduction*. London.

Lesky, A. 1931. 'Medeia' *RE* 15, 29–65.

—— 1972. *Die tragische Dichtung der Hellenen*. 3rd edn. Göttingen.

Leutsch, E.L. von and Schneidewin, F.G. 1839–51. *Corpus Paroemiographorum Graecorum*. 2 vols. Göttingen.

Levi, C. 1945. *Cristo si è fermato a Eboli*. Rome.

—— 1947. *Christ Stopped at Eboli*. New York. English trans. of Levi 1945. Text cited by pages of the 1982 Penguin edition, London.

Lewy, H. 1978. *The Chaldaean Oracles and Theurgy*. 2nd edn. Paris.

Lexicon Iconographicum Mythologiae Classicae 1981–. 9 + vols. Zurich and Munich. [*LIMC*]

Lightfoot, J.L. 1999 *Parthenius of Nicaea*. Oxford.

Lipinski, E. 2000. *The Aramaeans: Their Ancient History, Culture, Religion*. Leuven.

Lipsius, R.A. and Bonnet, M. eds 1891–1903. *Acta apostolorum apocrypha*. 2 vols in 3 parts. Leipzig.

Llamosas, V.M. 2002. '*De morbo sacro* 1,23 o la vision negative del mago' in Peláez 2002, 155–66.

Longo, V. 1969. *Aretalogie nel mondo greco*. i. *Epigraphi e papiri*. Genoa.

Lopez Jimeno, M.d. A. 1991. *Las tabellae defixionis de la Sicilia griega*. Amsterdam.

—— 1999. *Nuevas* tabellae defixiones *áticas*. Amsterdam.

—— 2002. 'La magia maléfica en la Antigüedad Griega: Las *Tabellae defixionis* de época clásica y de época imperial' in Peláez 2002, 121–32.

Lord, A.B. 1960. *The Singer of Tales*. Cambridge, MA.

Luck, G. 1962. *Hexen und Zauberei in der römischen Dichtung*. Zurich.

—— 1999. 'Witches and Sorcerers in Classical Literature' in Flint *et al.* 1999, 91–158.

—— 2006. *Arcana Mundi. Magic and the Occult in the Greek and Roman Worlds*. 2nd edn. Baltimore, MD. (1st edn. 1985).

Ludwich, A., ed. 1897. *Eudociae Augustae reliquiae*. Leipzig.

MacDowell, D.M. trans. and ed. 1982. *Gorgias. Encomium of Helen*. Bristol.

Macleod, M.D. 1979. 'Lucian's Activities as a *misalazōn*' *Philologus* 123, 326–8.

Mainoldi, C. 1984. *L'image du loup et du chien dans la Grèce ancienne d'Homère à Platon*. Paris.

Majercik, R. 1989. *The Chaldaean Oracles: Text, Translation and Commentary*. Leiden.

Mallory, J.P. and Adams, D.Q. 2006. *The Oxford Introduction to Proto-Indo-European and the Proto-Indo-European World*. New York.

Mankin, D. 1995. *Horace. Epodes*. Cambridge.

Manning, C.E. 1970. 'Canidia in the *Epodes* of Horace' *Mnemosyne* 23, 393–401.

Marinatos, N. 1995. 'Circe and Liminality: Ritual Background and Narrative Structure' in Andersen, Ø. and Dickie, M., eds, *Homer's World: Fiction, Tradition and Reality*. Bergen, 133–40.

—— 2000. *The Goddess and the Warrior: The Naked Goddess and the Mistress of Animals in Early Greek Religion*. London.

Martin, M. 2005. *Magie et magiciens dans le monde gréco-romain*. Paris.

Martindale, C.A. 1980. 'Lucan's *nekuia*' in Deroux, C., ed., *Studies in Latin Literature and Roman History* Coll. Latomus 168. Brussels, 367–77.

Mason, H.J. 1999. '*Fabula graecanica*: Apuleius and his Greek sources' in Harrison, S.J., ed. *Oxford Readings in the Roman Novel*. Oxford, 217–36.

Massoneau, E. 1934. *La magie dans l'antiquité romaine*. Paris. Re-edited version of the same author's *Le crime de la magie dans le droit romain*. Paris, 1933.

Masters, J. 1992. *Poetry and Civil War in Lucan's Bellum Civile*. Cambridge.

Mastronarde, D.M. 2002. *Euripides. Medea*. Cambridge.

Meier, G. 1937. *Die assyrische Beschwörungs Sammlung Maqlû*. Archiv für Orientforschung Beiheft ii. Berlin.

Meiggs, R. and Lewis, D. eds 1988. *A Selection of Greek Historical Inscriptions to the End of the Fifth Century BC*. 2nd edn. Oxford.

Merkelbach, R. 1954. *Die Quellen des griechischen Alexanderromans*. Munich.

Méthy, N. 2000. 'Magie, religion et philosophie au second siècle de notre ère. À propos du dieu-roi d'Apulée' in Moreau and Turpin 2000, iii, 85–108.

Meuli, K. 1921. *Odyssee und Argonautika*. Berlin. Reprinted at his *Gesammelte Schriften*. Basel, 1975, ii, 593–676.

Meyer, M. and Mirecki, P., eds 1995. *Ritual Power in the Ancient World*. Leiden.

Meyer, M. and Smith, R., eds 1994. *Ancient Christian Magic. Coptic Texts of Ritual Power*. San Francisco.

Migne, J.-P. ed. 1841–64. *Patrologiae Cursus, Series Latina*. Paris.

—— ed. 1857–66. *Patrologiae Cursus, Series Graeca*. Paris.

Molt, M. 1938. *Ad Apulei Madaurensis* Metamorphoseon *librum primum commentarius exegeticus*. Groningen.

Mommsen, T. ed. 1894. *Isidore Chronica at Monumenta Germaniae Historica, Auctores Antiquissimi* 11.2. Berlin, 424–81.

Moreau, A. 1994. *Le mythe de Jason et Médée. Le va-nu-pied et la sorcière*. Paris.

Moreau, A. and Turpin, J.-C., eds 2000. *La magie*. 4 vols. Montpellier.

Moret, J.-M. 1991. 'Circé tisseuse sur les vases du Cabirion' *Revue archéologique* 1991, 227–66.

Morgan, J.R. 1996. 'Heliodorus' in Schmeling, G., ed. *The Novel in the Ancient World*. Leiden, 417–56.

Moss, L.W. and Cappannari, S.C. 1960. 'Folklore and Medicine in an Italian Village' *The Journal of American Folklore* 73, 95–102.

Motte, A. 2000. 'À propos de la magie chez Platon: l'antithèse sophiste-philosophe vue sous l'angle de la pharmacie et de la sorcellerie' in Moreau and Turpin 2000, i, 267–92.

Moyer, I. 2003. 'Thessalos of Tralles and Cultural Exchange' in Noegel, S., Walker, J. and Wheeler, B. eds. *Magic in History: Prayer, Magic, and the Stars in the Ancient and Late Antique World*. University Park, TX, 39–56.

Müller, L., ed. 1932. *In Luciani Philopseuden commentarius*. Eus Supplement vol. 13. Leopoli.

Muro, P. 2002. 'Sobre las magas romanas' in Peláez 2002, 233–43.

Myers, S.K. 1996. 'The Poet and the Procuress: the *lena* in Latin Love Elegy' *Journal of Roman Studies* 86, 1–21.

Nagy, G. 1974. *Comparative Studies in Greek and Indic Meter*. Cambridge.

—— 1990. *Greek Mythology and Poetics*. Ithaca, NY.

Nardi, E. 1960. *Case 'infestate da spiriti' e diritto Romano e moderno*. Milan.

Nenci, G. 1994. *Erodoto. Le storie v*. Verona.

Nock, A.D. 1950. 'Tertullian and the *ahori*' *Vigiliae Christianae* 4, 129–41. Reprinted in his *Essays on Religion and the Ancient World*, ed. Stewart, Z. 2 vols. 1972. Oxford.

Novara, A. 2000. 'Magie, amour et humeur chez Properce' in Moreau and Turpin 2000, iii, 15–44.

O'Connor, E.M. 1989. *Symbolum Salacitatis. A Study of the God Priapus as a Literary Character*. Studien zur klassischen Philologie, Band 40. Frankfurt am Main.

Oesterreich, T.K. 1930. *Possession, Demonical and Other: Among Primitive Races in Antiquity, the Middle Ages and Modern Times*. London. Translation of *Die Besessenheit*. Langsalza, 1921.

Ogden, D. 1999a. 'Binding Spells: Curse Tablets and Voodoo Dolls in the Greek and Roman worlds' in Flint *et al.* 1999, 1–90.

—— 1999b. *Polygamy, Prostitutes and Death. The Hellenistic Dynasties*. London.

—— 2000. Combined Review of Faraone 1999 and Giordano 1999, *Classical Review* 50, 476–8.

—— 2001. *Greek and Roman Necromancy*. Princeton, NJ.

—— 2002a. *Magic, Witchcraft and Ghosts in the Greek and Roman Worlds. A Sourcebook*. New York.

—— 2002b. Combined Review of Dickie 2001 and Moreau and Turpin 2000, *Classical Review* 52, 129–33.

—— 2002c. 'Lucan's Sextus Pompeius Episode: Its Necromantic, Political and Literary Background' in Powell, A. and Welch, K., eds, *Sextus Pompeius*. London, 249–71.
—— 2002d. 'Three Evocations of the Dead with Pausanias' in Hodkinson, S., ed., *Beyond the Spartan Mirage*. London, 111–33.
—— 2004. 'Eucrates and Demainete' *Classical Quarterly* 54, 484–93.
—— 2005. 'The Function of the Pellichus Sequence at Lucian *Philopseudes* 18–20' *Scripta Classica Israelica* 24, 1–19.
—— 2006a. 'Lucian's Tale of the Sorcerer's Apprentice in Context' in Szpakowska, K., ed. *Through a Glass Darkly. Magic, Dreams and Prophecy in Ancient Egypt*. Swansea. 121–43.
—— 2006b. 'Defixiones' in Golden, R.M., ed. *Encyclopedia of Witchcraft: The Western Tradition*. 4 vols. Santa Barbara, CA, i, 255.
—— 2006c. 'Greek Magical Papyri' in Golden, R.M., ed. *Encyclopedia of Witchcraft: The Western Tradition*. 4 vols. Santa Barbara, CA, ii, 456–7.
—— 2007a. *In Search of the Sorcerer's Apprentice. The Traditional Tales of Lucian's* Lover of Lies. Swansea.
—— 2007b. 'Magic in the Severan period' in Swain, S., Elsner, J. and Harrison, S.J., eds *Severan Culture*. Cambridge, 454–65.
—— 2008. *Perseus*. London.
—— forthcoming a. 'How to Marry a Courtesan in the Macedonian courts' in Erskine, A. and Llewellyn-Jones, L., eds *Creating a Hellenistic World*.
—— forthcoming b. 'A War of Witches at the court of Philip II?' *Archaia Makedonia/Ancient Macedonia* 7, 425–37.
Olivieri, A. *et al.*, eds 1898–1936. *Catalogus codicum astrologorum graecorum*. 12 vols. Brussels.
Ortoli, F. 1883. *Les contes populaires de l'Ile de Corse*. Paris.
Otto, W.F. 1923. *Die Manen oder Von den Urformen des Totenglaubens*. Berlin.
Paetz, B. 1970. *Kirke und Odysseus*. Berlin.
Page, D.L. 1938. *Euripides. Medea*. Oxford.
—— 1942. *Greek Literary Papyri*. i. Loeb's Classical Library, Cambridge, MA.
—— 1973. *Folktales in Homer's* Odyssey. Cambridge, MA.
Parker, W.H. 1988. *Priapea: Poems for a Phallic God*. London.
Parry, H. 1992. *Thelxis: Magic and Imagination in Greek Myth and Poetry*. Lanham, MD.
Parry, M. 1971. *The Making of Homeric Verse. The Collected Papers of Milman Parry*. Oxford.
Patrologia Orientalis 1903–. Paris.
Pauly, A., Wissowa, G. and Kroll, W. eds 1894–1972. *Real-Encyclopädie der klassischen Altertumswissenschaft*. Multiple volumes and parts. Stuttgart.
Peláez, J., ed. 2002. *El dios que hechiza y encanta*. Córdoba.
Penglase, C. 1994. *Greek Myths and Mesopotamia. Parallels and Influence in the Homeric Hymns and Hesiod*. London.

Perry, B.E. 1967. *The Ancient Romances*. Berkeley, CA.

Pharr, C. 1932. 'The Interdiction of Magic in Roman law' *Transactions of the American Philological Association* 63, 269–95.

Phillips, C.R., III, 1991. '*Nullum crimen sine lege*: Socioreligious Sanctions on Magic' in Faraone and Obbink 1991, 260–76.

Pinch, G. 1994. *Magic in Ancient Egypt*. London.

Pirenne-Delforge, V. 1993. 'L'iynge dans le discours mythique et les procédures magiques' *Kernos* 6, 277–89.

Pralon, D. 2000. 'Théocrite, *La magicienne*' in Moreau and Turpin 2000, i, 307–26.

Preisendanz, K. 1935. 'Nekydaimon' *RE* 16.2, 2240–66.

—— 1972. 'Fluchtafel (Defixion)' *Reallexikon für Antike und Christentum* 8, 1–29.

Preisendanz, K. and Henrichs, A., 1973–4. *Papyri Graecae Magicae. Die griechischen Zauberpapyri*. 2nd edn. 2 vols. Stuttgart. [*PGM*]

Price, D. de S. 1974. 'Gears from the Greeks: The Antikythera Mechanism – A Calendar Computer from *c*. 80 BC' *Transactions of the American Philological Association* 64, 1–70.

Puiggali, J. 1986. 'Une histoire de fantôme (Xénophon d'Ephèse V 7)' *Rheinisches Museum für Philologie* 129, 321–8.

Radermacher, L. 1915. *Die Erzählungen der Odyssee*. Sitzungberichte der Akademie der Wissenschaft in Wien clxxviii. Vienna.

—— 1927 *Griechische Quellen zur Faustsage. Der Zauberer Cyprianus. Die Erzählung des Helladius. Theophilus*. Sitzungberichte der Akademie der Wissenschaft in Wien 206.4. Vienna.

Reinach, T. 1907. 'Hérodote et le Talmud' *Revue des études juives* 54, 271–3.

Reiner, E. 1966. 'La magie babylonienne' in *Le monde du sorcier*. Sources orientales 7. Paris, 69–98.

—— 1987. 'Magic Figurines, Amulets and Talismans' in Porada, E., hon., Farkas, A.E. *et al.* eds, *Monsters and Demons in the Ancient and Medieval Worlds*. Mainz, 27–36.

Reitzenstein, R. 1906. *Hellenistische Wundererzählungen*. Leipzig.

Renehan, R. 1992. 'The Staunching of Odysseus' Blood: The Healing Power of Magic' *American Journal of Philology* 113, 1–4.

Richer, N. 1994. 'Aspects des funérailles à Sparte' *Cahiers du Centre G. Glotz* 5, 51–96.

Richter, A. 1970. *Virgile, la huitième bucolique*. Paris.

Ritner, R.K. 1993. *The Mechanics of Ancient Egyptian Magical Practice*. Chicago.

Robert, L. 1980. *À travers l'Asie Mineure. Poètes et prosateurs, monnaies grecques, voyageurs et géographie*. BÉFAR 239. Paris.

—— 1981. 'Le serpent Glycon d'Abōnouteichos à Athènes et Artémis d'Ephèse à Rome' *Comptes-rendus de séances de l'Académie des Inscriptions et Belles*

Lettres lettres 513–35; reprinted in his *Opera minora selecta*. Amsterdam, 1989. v, no. 127.

Roccati, A. and Siliotti, A, eds 1987. *La magia in Egitto ai tempi dei Faraoni*. Modena.

Rohde, E. 1925. *Psyche. The Cult of Souls and Belief in Immortality among the Greeks*. London. Translated from the 8th German edition.

Römer, F. 1987. 'Vom Spuk zur Politik: Der Gespensterbrief des Jüngeren Plinius' *Wiener humanistische Blätter* 29, 26–36.

Roscher, W.H., ed. 1884–1937. *Ausführliches Lexicon der griechischen und römischen Mythologie*. 7 vols. Leipzig.

Russell, W.M.S. 1981. 'Greek and Roman Ghosts' in Davidson, H.R.E. and Russel, W.M.S., eds, *The Folkore of Ghosts*. Cambridge, 193–213.

Ryan, R.J. 1993. *The Golden Legend. Readings on the Saints* (trans. Jacobus de Voragine). Princeton, NJ.

Sandy, G. 1997. *The Greek World of Apuleius. Apuleius and the Second Sophistic*. Leiden.

Schalit, A. 1969. *König Herodes. Der Mann und sein Werk*. Berlin.

Schmeling, G. ed. 1996. *The Novel in the Ancient World*. Leiden.

Schmidt, M. 1992. 'Medeia' *LIMC* vi. 1, 386–98.

Scholl, A. 1994. 'Πολυτάλαντα μνημεία. Zur literarischen und monumentale Überlieferung aufwendiger Grabmäler im spätklassischen Athen' *Jahrbuch des deutschen archäologischen Instituts* 109, 239–71.

Schotes, H.-A. 1969. *Stoische Physik, Psychologie und Theologie bei Lucan*. Bonn.

Schuster, M. 1930. 'Der Werwolf und die Hexen' *Wiener Studien* 48, 149–78.

Schwartz, J., ed. 1951. *Lucien de Samosate. Philopseudès et De morte Peregrini, avec introduction et commentaire*. Textes d'études. Publ. fac. lettres Univ. Strasbourg, no. 12. Paris. 2nd edn, Paris 1963.

—— 1981. 'Papyri Graecae Magicae und magische Gemmen' in Vermasseren, M.J., ed., 1981. *Die orientalischem Religionen im Römerreich*. EPRO 93. Leiden, 485–509.

Schweizer, H. 1937. *Aberglaube und Zauberei bei Theokrit*. Basel.

Scobie, A. 1969. *Aspects of the Ancient Romance and its Heritage. Essays on Apuleius, Petronius and the Greek romances*. Beiträge zur klassischen Philologie. Heft. 30. Meisenheim am Glan.

—— 1975. *Apuleius Metamorphoses I. A commentary*. Meisenheim am Glan.

—— 1978. 'Strigiform Witches in Roman and Other Cultures' *Fabula* 19, 74–101.

—— 1983. *Apuleius and Folklore. Toward a History of ML 3045, AaTh 567, 449A*. London.

Scurlock, J.A. 1995. 'Magical Uses of Ancient Mesopotamian Festivals of the Dead' in Meyer and Mirecki 1995, 93–107.

Segal, C.P. 1968. 'Circean temptations' *Transactions of the American Philological Association* 99, 419–42.

—— 1973. 'Simaetha and the *iunx* (Theocritus *Idyll* ii)' *Quaderni urbinati di cultura classica* 17, 32–43.
Shelley, M.W. 1818. *Frankenstein* or *The Modern Prometheus*. London.
Smith, J.Z. 1978. *Map is not Territory. Studies in the History of Religions*. Leiden.
Smith, K.F. 1894. 'An Historical Study of the Werewolf in Literature' *Publications of the Modern Language Association of America* 9.1, 1–42.
Smith, M. 1978. *Jesus the Magician*. San Francisco.
—— 1979. 'Relations between Magical Papyri and the Magical Gems' *Papyrologica Bruxellensia* 18, 129–36.
Smith, W.D. 1965. 'So-called Possession in pre-Christian Greece' *Transactions of the American Philological Association* 96, 403–26.
Snell, B. 1964. *Scenes from Greek Drama*. Berkeley, CA.
Snell, B., Kannicht, R. and Radt, S. eds 1971–2004. *Tragicorum Graecorum Fragmenta*. 5 vols. Göttingen. [*TrGF*]
Solin, H. 1968. *Eine neue Fluchtafel aus Ostia*. Commentationes humanarum literarum. Societas scientiarum Fenica 42.3. Helsinki. NB pp. 23–31: 'Eine Übersicht über lateinische Fluchtafeln, die sich nicht bei Audollent und Besnier finden'.
Solmsen, F. and Fraenkel, E., eds 1966. *Inscriptiones Graecae ad inlustrandas dialectos selectae*. Stuttgart.
Stadler, H. 1913. 'Hippomanes' *RE* viii.2, 1879–82.
Stern, J. 1989. 'Demythologisation in Herodotus' *Eranos* 87, 13–20.
Stramaglia, A. 1999. *Res inauditae, incredulae. Storie di fantasmi nel mondo greco-latino*. Bari.
Strohmaier, G. 1976. 'Übersehenes zur Biographie Lukians' *Philologus* 120, 117–22.
Strubbe, J. 1997. *'APAI' 'EΠITY'MBIOI. Imprecations Against Desecrators of the Grave in the Greek Epitaphs of Asia Minor. A Catalogue*. Bonn.
Susanetti, D. 1999. 'Amori tra fantasmi, mummie e lenoni: Sicilia e Magna Grecia nel romanzo di Senofonte Efesio' in Avezzù, G. and Pianezzola, E., eds *Sicilia e Magna Grecia. Spazio reale e spazio immaginario nella letteratura greca e latina*. Padua. 127–69.
Swain, S. 1996. *Hellenism and Empire. Language, Classicism and Power in the Greek World, AD 50–250*. Oxford.
Szpakowska, K., ed. 2006. *Through a Glass Darkly. Magic, Dreams and Prophecy in Ancient Egypt*. Swansea.
Tavenner, E. 1916. *Studies in Magic from Latin Literature*. New York.
—— 1933. 'Iynx and Rhombus' *Transactions of the American Philological Association* 64, 109–27.
Thompson, S. 1955–8. *Motif-Index of Folk-Literature*. 2nd edn. 6 vols. Bloomington, IN.
Thraede, K. 1967. 'Exorzismus' *Reallexikon für Antike und Christentum* 7, 44–117.

Tomlin, R.S.O. 1988. 'The curse tablets' in Cunliffe, B., ed., *The Temple of Sulis Minerva at Bath* ii. *The Finds from the Sacred Spring.* OUCA monograph no. 16. Oxford. 59–277. Also published separately (but preserving original pagination) as *Tabellae Sulis: Roman Inscribed Tablets of Tin and Lead from the Sacred Spring at Bath* (fascicule 1 of OUCA monograph no. 16).

Totti, M. 1985. *Ausgewählte Texte der Isis- und Sarapis-Religion.* Studia Epigraphica 12. Hildesheim.

Touchefeu-Meynier, O. 1961. 'Ulysse et Circé' *Revue des études anciennes* 93, 264–70.

Tropper, J. 1989. *Nekromantie: Totenbefragung im Alten Orient und Alten Testament (AOAT)* 223. Neukirchen-Vluyn.

Trumpf, J. 1958. 'Fluchtafel und Rachepuppe' *Mitteilungen des deutschen archäologischen Instituts. Athenische Abteilung* 73, 94–102.

Trzcionka, S. 2007. *Magic and the Supernatural in Fourth-Century Syria.* London.

Tupet, A.-M. 1976. *La magie dans la poésie latine: i: des origins à la fin du règne d'Auguste.* Paris.

—— 1986. 'Rites magiques dans l'antiquité romaine' *Aufstieg und Niedergang der römischen Welt* ii 16.3. 2591–675.

—— 1988. 'La scène de magie dans la Pharsale: essai de problématique' in Le Bonniec, H., hon., Porte, D. and Néraudau, J.-P., eds, *Hommages H. Le Bonniec.* Brussels, 419–27.

van der Paardt, R.T. 1971. *Apuleius. The Metamorphoses* III. Amsterdam.

van Thiel, H. 1972. *Der Eselroman.* Zetemata 54. 2 vols. Munich.

Vermeule, E. 1979. *Aspects of Death in Early Greek Art and Poetry.* Berkeley, CA.

Versnel, H.S. 1985. ' "May he not be able to sacrifice...": Concerning a Curious Formula in Greek and Latin curses' *Zeitschrift für Papyrologie und Epigraphik* 58, 247–69.

—— 1991. 'Beyond Cursing: The Appeal to Justice in Judicial Prayers' in Faraone and Obbink 1991, 60–106.

Viansino, G. 1995. *Marco Anneo Lucano. La guerra civile (Farsaglia). Libri VI–X.* Verona: Mondadori.

Victor, U. 1997. *Lukian von Samosata. Alexandros oder der Lügenprophet.* Leiden.

Villeneuve, R. 1963. *Loups-garous et vampires.* Paris.

Volpilhac, J. 1978. 'Lucain et l'Égypte dans la scène de nécromancie de la *Pharsale* vi. 413–830 à la lumière des papyri grecs magiques' *Revue des études latines* 56, 272–88.

Voutiras, E. 1998. Διονύσοφῶ~ντος γάμοι. *Marital life and magic in fourth-century Pella.* Amsterdam.

—— 1999. 'Euphemistic Names for the Powers of the Nether World' in Jordan et al. 1999, 73–82.

Vrugt-Lentz, J.T. 1960. *Mors immatura*. Groningen.
Waegeman, M. 1987. *Amulet and Alphabet: Magical Amulets in the First Book of Cyranides*. Amsterdam.
Walcot, P. 1966. *Hesiod and the Near East*. Cardiff.
Ward, J.O. 1981. 'Women, Witchcraft and Social Patterning in the Later Roman Law Codes' *Prudentia* 13, 99–118.
Waszink, J.H. 1954. 'Biothanati' *Reallexikon für Antike und Christentum* 2, 391–4.
Watkins, C. 1995. *How to Kill a Dragon. Aspects of Indo-European Poetics*. Oxford.
Watson, L.C. 1993. 'Horace *Epode* 5: Theme and Purpose' in Pinsent, J., hon., Jocelyn, H.D. and Hurt, H., eds, *Tria Lustra: Essays and Notes Presented to John Pinsent* Liverpool Classical Papers, no. 3. Liverpool, 269–82.
—— 2003. *A Commentary on Horace's* Epodes. Oxford.
Weinreich, O. 1909. *Antike Heiligungswunder: Untersuchungen zum Wunderglauben der Griechen und der Römer* RGVV 8.1. Giessen.
—— 1921. 'Alexander der Lügenprophet und seiner Stellung in der Religiosität des zweiten Jahrhunderts nach Christus' *Neue Jahrbücher für das klassiche Altertum* 47, 129–51.
Wells, H.G. 1896. *The Island of Dr Moreau*. London.
Wendland, P. 1911. 'Antike Geister- und Gespenstergeschichten' in Siebs, T., ed., *Festschrift zur Jahrhundertfeier der Universität zu Breslau, im Namen der schlesischen Gesellschaft für Volkskunde*. Breslau.
West, M.L. 1966. *Hesiod. Theogony*. Oxford.
—— 1997. *The East Face of Helicon. West Asiatic Elements in Early Greek Poetry and Myth*. Oxford.
—— 2002. 'Eumelos: A Corinthian Epic cycle?' *Journal of Hellenic Studies* 122, 109–33.
—— 2003. *Greek Epic Fragments*. Loeb's Classical Library. Cambridge, MA.
—— 2007. *Indo-European Poetry and Myth*. Oxford.
Whitmarsh, T. 2001. *Greek Literature and the Roman Empire. The Politics of Imitation*. Oxford.
Wide, S. 1909. "*Aōroi biaiothánatoi*' *Archiv für Religionswissenschaft* 12, 224–33.
Wildhaber, R. 1951. 'Kirke und die Schweine' in Meuli, K., hon., *Festschrift K. Meuli* Basel, 233–6.
Winkler, J.J. 1980. 'Lollianos and the desperadoes' *Journal of Hellenic Studies* 100, 155–81.
Wortmann, D. 1968. 'Neue magische Texte' *Bonner Jahrbucher* 168, 56–111.
Wünsch, R. 1897. *Defixionum tabellae [Atticae]*, *IG* iii.3 Appendix. Berlin. *Guide* no. 63 [*DTA*]. NB 'Atticae' is not part of the published title of this volume, but is conventionally added to distinguish it from Audollent 1904.
—— 1898. *Sethianische Verfluchungstafeln aus Rom*. Leipzig.

Xella, P. ed. 1976. *Magia. Studi di storia delle religioni in memoria di R. Garosi.* Rome.
Yarnall, J. 1994. *Transformations of Circe. History of an Enchantress.* Urbana, IL.
Ziebarth, E. 1934. 'Neue Verfluchungstafeln aus Attika, Boiotien und Euboia' *Sitzungberichte der Preussichen Akademie der Wissenschaften. Philologisch-historische Klasse* [no serial no.] 1022–34, with plates 1–3.
Zintzen, C. 1976. 'Geister (Dämonen)' *Reallexikon für Antike und Christentum* 9, 640–67.

Index

Abantiphocus 84
Abonouteichos *see* Alexander of Abonouteichos
abortionists 52, 179
Abra 132–3
Absoris 27, 29
Acastus 156
Acestor 142
Acheron 9, 148, 155
Achilles 112–13, 148, 151
Acts, Book of, 115
Admetus 157, 159
Aea 30
Aeacus 53
Aeaea 7, 30
Aeetes 27
Aegae (Cilicia) 109
Aegeus 29, 32–3
Aelian 65, 152
Aeschylus 24, 32, 36–7
Aeson 28–31, 34–6
Aesop 57, 65, 73
Aetolia 1, 64, 166
Agamede 29, 36, 42, 177
Agasibolos 142
Aglaidas 87, 138
Agrippa 85
Agrippina 154–5
agyrtes 24
Ahura-Mazda 78
Aigialeus 153
Alcestis 157, 159
alchemy 97
Alexander of Abonouteichos 105–9, 114

Alexander the Great 39, 78–9, 91, 93, 108, 135, 152, 155; see also *Alexander Romance*
Alexander Romance 91, 95, 109, 135, 152; *see also* Nectanebo
Alexicles 120
Aliano 71–5
Altenburg-Petronell 131
Ammon 92–3
Ammonion 137
Amorgos 143
amulets 3–4, 20, 26, 47, 71, 84, 86–7, 101–2, 104, 116, 126, 129–39, 144; *see also* rings
Anastasi, Giovanni 115
Androcles 153
Ansky 169
Antaura 131–4
Antheira 192
Anthia 167
Anthimus, St 89
Anticythera mechanism 94–5
Antinoopolis 116, 159
Antinous 116, 158–9, 167
Antioch 87
Antoninus Pius 86, 108
aornos 78
Aphrodite 13, 26, 32, 42, 129–30
Apollo 105–6, 108, 157, 163
Apollodorus 16, 20–1, 32
Apollonius of Rhodes 16, 20, 27, 31, 40, 75
Apollonius of Tyana 109–14, 117–19, 126, 151, 160–4, 167–8; Old Serving Woman of, 109–10, 117, 126

220 INDEX

Apsyrtus 16, 27
Apuleius 4, 18, 52, 60–6, 69, 71, 74–6, 95, 138, 153
Apusorus 84
Arabian Nights 17, 171
Arabos 24, 36, 174, 190
Arcadia, Arcadians 41, 57, 65, 142
Archonides 152–3
Ares 158, 166
aretalogy 59–61, 69, 146, 181
Argonauts 30; *see also* Apollonius of Rhodes, Jason, Medea
Ariadne 41, 136
Arignotus 59, 104–6
Ariminum 50
Aristomenes (Apuleius) 62–6
Aristomenes (comic poet) 174
Aristophanes 22, 26, 37
Armenians 155
Arnouphis 86
Arrhidaeus, lieutenant of Philip II 164
Arrhidaeus, son of Philip II 136
Artayctes 156–7
Artemis 28, 39, 40, 131, 133–4
Asclepius 60, 96, 105–7, 109, 187
asses 60–2, 125
Assyrians 42, 78–9, 84, 86, 91, 114
Asterius 89
astrolabe 94–5
astrology 78, 84–5, 92–6, 98, 116, 135; *see also* Chaldaeans, divination
Athenaeus 79, 155
Athene Chalkioikos 147
Athenians, Athens 4, 12, 22, 24–5, 29, 31, 34, 79, 86, 139, 147, 155–6, 158
Athenodorus 105
Atossa 24
Augustine, St 149
Augustus 59, 85, 108
Autolycus, sons of, 45
Avernus 51, 79, 147

Baal 78

Babylon, Babylonians 59, 78–86, 91, 93, 95, 110, 114, 155–6; *see also* Chaldaeans
Bacchis 90
Baiae 154
Bath 140
bawds 45, 50, 60, 70, 90; *see also* courtesans
beaver 63
Bedr Basim 171
Beirut 159–60
Belle dame sans merci 14
Bessa, old woman of, 90, 98–100
biaiothanatoi 168; *see also* restlessness
binding 1, 43, 47, 49, 63, 66, 70, 72, 75, 94, 118, 126, 129–30, 137–44, 158; *see also* curses
birds 119–20; birdlessness 79, 155
Bitos, Bitys 189
Black Sea 27, 44, 91, 108, 147
Boccaccio 69
Body-parts 16, 45–6, 51–2, 66, 68–9, 75
Bolus of Mendes 83, 97
Brahmins 110
breath 46, 49, 55, 59, 81–3, 89, 119
Byrrhena 66

Caesar 51–2, 55
Caesarea Trocetta 108
Cain 88
Calasiris 98–9
Callisthenes see *Alexander Romance*
Calypso 11–12, 18–19, 23, 65
Canidia 46–51, 62, 75, 77, 160
cannibalism 17, 48, 54
Cappadocians 58, 109
Caracalla 109
Carnuntum 131
Caterina, Donna 72
Cato 44–5
Catullus 50
cauldrons 8, 28, 30–1, 35–7, 45, 46, 180

INDEX

Celsus 103–4, 113
Cerberus 120, 150–1
Ceryx 121–3
Chalcedon 105
Chaldaeans 34, 37–8, 77–86, 103–4, 114; Chaldaean Oracles 85; see also Babylonians
Charicleia 98–9
charioteers 139
Charito 164–6
Charon 53, 80
Charybdis 11–12
Child-sacrifice 47–9, 158–60, 166
Choaspes 80
Christ 87–8, 101–4, 109, 111–14, 132–3; anti–Christ 103
Christ stopped at Eboli 71–6
Christians, Christianity 3, 82–3, 85, 89–90, 97, 100–4, 107, 111, 113–15, 128, 131–4, 149–50, 163
Christmas Day 73
Chrysis 120, 138
Cicero 65, 160
Cillus 149
Circe 7–27, 30, 32, 34–6, 41–2, 44–5, 48–9, 62, 65, 77, 95, 111, 148, 164
Claudius 85
Clement of Alexandria 23
Clement of Rome 97, 159
Cleodemus 59, 120
Cleomenes I of Sparta 152–3
Cleonice 146–7, 155
Cleopatra 39
Clodia 50
cockerel 143
Colchis 27, 29–31, 33, 78
Commodus 86
confession 59–60
Constantius II 85
Constantius of Lyon 105
Constanza 108
cooking 35; see also cauldrons
Coptic 115

Coptus 122
Corcyra, Corcyreans 111
Corinth 28–9, 31, 36, 104, 148, 153, 155, 161, 163, 167
Cornelius Hispalus 84
Corsica 14
Cos 39
courtesans 12, 43, 45, 70, 90, 139, 156, 167, 191; see also bawds
cranes 107
Crateia 154
Craterus 164, 196
Creon 28–9, 31, 33, 36, 47
Creophylus 31, 36
Cresimus 44
Crete 27, 153
Crop-charming 44
Culex 149
curses, curse tablets 3–4, 41, 47–8, 66, 70, 75, 89, 103, 115–16, 129–31, 136–45, 191; see also binding
Cyclops 7, 17, 59
Cynics 79, 161–2
Cyprian of Antioch 87–90, 184–5; *Cyprian and Justina* 87–90
Cyranides 20, 86–7, 101
Cyrene 176

Dactyls 24, 36–7
Daphnis 43–4
Datius, bishop of Milan 105
dead, restless 19–20, 52, 57, 75, 125, 147, 151, 158, 168; see also ghosts
deer 13, 53, 131, 133
defixiones 138; see also binding, curse tablets
Deianeira 49
Delphi, Delphians 55, 163
Delphis 39–45, 50, 136
Demaenete 150–1
Demeas 120
Demeter 139, 143–4
Democritus 83, 97

Demogorgon 54
demons 20, 59, 66, 70, 80, 85–89, 93, 97, 100–4, 109–12, 116–18, 120–2, 125, 131–4, 137–8, 141, 147, 159, 162–3, 168
Demostratus 164–6
Demotic 115
Dia 41
dichotomies, exhaustive 41, 141
Dickie, Matthew 21, 23, 25, 75
Dictynna 111
Dido 48, 100, 150
Dio Cassius 85, 109, 158–9
Diogenes Laertius 79, 104
Dionysophon 141–2
Dionysus 22, 28–9, 32
dislocation 44–5
Disney 123
divination 24–5, 36–7, 51–3, 55, 79, 85, 92, 94, 96, 99, 116, 124, 159–60, 179; *see also* necromancy
dogs 7, 12–13, 20, 40, 44, 47–8, 52–3, 56, 69, 105, 111–12, 117, 121, 132, 143, 150–1, 184
dolls 33–4, 36, 39–43, 47, 58–9, 94, 99, 116, 119–20, 135, 140, 157, 178
Domitian 109, 160
Donatus, commentator on Terence 160–1
Donatus, St 83
dragons 2, 33–5, 82–4, 100, 163, 183; *see also* serpents
dreams 24, 37, 64, 70, 87, 92–4, 116, 119, 121, 125–6, 148–9, 151, 153, 157; dream–interpreters 92–3
drugs 7–8, 11, 15, 17, 20, 26–37, 41–2, 45–7, 67, 71–2, 86, 88, 91, 95–6, 100, 119, 136, 153; see also *pharmaka*, poison, roots
Drusus 48–9
Dukas 123
Dybbuk, The 169

echenais 53
Egypt, Egyptians 11, 27, 39, 67–9, 78, 83, 86–7, 89, 91–100, 102, 104–5, 109–10, 114–15, 118, 121–4, 130, 135–9, 149, 152–3, 159
eisagogeus 124
Elaios 157
Eleazar 101–2
Eleusis 110
Elpenor 9–10, 19–20, 148
empousas 162–4
Endor, Witch of 179
Endymion 64
Epaphroditus 143–4
Ephesus 102, 111, 167
Epictesis 143–4
epilepsy 4, 167, 184
epitaph 48
epoidos 3, 22
Eratomenes 142
Erictho 19, 50–6, 62, 66, 75, 79, 100, 126, 142
Eros 40, 119–20; *see also* magic, erotic
Erotion 119–20
Esquiline 46, 49
Ethiopia, Ethiopians 63, 98, 100, 127–8, 159–60
Etruria 30, 119
Eubatides 104–5
Eucrates 59, 122–3, 130, 150–1
Eudocia, Empress 184–5
Eumaeus 172
Eumenides 166
Euripides 22–3, 27, 32–3, 37–8, 64, 148, 156–7
Eurydice 157, 166, 195
Eurylochus 7–9, 15, 21
Eusebius of Caesarea 113
Eve 88
excantatio cultorum 44
exorcism 20, 59, 74, 78, 89, 100–4, 111–14, 132, 163, 168–9
eye, evil 28, 32, 34, 37, 71

fart 47
Faust 90
Faustina 86
Feralia 75
fire 29, 33, 39–40, 42, 47, 49, 55, 82–3, 90, 99, 103, 112, 118, 121, 132–3, 144, 157
flies 66
Folia 47, 50, 160
folktales 2–3, 14–15, 34–5, 56, 62, 76, 146, 169; *see also* traditions, folk
Foulon, John 159–60
Frankenstein 2, 55–6, 180
frog 63
Fundanius 46
Furies 47–8, 51, 53–4, 57, 80, 155
Furius Scribonianus 85

Gabriel 90
Gadara 104, 134
Gagliano 71–5
Galen 108
Ganymede 64
garlic 20, 46
Gaza 89
genie 117
George, St 82, 183
Gerasa, demons of 101
Germanus, St 105
ghosts 1–3, 9–10, 19–21, 24–5, 36–7, 45–8, 51–7, 59–60, 62–3, 65–7, 69–70, 73, 78–81, 84, 91, 96–8, 100, 102–5, 110–13, 116, 124–6, 138–142, 144, 146–69; *see also* house, haunted, restlessness
Gibiliscos 72
Gilgamesh 13
gladiator 86
Glauce 28–9, 33, 47
Glaucias 120, 138
Glaucus 153
Glycon 107–8, 187
gnat 149

Gnomes 73
goddesses 13–14, 25–6, 40, 59, 61, 75, 95, 117–21, 129, 137, 140, 143; *see also* Mistress of Animals
goetes 3, 4, 22, 24, 105, 109; *see also* sorcerers
Goethe 123, 167, 196
Golden Legend 90, 183, 185
Gorgias 22, 37
Gorgons 47, 118, 127–8
Graeae 118
Gratidia 50
gravedigger 73
Greek Magical Papyri 3, 6, 53–4, 89, 101–2, 104, 109, 114, 115–29, 134, 136, 144
Gregory the Great, St 105, 132
Gyges 130
Gyllis 50, 70

Habrocomes 153
Hades 9, 19, 23, 42, 53–4, 97, 150, 157–8; *see also* Pluto, underworld
Hadrian 158–9
Hag-witches 1, 45–70; *see also* Canidia, Erictho, Meroe
Hannan 169
Harnouphis 86
Harpalus 79, 155–6
Harpocration see *Cyranides*
haruspices 85
hawk 15, 93
healing 35, 37, 44–5, 74, 84, 87, 96, 106, 112–13, 133, 136
Hebrew 102, 139, 151–2
Hecabe 148
Hecate 27, 33–4, 36, 40–1, 44–5, 47, 53–4, 59, 80, 120, 130, 163
Helen 11, 22, 27, 36, 91
Heliodorus 98–9
Heracleia Pontica 147
Heracles 29, 49, 80, 112, 157
Heraclitus 23, 36, 78, 108

herbs *see* drugs, *pharmaka*, poison, roots
hermaphrodite 2, 166
Hermes 8, 18, 20, 26, 59, 86, 166
Herod the Great 151–2
Herodas 50, 70
Herodotus 22, 24, 34, 37, 57, 77–8, 86, 91, 103, 147–52, 155–7, 193
Hesiod 13, 30, 34, 36
Hesperides 100
Hierapolis 183
Hierocles 113
Hilarion, St 83, 89
Hipparchus of Amphipolis 164
Hipparchus of Nicaea 94
Hipparchus, wife of 61–2
Hippocrates 4, 22, 38, 78
Hippolytus 107
Hippomanes 41, 177
historiolas 41, 43, 131–8, 144
Hittite 45
Homer 7–13, 15, 17–30, 34–6, 42, 45, 53, 65, 91, 116, 129, 148, 151, 156, 158, 164, 166
homosexuality 62, 111, 168–9
honey 8–9, 80, 84, 99, 136, 152–3
Horace 46–50, 75, 160
house, haunted 2, 59, 104–5, 155; *see also* ghosts
Hydaspes 79, 155
Hydra 49
hyena 53, 83–4
Hyginus 153, 156
Hylax 144
Hyllus 166
Hypata 62–5, 74
Hyperboreans 59, 78, 89, 120, 138,

Iamblichus 81
ichor 28
immortality 22–3, 28, 31, 37, 97; *see also* reanimation, rejuvenation
impotence 129–30

incantations 19, 22–3, 36–7, 39, 43–5, 49, 53–4, 64, 72, 74, 80–2, 90, 93, 98, 99, 101, 110, 122–3, 129, 158; *see also* prayers
incest 154–5
India, Indians 17, 63, 109, 112, 163, 168
initiation 22–3, 36, 38, 110, 116, 122, 161, 164
innkeepers 56–7, 62–6, 69, 122, 150
intaglios 130–1
invisibility 14, 18, 23, 58, 121, 130
Iolcus 27–8, 30–1
Ion 81–2, 103
Iphigenia 22, 37
Irdakurraddus 24
Ishtar 13–14
Isis 61, 65, 95, 136–7, 189
Italy, modern, 71–6
Iucundus 48–9
Iynx-wheel 32–4, 37, 40, 42

Jacobus de Voragine 90, 183, 185
Jason 16, 27–37, 39, 42
Jerome 83, 89
Jews, Judaism 59, 86, 88–9, 100–4, 111, 114, 116, 138, 149–52, 163, 165, 169
Josephus 101, 151
Julia Domna 109
Julian the Chadaean 85
Julian the Theurge 85
Justina 87–90

katadesmoi 138, 143; *see also* binding, curses
kestos himas 26, 129
kolossoi 140; *see also* dolls

Lab, Queen 171
Laestrygonians 7, 12, 17, 59
lamellas 102, 116, 131, 138; *see also* amulets, curses

INDEX

lamashtu 162, 196
lamias 112, 162–4, 167
Laodameia 156–7
Larissa 66, 135
Leah 169
lecanomancy 79, 94, 96, 124
Legion 101
Levi, Carlo 71–6
libations 9, 24, 80, 99, 111
Libo Drusus 85
lions 7, 9, 13, 15–17, 21, 25, 80, 85, 105, 112, 126, 150
liver 48, 160
Livilla 48–9
Lucan 19, 50–6, 71, 75, 79, 126
Lucania 71–6
Lucian 50, 58–9, 60–1, 79, 81–3, 89–90, 95, 98, 102–9, 119–20, 122–4, 130, 138, 150–1; *Philopseudes (Lover of Lies)* 58–60, 78, 81, 85, 102, 104, 119, 122, 130, 150
Lucius (Apuleius) 61–2, 65, 69, 74
Lucius of Patras 61, 181
Luke, Book of 101
Lupus 62, 65
lycanthropy *see* werewolves
Lycas, Hero of Temesa 21, 57
Lydney Park 130

Macarius, St 89, 149–50
Macedon 39, 63, 92, 135, 14, 196
Machatas 196
Machates 164–7
Macron 141
Madaura 60
mageia 4, 105, 135
mages 3–4, 21–7, 29–31, 34–8, 59, 62, 77–93, 97, 103–5, 109–10, 113, 120, 125–6, 129–30, 135, 138, 144, 155, 158–9
magia 104
magic *passim*; definition of, 3–6; erotic magic 18–19, 25–6, 32–4, 36, 39–45, 47, 49–60, 60, 63, 75, 89–90, 94, 116, 126, 130, 135, 137, 139, 143, 155, 157, 159, 163, 169; sympathetic magic 40, 42, 47, 138–9, 142, 192; *see also* mages
magos 3–4, 22–4, 36, 109, see also mages
magus 3–4
Malalas, John 127–9
Marcus Aurelius 85
Maria 72
Maria C 71
Mariamme 151–2
Mark, Book of 101
Marmarus 84
marrow 45, 48, 53, 84, 132, 160
Massylians 100
mathematici 84–5; *see also* astrologers
Medea 16, 18, 20, 27–37, 39, 41–2, 44–7, 64, 75, 77–8, 91, 100; Metaia 30
Medeios 30, 34, 36
Medes 30, 34, 77, 78–9, 84, 86, 113, 127; *see also* Persians
Megaera 54
Megara 65, 142
Melissa of Corinth 148–52, 155
Melissa of Tarentum 56
Melitta 90
Memphis 89, 95, 97, 122
Menander 160–1
Menippus of Gadara 79–81
Menippus of Lycia 161–4, 167
mermaid 131
Meroe 1, 18, 62–6, 71, 76
mice 66
Midas 81–3, 103
migraine 131–4
Miletos, son of Glycon 108
miller 69–70
Mimnermus 30, 36
Minos 153
Mistress of Animals 13–14, 26

Mithrobarzanes 79–80
Moeris 91, 177
Moiragenes 109
moly 8, 20, 32
moon 22–3, 37, 40, 43, 45–7, 49, 53, 56, 59, 80, 94–5, 99, 103, 120, 163, 174
Moreau, Island of Dr, 2, 16
Moses, Eighth Book of, 101
mullein 20
Murnau 54
Muta Tacita 75
Mysteries of Eleusis 110

Naples 50
narratives 2–3 and *passim*; *see also* folktales
Naupactia 31
Nausicaa 11
Nechepso 96, 124
necromancy 19, 46, 53, 55, 79, 81, 96, 97, 100, 107, 112, 124, 148–9, 151–3, 155, 159–60; *see also* divination
necrophilia 147–56
Nectanebo II 91–5, 98, 109, 135
Neophanes 142
Neophron 33
Nephotes 124
Nephthys 117–18, 189
Nero 56, 76, 109, 154–5
Nerva 109
New Testament 82, 101
Niceros 56–8, 75
Night, personified, 47
Nile 122
Nodens 130
Nosferatu 54
Nostoi 31, 36

Odysseus 7–25, 32, 35, 45, 48–9, 59, 64–5, 79, 80, 129–30, 137, 148, 166
Oedipus 24
Olympias 92–4, 135–6

Ophianoi 83
Optatus 87
oracles 55, 80, 85, 106–7, 127; oracles of the dead 79, 147–8, 155; *see also* divination, necromancy
Origen 104, 113
Orlok 54
Orpheus 80, 157, 166, 195
Ortoli 14
Osiris 124, 126, 137
Osrael 102
Ostanes the Elder 97–8, 125–6, 129
Ostanes the Younger 97–8
Ovid 20, 75, 1–3
oxen 82, 107, 120, 131, 133

Palladius 89
Palaestine 86, 102–4, 114
Palaestra 62
Pamphile 52, 62, 65, 138
Pancrates 95, 98, 122–3
Panthia 1, 62–4, 76
Paphlagonia, Paphlagonians 105–6, 108
Paris, Great Magical Papyrus in, 116, 124–5
Parthenius 154
Pasianax 142, 192
Patroclus 148
Paul, St 102
Pausanias periegete 21
Pausanias regent 146–7, 155
Peliades 28, 32, 37
Pelias 28–32, 36–7
Pella 92–3, 106, 108–9, 141, 164
Pellichus 58–9
Pelops 149
Penelope 11, 137
periamma, periapta 129; *see also* amulets
Periander 148–56, 193
Perimede 41–2, 177
Peripatetics 120
Perse(is) 7, 10, 34

INDEX

Persephone 9, 53–4, 80, 157
Persepolis 24
Perseus 106, 118, 127–9
Persia, Persians 17, 22, 24, 29, 34, 36–7, 77–91, 97, 109, 113, 118, 126–9, 146–7, 156–7; *see also* Medes
pestle 122–3
Petronius 56–9, 71, 74–6, 129–30
Phanias 90
pharmaka 7, 15, 23, 26, 29, 31–3, 135–6; *see also* drugs, poison, roots
pharmakeus 3, 22; *see also* sorcerers
pharmakeutria 26, 39; *see also* witches
pharmakis 2, 22, 26–7, 90; *see also* witches
Pherae 157
Pherecrates 22, 37
Pherecydes 24, 32, 37, 158
Phigalia 147
Phila 141–2, 196
Philemon 105
Philinna 134–6, 196
Philinnion 164–7
Philinus 39
Philip II of Macedon 92–3, 135–6, 164, 196
Philip, St 83
Philippi 102
Philista 40, 43
Philocles 78
Philostratus 109–14, 151, 160–1, 163, 167
philtres, love, 41, 71–2, 75
Phlegon of Tralles 164–7
Phoenicians 161
Phorcides 117
Phoronis 24, 36
Photis 62, 65, 138
Physica et Mystica 97
Pibechis 89, 102
Picus 21, 127–8
pigs 8–9, 15–17, 21, 23, 25, 35, 101, 108, 119, 172

Pindar 31–2, 37
Piso 44
Pitys 125–9, 135
plague 111–12
Plato 4, 61, 81, 103, 130, 150, 169
Platonism 81, 102–4
Plautus 105
Pliny the Elder 4–5, 57, 83–4, 86, 116,
Pliny the Younger 105, 130, 155
Plotius Crispinus 181
Pluto 80; *see also* Hades
Pnouthi(o)s 121–4, 135
Podaleirios 108
Poenae 53, 80
poison 11, 15, 20, 22, 29, 32, 34, 37, 41, 45–9, 53, 67, 69, 71–2, 81–3, 85, 137; *see also* drugs, *pharmaka*, roots
Polites 7, 16, 21, 26, 57
Polycrates 104
Polycritus 1, 166
Polydamna 11, 27, 36, 91
Polydorus 148
Polyidus 153
polypharmakos 15, 26–7
Pompey the Great 51–2, 55
Poppaea Sabina 154–5
prayer 9, 23, 33, 36, 40–1, 67, 87–9, 95, 106, 116, 132–3, 136; prayers for justice 130, 140, 143; *see also* incantations
Praylius 87
Priapus 46–7
Prometheus 180
prostitutes *see* courtesans
Protesilaus 156–7, 195
Proto-Indo-European 10, 44–5
Psammetichus 124
psychagogoi 147
Ptolemais 116
Ptolemy II Philadelphus 39
purifications 16, 22–3, 37, 80–1, 83, 96, 105

Pygmalion of Tyre 150
Pyriphlegethon 9, 80
Pythagoras 79, 104, 110–11
Pythagoreans 59, 77–8, 104–14
Pythionice 79, 155–6
Python of Catana 79

Quadi 85
Quintilian 157–8

rams *see* sheep
reanimation 1, 19, 53–6, 67, 69, 79, 81–3, 95, 98–100, 126, 180; *see also* immortality, rejuvenation
rejuvenation 18, 23, 28–37, 180; *see also* immortality, reanimation
restlessness, ghostly 19–20, 52, 57, 75, 125, 147, 151, 158, 168; *see also* ghosts
revenants 70, 147, 158, 166
rings 14, 20, 30, 59, 71, 101, 126, 130–1, 164–6; *see also* amulets
rivalry 20, 28, 33, 41, 49–50, 90, 135–6, 139, 147, 151
rhombos 40–1, 90
roots 8, 29, 33, 47, 101; *see also* drugs, *pharmaka*, poison, roots

saga 3, 27, 46, 48, 66
Sagana 46–7, 160
Samos 104
Sanksrit 10, 45
Sappho 133
Sarapammon 16
Sarapis 124
scapegoats 101
Sceva, sons of, 102
Scylla 12, 20
Selinus 138–9
Senicianus 130–1
Septimius Severus 109
Septuagint 102

serpents 12, 27, 29–30, 32, 36–7, 47, 53, 72, 82–4, 88, 94, 118, 162–3, 184; *see also* dragons
Seth-Typhon 117, 189
Sextus Pompey 19, 51–3
Shakespeare *Macbeth* 2
sheep 9, 18–19, 23, 28–9, 31, 34–6, 46, 65, 80, 92, 112, 137
Shelley, Mary 55–6
Sibyl 19
Siduri 171
Silas 102
Silchester 130–1
Silvianus 130–1
Simaetha 26, 39–45, 50, 75, 77, 86, 91, 136
Simon Magus 159
Simonides 31, 36
Sinai, Mt 132
Sinbad 17, 171–2
Sinopium 95
Sirens 12, 16, 19
Sisyphus 158
skulls 52–3, 107, 116–18, 125–8, 179
snakes *see* serpents
Socrates (Apuleius) 1, 18, 62–5, 86
Socrates (philosopher) 19
Solomon 101–2
Sophocles 24, 32–4, 36–7, 46, 78
Sophron 176
sorcerers 2–5, 21–7, 35–8, 49, 57, 69, 77–114, 119, 120, 122, 124, 126, 130, 144, 168; *Sorcerer's Apprentice* 59, 95, 122–4; *see also* mages
Sozomen 83
Sparta, Spartans 11, 146–7, 152–3
sponge 1, 63–4
sport 139
Strabo 79
stuff 90, 121, 138,
Styx 53–4
Suda 85, 103
Suetonius 59, 155

INDEX

Sulis Minerva 140
sun 7, 22–3, 29, 45, 54, 56, 67, 74, 80, 9–5, 111
Susa 110
Sychaeus 150
Syria, Syrians 37,50, 78, 86–7, 90, 98, 102–3, 114, 134; Syrians from Palaestine 78, 86, 102–3, 114; see also Assyrians

Tainaron 51
Talmud 150
Talos 28–9, 32, 37
Tantalus 162
Tarmoendas 84, 86
Temesa 21, 57
Terence 160–1
Tertullian 4
Thanatos 32, 158
Theagenes 98
Thebes (Boeotia) 29, 96
Thebes (Diospolis, Egypt) 115, 159
Thelxinoe 153
Thelyphron 65–9, 95, 153
Theocritus 26, 39–44, 50, 75, 86, 136
Theodotis 137
Theonnastos 192
Theophilus 90
Theophrastus 20
Theopompus 149
Theseus 29, 32, 37, 41, 136
Thesprotia 148
Thessalians, Thessaly 1, 22, 37, 45, 51, 53, 62–3, 65–6, 68–9, 75–6, 112, 125–6, 129, 134–6, 151, 157
Thessalus of Tralles 96–8, 124
Thestylis 39–42
Thetima 141–2
Thomas, St 83
Thon 27, 91
Thoth 91
Thrace 107, 157
Timandridas 142

Tiresias 9–10, 19–20, 24, 79–80
Tiridates 155
Tisiphone 47
toads 71
tombs 29, 47, 51–2, 56, 59, 74, 81, 91, 101, 115, 126, 130, 141–2, 149, 151, 153, 155–7, 164–5, 167
Tomi 108
traditions, folk, 71–6
transformation 14–25, 28, 35, 43, 56–7, 61–3, 65–6, 68–9, 73, 89–91, 93, 105, 120–1, 140, 163, 167
Trimalchio 56, 58–60, 75
Trojans, Troy 7, 24, 112–13, 151, 156–7
Trophonius 80–1, 110
Twelve Tables 44
Tychiades 59, 78, 82, 102–3
Typhon 117
Tzetzes 156

underworld 4, 9. 19, 23, 40, 47, 51, 53–4, 59, 67, 79–81, 88, 130, 138–41, 147, 150, 156–8, 163, 166–7; *see also* Hades

vampires 2, 112, 162–7
Varus 47–8
Vatinius 160
Veia 47, 160
venefica 3
veneficus 3
Venere, Giulia, 72, 75
Venus 130; *see also* Aphrodite
Virgil 19, 43–4, 45, 48, 50, 91, 100, 149–50
Vitellius 85
voodoo *see* dolls

war 52
weasels 67, 79
weather, control of, 22–3, 36–8, 45

werewolves 2, 21, 56–7, 65, 73, 75, 91; *see also* wolves
wheel, magic, see *iynx*
Willson, Meredith 182
witches 1–4, 7–78, 86, 90–1, 98, 100, 113, 129, 135–6, 138, 144, 146, 160 and *passim*
wizards *see* sorcerers
wolves 7, 9, 13, 15–17, 21, 24–5, 45, 47–8, 52–3, 57, 65, 71, 73, 75, 91, 134; *see also* werewolves
womb 63
woodpecker 21

Xanthus of Lydia 37, 77, 174
Xenophon of Ephesus 153, 167
Xerxes 24, 78, 129, 174

Zacharius the Scholastic 159–60
Zaratas 84
Zatchlas 67–9, 95, 100, 153
Zeeraj 150
Zeus 108, 127–8, 166; Zeus Bel 78
Zoilos 192
zombie 2; *see also* reanimation
Zoroaster 37, 79, 84, 174
Zurvan 78